LOGIC
SELF-TAUGHT

WORKBOOK

Basic Concepts
and Symbolization
in Propositional Logic

2022

Logic Self-Taught Workbooks

1. Basic Concepts and Symbolization in Propositional Logic (2022)
2. The Truth-Table Method (2022)
3. Natural Deduction in Propositional Logic (2022)
    Thin Edition
    Full Edition (with supplementary units)
    Extra Full Edition (with supplementary units and extra exercises)
4. Basic Concepts and Symbolization in Monadic Predicate Logic (2nd ed., 2024)
5. Natural Deduction in Monadic Predicate Logic (2024)
    Full Edition
    Extra Full Edition (with extra exercises)
6. Symbolization and Natural Deduction in Quantifier Logic (in preparation)
7. Symbolization and Natural Deduction in Quantifier Logic with Identity (in preparation)

If you have comments or suggestions, let me know at
dr.phi.logic@gmail.com

Logic Self-Taught Workbook 1
Basic Concepts and Symbolization in Propositional Logic

ISBN: 979-8-35-590624-5 (paperback)
ISBN: 979-8-32-646244-2 (hardcover)

Table of Contents

Introduction to *Logic Self-Taught*
(All Workbooks)

Who Are the Workbooks for?

If you answered any of Logi's questions positively, the Workbooks may help you learn logic.

The Workbooks are prepared for students who do not have formal minds (i.e., the great majority of us). Having a formal mind differs from being intelligent. There are very intelligent, even outstanding, students who barely pass logic with a good grade. The Workbooks can help students with a GPA of around 2 get a very good grade on the condition that they stick to the instructions. The Workbooks are not textbooks of logic. They are meant to supplement a logic textbook.

The Workbooks will be useless or irritating to students with a formal mind.

"How to Swim?" or the Method

Logic Self-Taught Workbooks are based on the insight that understanding logic is not sufficient for learning logic, just as understanding how to swim is not sufficient for learning to swim and understanding the grammar of a foreign language is not sufficient for learning that language. You need to practice and take an active part in self-teaching.

(1) **Learning logic is like learning to swim.** Learning introductory logic involves developing certain skills: precise logical thinking, symbolization, truth-value calculation, proofs, etc. You cannot develop such skills in a lecture. Even if a lecturer were to explain how to swim (which muscles to contract, which to relax, and in what order) in the most captivating and witty way, the lecture would not only be boring but ineffective. A student thrown into deep water at the end of the term will simply drown. The same is true of logic lectures. They are boring to death. Moreover, most students drown on the final exam.

Of course, we do not teach swimming in a lecture room but in a swimming pool, where students practice, practice, practice under instruction. You guessed it! The method consists of practicing, practicing, practicing under the instructions of the Workbook.

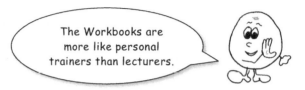

The Workbooks are more like personal trainers than lecturers.

(2) **You have to teach yourself**. You may think that it is obvious that you have to teach yourself. Perhaps you can appreciate that it is not so obvious if you have already attended logic classes but could not pass the exams, barely passed them, or were frustrated ("So little material... but how do I learn it?").

The Workbooks are designed to help you with the self-teaching process. However, you need to understand *how* and *how not* to use them.

The belief that students must teach themselves (rather than be taught) is the foundation of the best system of higher education, namely the Oxford system. In Oxford, there are no course lectures that present knowledge to students, which students then present on the exams. Instead of lectures, students attend the so-called tutorials, approximately two per trimester. Such a tutorial is usually devoted to some field of study, e.g., social psychology, educational psychology, introduction to logic, advanced logic, etc. It consists of eight weekly meetings with the tutor, for which the students work through the assigned material (depending on the subject, they may read from 100 to 400 pages). They solve problems or write an essay that critically discusses a given segment of the material. The solutions or the essay are discussed during the meeting with the tutor. Doubts and misunderstandings are cleared up. In addition, students may, but do not have to, attend lectures that are often devoted to topics other than the topic of a given tutorial.

The point is that students are alone with the knowledge contained in books and specialized articles. They have to actively seek to acquire knowledge. Finally, they are tested on very difficult exams that take place only at the end of their three-year studies.

How (Not) to Use the Workbooks

The Workbooks will be **useless** if you **read** them **cover to cover**.

Just as understanding how to lose weight is not sufficient for losing weight, so **understanding** logic is **not sufficient** for learning it. You can dream of losing weight only if you follow the proposed method. (And you will lose weight if the method is good.) The method proposed in the Workbooks is good, but you will learn logic only if you **stick to the rules**, particularly those **about exercises**.

Six Rules about Exercises

The Workbooks are composed of units. Each unit is composed of sections. Exercises follow most sections in the units. They are designed to help you digest what you have been reading about. Moreover, they are designed to help you acquire the logical skills necessary to move on. You must do those **exercises immediately after** going through a given section. Do not wait until you have read the whole unit.

You should also **check** that you have done an exercise correctly immediately after you finish it. The solutions are located at the end of each Workbook. If you have made **mistakes**, you need to understand why. You must **rework** the section. You should also **retake the exercises** until you make no mistakes.

Beware of peeking at the Solutions, however. If you do, you will destroy your learning process.

Here are the rules you should obey:

1. You must do *all the exercises*.

2. You must do them *in the **order*** in which they are presented.

3. You must do them *at the **right time***.

4. You must ***immediately check*** your answers *against the Solutions*.

5. You must repeat the exercises *until you do them **100% correctly***.

6. You must do the exercises ***one by one***.

There are good reasons why you should obey them.

Q: **Why should I do** *all the exercises*?

A: The exercises are designed to help you develop the relevant skills. Just like learning to swim involves repeating certain motions, so does learning logic.

The skills you develop should become second nature. It is not enough for you to know how to move your arms; you must actually be able to move them. Likewise, it is not enough for you to understand how to do the exercises; you must actually do them until they feel like a breeze and until you make no mistakes.

The exercises are designed to be intellectually enjoyable but not overly stressful. Think of them as puzzles.

Q: **Why should I do the exercises** *in the order* **they are presented?**

A: Learning logic is highly cumulative. So are the skills you will learn. Most of them presuppose you have *mastered* earlier skills.

Q: **Why should I do the exercises** *at the right time*?

A: You should do the exercises immediately after working through a section for a similar reason: learning logical skills is highly cumulative. You need to master certain skills before even reading on!

If you are in the habit of reading a whole chapter to get a general idea, you must break that habit. Read a section. Try to understand it. Do all the exercises that follow the section *immediately*. Remember that the Workbooks are designed to help you acquire *skills*, not mere understanding!

Q: **Why should I check my answers against the Solutions** *immediately*?

A: You should check the Solutions immediately after completing the whole exercise. To master a skill, you must do the exercises correctly—in fact, 100% correctly. It is thus crucial that you check your answers against the Solutions.

If you made mistakes, you need to go back to the section. You need to figure out what went wrong. You need to find ways of teaching yourself not to make such a mistake again. Then, redo the exercise (without peeking at the Solutions).

Q: **Why should I repeat an exercise** *until I do it 100% correctly*?

A: You need to recalibrate your expectations of yourself to 100% correctness. Learning logical skills is highly cumulative. Unfortunately, insufficient grasp of the material and proneness to making errors are also highly cumulative.

If your answers are 90% correct, you have not fully mastered the skill. This can actually block you from acquiring further skills. If you let yourself be satisfied with 90% correct answers at an early point, chances are that you will eventually end up with 0% correct answers on the final exam. This is why you should repeat the exercises until you can do them 100% correctly (without peeking).

Q: **Why should I do the exercises *one by one*?**

A: The exercises usually presuppose that you have mastered the skill at the level of an earlier exercise. You will waste your time and get frustrated if you do all the exercises at once. You need to check how you are doing before proceeding.

 I strongly advise that you stick to the rules, especially at the beginning, especially with hard or confusing topics. Such pedantic adherence to these rules will not always be necessary. However, any deviation is your own responsibility! 0.001% of people do not need to do the exercises at all. Their minds already work formally. The exercises are a must for most of us (myself included)!

Some Further Advice

The Workbooks are really **notebooks**. You should work along. Work through the examples on your own. Write in the solutions. The exercises are presented in a graphically accessible way so that you can write in the solutions easily. You do not have an excuse for not having time to rewrite the exercise.

Work along.

Never peek at the solutions!

Beware of peeking! The Workbook is full of exercises and solutions to them. Sometimes, you will be tempted to study the solutions to the exercises in depth rather than go through the pain of doing the exercises. Beware! You will learn nothing this way. The exercises are meant to develop skills! Understanding is not sufficient to develop the skills.

Studying solutions to exercises (rather than solving them yourself) is like…

… watching how effectively the diet works on a friend.

Learning logic means **learning from *your* mistakes**. That someone can lose weight or solve exercises does not mean you can. Remember that the purpose of the exercises is to develop skills. There are **no shortcuts here.**

If parts of the material seem particularly hard for you or you made many mistakes, it is a good idea to take a break and redo the exercises on another day, for example. At the very least, take a walk or do your favorite physical exercises before continuing.

Spread your work out! Don't do it in one sitting.

Mistakes are your best friends. Do not get discouraged if you make mistakes. On the contrary, be happy that you made them—they indicate *what* you must work on. Remember, however, that you must understand the source of the problem. Moreover, you must find ways of teaching yourself not to make those mistakes. At the end of the process, you must complete the exercises flawlessly without making any mistakes.

There are lots of visual metaphors in the Workbooks. They are designed to help you grasp the material. **Visualization** is often crucial in learning logic. Sometimes, I ask you to use color markings (like in the first grade). Do not laugh! Do it! There is a reason why
your first-grade teacher asked you to use colors. Moreover, to learn proofs (Workbooks 3, 5, 6, and 7), one must be able to recognize certain complex substructures within complex structures. You won't learn proofs unless you virtually "see" the relevant substructures. To do so, you must train your eyes to recognize them. This is what the exercises are for.

But in the end, it is all about practice. Through systematic work with the Workbooks, you will build self-confidence. You can learn logic, even its hardest parts.

About the Workbooks

The Workbooks evolved over many years of my teaching logic. The idea came somewhat by accident. In 2000, prof. Forrest Wood, then chair of the Department of Philosophy and Religion at the University of Southern Mississippi, asked me to teach a logic course exclusively online. (In 2000, the software for online teaching was at its baby stage.) The course would be offered to prospective nursing students with very poor formal preparation. My first thought was that such a course was impossible. However, the course was created. It not only taught future nurses logic, but it also taught me how to teach it.

The Workbooks have grown out of these experiences. The prototypes were course materials that USM students used. As it was impossible to do video lectures back then, the students had to take responsibility for their education. Oxford education was my model. I envisaged my task as that of creating optimal conditions for the students. This is, in fact, a key element of the Workbooks method.

A significant step in the development of this method was the realization that teaching logic should be modeled on teaching a foreign language (see my "Teaching Logic as a Foreign Language Online," *Teaching Philosophy* 27, 2004: 117-125). Teaching a foreign language involves developing appropriate mental structures, mainly syntactic ones. They are best developed by (repetitive) reading out loud of sentences with a given syntactic structure on various examples. The Workbooks are based on relatively easy exercises. The point is to carry them out until they become second nature. Their difficulty is thus increased slowly.

As I saw how the students reacted to the early versions, I have tried to prevent the problems they encountered in subsequent versions. I also relied on and developed various ideas presented in some excellent logic textbooks, including:

- Virginia Klenk, *Understanding Symbolic Logic* (Prentice Hall, Pearson);
- Irving M. Copi, Carl Cohen, *Introduction to Logic* (Prentice Hall);
- Merrie Bergmann, James Moore, Jack Nelson, *The Logic Book* (McGraw Hill).

I would like to thank the numerous students who went through the various stages of the Workbooks. They helped correct many mistakes and made me aware of various shortcomings. One student thought I was intentionally placing errors for teaching purposes, but she did not appreciate the trouble of editing such exercises. I can only guarantee that there are no intentional errors in this release.

The Workbooks are dedicated to my great teachers: the memory of Hanna Maszewska (Primary School No. 69 in Poznań, Poland), an excellent teacher of mathematics, to whom even the weakest students were grateful in their subsequent education; Colin D.O. Jenkins (Atlantic College, Wales), a wonderful biology teacher who would convince even the most romanticizing student that memorization is sometimes useful and not detrimental to creativity; Michael Treisman (Oxford University), a psychology professor who did not hesitate to waste his time for students like myself; Kenneth Manders (University of Pittsburgh), a philosopher and a historian of mathematics, as well as a wonderful logic teacher whose impossible homework could teach so much.

Unit 1.1

Propositions, Arguments, and Their Properties

Overview

Logic is the study of thinking. Unlike psychology, however, it is concerned with *correct* thinking. Furthermore, logic is not only a study of thinking but teaches us to think and argue correctly.

In this unit, you will learn:
- what the subject matter of logic is (in a preliminary and informal way),
- the distinction between deductive and non-deductive arguments,
- what the logical form of an argument is (in a preliminary and informal way),
- what a valid argument is (in a preliminary and informal way),
- what a sound argument is,
- what an enthymematic argument is,
- what a fallacy is.

In this unit, you will learn how to:
- distinguish between sentences and propositions,
- recognize arguments and their elements.

Time:	2-3 hours
Difficulty:	●○○○○○○
Status:	**Essential**/Recommended/Optional
Number of exercises:	9
Prerequisites:	Introduction

A. Sentences and Propositions (Statements)

When we reason, we use sentences. The sentence "The girl who is in love with Fred offended most of her classmates" implies, among other things, the sentence "Some girl offended most of her classmates" as well as the sentence "Some girl is in love with Fred." Someone who accepts the first sentence must also accept the second and third sentences.

However, not all sentences can enter into inferential relations with other sentences. For example, nothing follows from the question, "What's the time?" Someone might want to know what time it is, or someone might remind another person that it's time to change turns at their favorite computer game, or someone might want to give an example of a question, etc. Nothing follows from the exclamation "Heyah!" (someone might be greeting another person in this way, or someone might be calling another, or someone might be explaining to another how to say the equivalent of "Ciao!" in English, etc.). They contain too little information to draw any conclusions.

Logicians distinguish between sentences and propositions (or statements). Sentences are identified with grammatically correct sentences. A **proposition** (**statement**) is what an unambiguous declarative sentence asserts. It is useful to think of a proposition as the meaning of such a sentence.

Different sentences may express the *same proposition*. Consider the following English sentences:

> Logic is the most boring class Jane has ever taken.
> The most boring class Jane has ever taken is logic.

They say the same thing. The same proposition can also be expressed by different sentences in other languages (I have used Google Translate for languages I do not speak):

Logic is boring. [in English]	La logique est ennuyeuse. [in French]
Logika je nuda. [in Czech]	La lógica es aburrida. [in Spanish]
Logika jest nudna. [in Polish]	La logica è noiosa. [in Italian]
логіка нудна [in Ukrainian]	Logik ist langweilig. [in German]
логіка сумная [in Byelorussian]	Logica is saai. [in Dutch]
Логика скучная. [in Russian]	Logikk er kjedelig [in Norwegian]
Logika nuobodi. [in Lithuanian]	Logik är tråkigt. [in Swedish]
Loġika ir garlaicīga. [in Latvian]	Logiikka on tylsää. [in Finnish]
Loogika on igav. [in Estonian]	A logika unalmas. [in Hungarian]

The same sentence may express *different propositions*. For example, ambiguous sentences or sentences that use indexicals can be used to express different propositions. Consider:

> I am here now.

This sentence will express different propositions depending on who, where, and when utters it.

Propositions are either true or false. As logicians put it, propositions bear **truth values**. In classical logic, there are only two truth values: ***true*** and ***false***.

We thus have two characterizations of propositions:

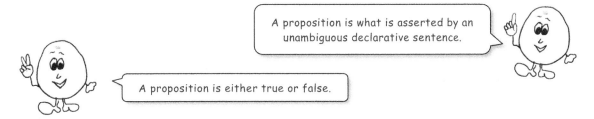

Let us see how these two characterizations are related to one another. We will ask whether non-declarative sentences, in particular exclamations and questions, can be true or false (cf. (a), (b)) and whether ambiguous declarative sentences can be true or false (cf. (c), (d)).

(a) No exclamations are propositions.

    (1) Come here!
    (2) Don't smoke!

Exclamations like (1) or (2) are not propositions. They are neither true nor false, and they cannot be used to assert anything at all.

 (b) **No questions are propositions.** Consider the questions:

    (3) What is the time?
    (4) How are propositions characterized?

What would you say if someone asked you whether questions (3) or (4) are true or false? It is good if you are puzzled. This is because no question can be true or false. The answers to these questions can be true or false but not the questions themselves.

    Again, we do not assert anything with a question.

(c) No ambiguous declarative sentences are propositions. Let's consider another sentence, this time a declarative sentence:

    (5) The deans did not permit the students to demonstrate since they were skinheads.

It might look as if whoever makes this statement says something that is either true or false. However, the impression is mistaken because sentence (5) is ambiguous. It is unclear whether "they" refers to the deans or the students. The following two sentences capture propositions that disambiguate (5):

    (5a) The deans did not permit the students to demonstrate since the deans were skinheads.
    (5b) The deans did not permit the students to demonstrate since the students were skinheads.

Here is another example of ambiguity.

(6) Susan walked the dog in pajamas.

This sentence is again ambiguous. It is unclear who was in the pajamas: Susan or the dog.

(6a) Although Susan wore pajamas, she walked the dog.
(6b) The dog Susan walked wore pajamas.

(d) No declarative sentences with indexical expressions are propositions. There is a class of sentences that contain so-called "*indexical*" expressions (like "I," "he," "she," "there," "now," etc.). Indexical expressions change their referent depending on the context, in which they are uttered. This makes sentences that use such expressions notoriously ambiguous.

Consider the sentence:

(7) I am in Warsaw now.

One might think that the sentence is true (in fact, I am in Warsaw now). However, let us consider what is asserted by this sentence. When *I* use the sentence, *I* mean by it:

(7a) Dr. φ is in Warsaw on April 3rd, 2022.

Proposition (7a) is true. If you uttered sentence (7), you would mean:

(7b) [_____] is in Warsaw on [_____]
            your first and last name   today's date

Proposition (7b) is (most likely) false (unless you are currently in Warsaw). The point is that sentence (7) will express different propositions depending on who and when utters it.

Sentences and propositions thus differ from each other. In propositions, the content is stated as explicitly as possible. There is no room for contextual filling. *Propositions are independent of context.* In sentences, on the other hand, some of the content often depends on the context in which the sentence is uttered. Sentence (7) is a good example: its meaning depends on the context of its utterance. If I utter sentence (7) on April 3rd, 2022, I mean proposition (7a); if you utter the same sentence (7) today, you will mean proposition (7b). However, proposition (7a) is unaffected by the context in which it is uttered; it makes no difference who, where, or when says it; the truth value of (7a) remains constant. If the proposition "Dr. φ is in Warsaw on April 3rd, 2022" is true, it will be true on April 7th and at any other time. The same is true for (7b).

You will find that logicians often speak about propositions, statements, and claims interchangeably.

Exercise A.1 Propositions

Mark those sentences that express a proposition.

O   (a) Dick Cheney overcooked the cauliflower.

O   (b) No force could stop you.

O   (c) It was very dark there.

O   (d) My friends went to the forest to pick mushrooms.

O   (e) Henry Fonda sneaked into the kitchen.

O   (f) Hillary Clinton attached herself to the painted wall.

O   (g) If Fred Astaire were not a dancer, Greta Garbo would not be an actress.

O   (h) If only children knew more than their parents!

O   (i) Will Henry ever come to like girls?

O   (j) Bill Clinton is a woman.

Exercise A.2 Propositions

True or false?

(a) An unambiguous declarative sentence expresses a proposition.   O true   O false

(b) An ambiguous declarative sentence expresses a proposition.   O true   O false

(c) A non-declarative sentence expresses a proposition.   O true   O false

(d) All propositions are either true or false.   O true   O false

(e) All sentences are either true or false.   O true   O false

(f) One proposition can be expressed by means of more than one sentence. O true   O false

(g) One unambiguous declarative sentence expresses only one proposition. O true   O false

B. Arguments

WHAT IS AN ARGUMENT?

When we argue, we accept one proposition (**conclusion**) on the basis of other propositions (**premises**). The premises provide evidence or justification for the conclusion. The conclusion is said to *follow from* the premises.

> An **argument** is a group of propositions where one proposition (the conclusion) is taken to *follow from* the others (the premises).

Consider the following classic example of an argument:

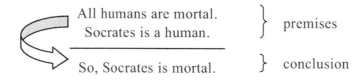

All humans are mortal.
Socrates is a human. } premises

So, Socrates is mortal. } conclusion

A horizontal line sometimes separates the premises and the conclusion.

An argument can have many premises, but it must have at least one. However, an argument must have one and only one conclusion.

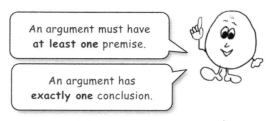

An argument must have **at least one** premise.

An argument has **exactly one** conclusion.

Note, however, that it is possible to draw more than one conclusion from the same premises. Consider, for example, the following set of premises:

P1. Whoever reads Dostoyevsky will not be able to look at the world in the same way.
P2. Everybody in Susan's class read Dostoyevsky.

There are a couple of conclusions we can draw from these premises. For instance, we can conclude that Susan (who is in Susan's class, of course) will not be able to look at the world in the same way:

C1. Susan will not be able to look at the world in the same way.

But given that all students in her class read Dostoyevsky (P2), we can also conclude:

C2. Nobody in Susan's class will be able to look at the world in the same way.

Logicians agreed to use the term "argument" in such a way that **one argument** has exactly **one conclusion**. An argument is thus an inference of *one* conclusion from a set of premises.

In the example above, we have made two arguments:

Whoever reads Dostoyevsky will not be able to look at the world in the same way.
Everybody in Susan's class read Dostoyevsky.

So, Susan will not be able to look at the world in the same way.

and:

Whoever reads Dostoyevsky will not be able to look at the world in the same way.
Everybody in Susan's class read Dostoyevsky.

So, nobody in Susan's class will be able to look at the world in the same way.

The two arguments have the very same premises. However, they are different arguments because they have different conclusions.

Exercise B.1 Arguments

True or false?

(a) All arguments have exactly one premise. ○ true ○ false

(b) All arguments have at least one premise. ○ true ○ false

(c) All arguments have at least two premises. ○ true ○ false

(d) An argument can have no premises. ○ true ○ false

(e) An argument can have only one premise. ○ true ○ false

(f) An argument can have only two premises. ○ true ○ false

(g) An argument can have one hundred premises. ○ true ○ false

(h) It is impossible for an argument to have exactly seven premises. ○ true ○ false

(i) All arguments have exactly one conclusion. ○ true ○ false

(j) All arguments have at least two conclusions. ○ true ○ false

(k) Some arguments can have no conclusions. ○ true ○ false

(l) Some arguments can have two conclusions. ○ true ○ false

(m) In an argument, one proposition is accepted on the basis of others. ○ true ○ false

(n) In an argument, one sentence is accepted on the basis of others. ○ true ○ false

HOW TO RECOGNIZE ARGUMENT PARTS?

 You have just learned what an argument is. I will usually present arguments in a standardized format. It will thus be clear what the premises and the conclusion are. However, most arguments occur in less perspicuous forms in real life. The more logic one learns the better one becomes at identifying arguments in practice. You should not expect this skill from yourself just yet. Still, it is useful to learn a few points.

First, you need to figure out what claim is argued for. In other words, you need to identify the conclusion of the argument. Second, you need to look for the premises (i.e., claims that serve as evidence for the conclusion).

There is no general foolproof recipe for identifying argument parts. The premises are often mentioned first. Sometimes, however, the conclusion appears first. Consider the following argument:

> God does not exist |because| the Bible, which is the sole evidence that God exists, was written by the Ancients. They were wrong on countless occasions.

Note the role that "because" plays in this argument. It marks out the conclusion from the premises. The conclusion of this argument is the proposition "God does not exist." The premises of the argument include the propositions: "The Bible is the sole evidence that God exists," "The Bible was written by the Ancients," and "The Ancients were wrong on countless occasions." We can write the argument in our standardized form thus:

The Bible is the sole evidence that God exists.
The Bible was written by the Ancients.
The Ancients were wrong on countless occasions.

God does not exist

It becomes easier to evaluate the argument once you identify its premises and conclusion. You can ask what sort of argument it is: deductive or inductive? You can ask whether the argument is complete or whether some premises are missing. You can ask whether the premises are true, etc. In the above argument, for example, one may be concerned that the Bible is not the sole evidence that God exists. For now, however, we will focus on how to recognize arguments and their minimal structure (their premises and conclusion).

In recognizing conclusions and premises, it is helpful to note words that typically indicate conclusions (also called "**conclusion indicators**") as well as words that typically indicate premises ("**premise indicators**"). Here are some examples of each.

Premise indicators (examples):

since	because	for
as	given that	for the reason that
inasmuch as	in that	seeing that
owing to	as indicated by	may be inferred from

Conclusion indicators (examples):

therefore	thus	consequently
accordingly	entails	hence
it must be that	follows	for this reason
implies that	so	as a result
in conclusion	we may infer	we may conclude

While many arguments include at least one of these indicators, not all do; consider the following example. The professor says:

Tim will not get an A in logic, I'm afraid. He did not study hard enough for logic. Only students who study very hard get an A in logic.

There are no conclusion or premise indicators in what she says. However, we find the conclusion easily. What is the claim argued for, established, defended, or explained? That Tim will not get an A in logic is the conclusion of her argument.

Once we have found the conclusion, it is easy to see that the remaining items serve as evidence for the conclusion, i.e., as premises of the argument. The teacher believes what she does because Tim did not study hard enough for logic. Moreover, she believes that only students who study very hard get an A in logic. These two propositions (the two premises) are the reasons why she believes that Tim will not get an A in logic.

We can represent the argument thus:

> Only students who study very hard get an A in logic.
> Tim did not study hard enough for logic.
> _____
> Tim will not get an A in logic.

However, this argument could be formulated in other ways. Here are some examples.

Mark the conclusion and premise indicators!

Note how the order of the premises and the conclusion may change!

"The reason why Tim will not get an A in logic is that he did not study hard enough and only students who study very hard get an A in logic."

"Only students who study very hard get an A in logic. Due to the fact that Tim did not study hard enough, he will not get an A in logic."

"Tim will not get an A in logic since he did not study hard enough, and only students who study very hard get an A in logic."

"It is quite well known that only students who study very hard get an A in logic. However, Tim did not study hard enough, so he will not get an A."

"Only students who study very hard get an A in logic, but Tim did not study hard enough. He will not get an A."

"Tim did not study hard enough for logic and, for this reason, he will not get an A. This is because only students who study very hard get an A in logic."

Exercise B.2 Argument Recognition (optional) Identify the premise(s) and the conclusion.

(a) All killing of innocent human beings is wrong. Abortion is the killing of an innocent human being. So, abortion is wrong.

(b) People have the right to decide what to do with their bodies. Nobody can be forced to save the life of a human being by giving them a kidney or even bone marrow or blood. So, women have the right to terminate an unwanted pregnancy.

(c) Human actions are either causally determined or mere random occurrences. If human actions are causally determined, there is no free will; if they are merely random events, there is no free will. Therefore, there is no free will.

(d) Nothing can cause itself since nothing can be prior to itself.

(e) We want our children to grow up strong and independent. We cannot buy a car for each of them. If we did, they would get spoiled and fail to become strong and independent.

(f) It is impossible to think of anything greater than God. Something that exists in reality is greater than something that exists only in the mind. If God did not exist in reality, it would be possible to think of something greater than God, i.e., a being just like God that, in addition, existed in reality. Thus, God exists in reality.

(St. Anselm)

(g) If an all-good, all-powerful, and all-knowing God existed, God would eliminate all evil. God does not exist because evil exists.

(Epicurus)

DEDUCTIVE ARGUMENTS VS. NON-DEDUCTIVE ARGUMENTS

There are two general types of arguments: deductive and non-deductive. Deductive arguments are logically valid in the sense that the conclusion cannot be false if the premises are true. In non-deductive arguments, there is always a logical gap between the premises and the conclusion. Such arguments are fallible, i.e., it is possible for the premises to be true while the conclusion is false. In non-deductive arguments, the conclusion is said to follow with some probability.

In a logically valid deductive argument, the truth of the premises **guarantees** the truth of the conclusion.

In a good non-deductive argument, the truth of the premises makes the truth of the conclusion **more probable**.

We have already considered some examples of deductive arguments. Let's bring them together:

Whoever reads Dostoyevsky will not be able to look at the world in the same way.
Everybody in Susan's class read Dostoyevsky.
_____
So, nobody in Susan's class will be able to look at the world in the same way.

Only students who study very hard get an A in logic.
Tim did not study hard enough for logic.
_____
So, Tim will not get an A in logic.

All humans are mortal.
Socrates is a human.
_____
So, Socrates is mortal.

Here are some examples of non-deductive arguments:

Tim is older than Jenny.
=========================
So, Tim is more experienced than Jenny.

In non-deductive arguments, the conclusion bar is a double line.

The majority of Americans live on the American continent.
George is an American.
===
So, George lives on the American continent.

Taking the "Introduction to Logic" course was a great experience for most students.
===
So, taking the "Introduction to Logic" course will be a great experience for

[your name]

The law of gravity applies to all observed physical objects.
==
So, the law of gravity applies to all physical objects.

All observed ravens have been black.
====================================
So, all ravens are black.

Sometimes non-deductive arguments are called "inductive arguments"; other times the term "inductive argument" is used more narrowly (the last two arguments are prime examples of this narrower usage).

   We will not be concerned with non-deductive arguments.

 You should not worry too much if you feel that you cannot distinguish between deductive and non-deductive arguments. It takes practice to be able to do so. You might take solace because you already have the power to reason deductively. Do the following exercise to convince yourself of it.

Exercise B.3 Deduction in Practice

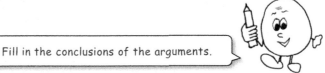

Fill in the conclusions of the arguments.

(a)   If the Philadelphia Eagles win the game against the Dallas Cowboys, they will enter the playoffs.
      The Eagles did not enter the playoffs.

So, [did the Eagles win the game?]

(b)   You can't go wrong with this salad: if you follow the recipe, it will be perfect.
      The salad was not perfect.

So,

(c)   If it rains, Abe always takes an umbrella.
      If Abe takes an umbrella, he's uncomfortable.
      Yesterday, Abe was not uncomfortable.

So, [did it rain?]

(d)   If you get either 85 or 86 points on a quiz, you get a B.
      Al got 85 points on a quiz.

So,

(e)   If it either rains or snows, Joe never goes out.
      Joe did go out yesterday.

So,

(f)   All metals conduct electricity.
      But no sotones conduct electricity.

So, [are any sotones metals?]

LOGICAL FORM OF ARGUMENTS

Consider the innocently looking case (f) from the last exercise (Exercise B.3 Deduction in Practice).

All metals conduct electricity.
But no sotones conduct electricity.

So, [Are any sotones metals?]

You have surely written down the conclusion that no sotones are metals. (It stands to reason: If all metals conduct electricity, and sotones don't, they can't be metals.)

You came to the right conclusion, even though you did not know what sotones are. How do I know that you do not know what sotones are? Well, because I don't either. It's a term I invented... And yet (this is quite incredible!) we could reason about sotones! This is all because reasoning is formal.

Reasoning is *formal*. What matters to an argument is not so much the content of a proposition as its logical structure, i.e., its **logical form**. Arguments are valid (or invalid) in virtue of their logical form. This is why you can sometimes reason correctly about things (like sotones) that do not even exist or that you have no idea about.

We will later see how different logical theories understand logical form. For now, you need to get an intuitive grasp of what logical form is. Please fill in the conclusions of the following arguments:

(i)   John will turn right or left.
      John did not turn left.

(ii) Kay will have fruit or ice cream.
      Kay did not have ice cream.

(iii) Tim will get a rabbit or a hamster.
      Tim did not get a hamster.

(iv) Rose will go to the movies or theater.
      Rose did not go to the theater.

Although all these arguments are different, they nonetheless share something. They have the same logical form. Let us write one of the examples in a more detailed fashion so that we can explicitly see all the propositions involved.

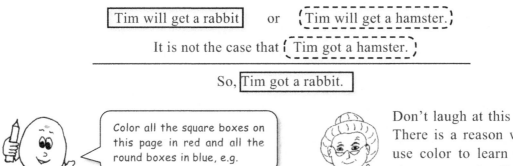

 Color all the square boxes on this page in red and all the round boxes in blue, e.g.

 Don't laugh at this request. There is a reason why you use color to learn math in elementary school!

All of the above arguments have a common structure, which can be represented thus:

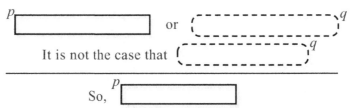

Different boxes stand for different propositions (note that the same proposition must always go into the same box). What you see outside the boxes, i.e., the phrases "or" and "it is not the case that," are called (propositional) **connectives**. One of the main tasks of propositional logic is to study how connectives behave in language.

Since it would be hard for logicians to use differently colored or differently shaped boxes, they have adopted the convention of using so-called **propositional variables**. Propositional variables can be thought of as **names for such boxes**, i.e., names for places where propositions can be inserted.

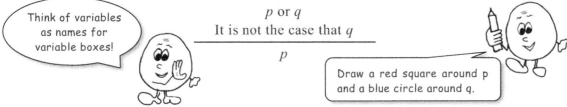

By convention, propositional variables are written using small letters of the alphabet, starting with p, q, r, etc. The logical form of the above arguments is thus:

$$\frac{p \text{ or } q}{\text{It is not the case that } q}$$
$$p$$

Think of variables as names for variable boxes!

Draw a red square around p and a blue circle around q.

This argument form has a Latin name. It is called *modus tollendo ponens* though it is better known as **disjunctive syllogism**. It is important for you to see how the above arguments (i)-(iv) fit this form. When an argument fits a certain logical form, we say that the argument **instantiates** or **exhibits** this logical form. Arguments (i)-(iv) all instantiate the logical form of disjunctive syllogism. We can also say that arguments (i)-(iv) are all **instances** of disjunctive syllogism. Do the following exercise.

Exercise B.4 Logical Form – Disjunctive Syllogism

(a) Color the square boxes in red, the round boxes in blue. (b) Write in arguments (i)-(iv) from p. 13 in the boxes. Make sure that each box contains a complete proposition (cf. p. 14).

Note! You will need to rephrase the statement "John will turn right or left" into the logically more perspicuous "John will turn right or John will turn left."

(i)

[ ] or [ ]

It is not the case that [ ]

So, [ ]

(ii)

[ ] or [ ]

It is not the case that [ ]

So, [ ]

(iii)

[ ] or [ ]

It is not the case that [ ]

So, [ ]

(iv)

[ ] or [ ]

It is not the case that [ ]

So, [ ]

C. Validity, Invalidity, and Logical Form

Now that you know what logical form is, you are prepared to learn about an important fact but not yet to fully understand it.

> Arguments are valid (or invalid) in virtue of their logical form.

This means that an argument (instance) is valid if and only if its argument form is valid. This in turn means that *all instances of that argument form* will be valid. (The same is true for invalidity.)

If you think about it, this is quite an incredible fact! After all, there are an infinite number of instances of any given logical form! In principle, though not in practice, we can form an infinite number of statements.

One question that you might ask yourself is, "How on Earth could we know such a fact?" Believe it or not, we will find an answer to this question when we introduce the truth table method (Workbook 2).

INVALIDITY OF ARGUMENTS

An argument is invalid when its conclusion does not follow from the premises. For example:

> Some women are mothers.
> Jane is a woman.
> _____
> So, Jane is a mother.

The argument is invalid: from the fact that *some* women are mothers, it does not follow that a particular woman is a mother. Jane may be a mother. Just as well, however, she may not be a mother.

How could we show that the argument is invalid? Well, we could pick a just-born baby girl named Susie. Susie is a woman, but she is not a mother. Or we could point out that numerous adult women are not mothers. Indeed, to show that an argument is invalid, we must find an argument (a so-called "counterexample") with the same argument form whose premises are all true but the conclusion is false.

We have shown that the original argument about Jane is invalid because there are some arguments of the same form that have all true premises but a false conclusion, e.g., the argument about Susie, the just-born baby girl:

> Some women are mothers. (T)
> Susie is a woman. (T)
> _____
> So, Susie is a mother. (F)

> **Definition of invalidity**
> An argument form is logically invalid if and only if it is possible for its conclusion to be false while its premises are true.

VALIDITY OF ARGUMENTS

In a (logically) valid argument, the conclusion follows (deductively) from the premises. If someone accepts the premises of a valid argument, they must accept the conclusion.

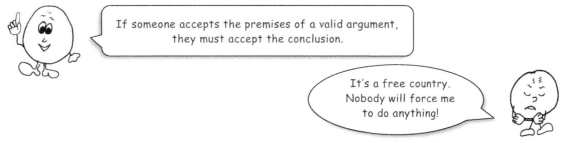

It will pay to pause a little to think about what this "must" means. Logic recognizes your right not to accept the conclusion of a valid argument, but *only if* you also refuse to accept one of its premises. If, on the other hand, you *do* accept all the premises of a valid argument, then you indeed *must* accept the conclusion of that argument. And if you see the argument as valid (i.e., if you see the conclusion as following from the premises), you will have no trouble seeing that someone who accepts the premises cannot but accept the conclusion.

Here are a couple of controversial but valid arguments to convince you of this. Those arguments are controversial because people disagree about whether the premises are true. Their validity is not questioned.

Example 1

Consider the following argument:

> If an omnipotent (all-powerful), omnibenevolent (all-good), and omniscient (all-knowing) being existed, there would be no evil in the world.
> There is evil in the world.
> _____
> So, an omnipotent, omnibenevolent, and omniscient being does not exist.

This is a logically valid argument in the sense that someone *who accepts* both premises *must accept* the conclusion.

As you probably know, this is the central argument in the long debate between theists and atheists, which has come to be known as the "problem of evil." The participants in the debate agree that the argument is logically valid. They disagree about whether the premises are true (and consequently also whether the conclusion is true). One can undermine the first premise by claiming that an omnipotent, omnibenevolent, and omniscient being might have good reasons to allow evil to exist. For instance, one might argue that such a being would want to endow humans with free will and that it would be impossible to create free human beings without allowing that there might be evil.

The important fact for us is that the only way to deny the conclusion of a logically valid argument is to deny one of its premises. Nobody who accepts the premises can deny the conclusion. For, in deductive arguments, the truth of the premises guarantees the truth of the conclusion.

Example 2

> It is morally wrong to kill innocent human beings.
> Abortion involves the killing of a fetus.
> A fetus is an innocent human being.
> _____
> So, abortion is morally wrong.

The argument is logically valid: someone who *accepts* the premises *must accept* the conclusion. Of course, we may deny the conclusion but only if we deny one of the premises.

Logical validity is a formal property of reasoning. An argument form is logically valid if and only if it is impossible for its conclusion to be false while its premises are true. We will come back to the definition of validity in later units (e.g., in Workbook 2).

> **Definition of validity**
> An argument form is logically valid if and only if it is impossible for its conclusion to be false while its premises are true.

D. Validity of Arguments and Truth of Premises and Conclusion

Let us step back a little to reflect on the relation between the validity of arguments, on the one hand, and the truth of the premises and the conclusion, on the other. The relation is interesting though not easy to grasp. We will study it more carefully in later units. For now, this is just a preliminary introduction to a rather complex concept.

We have already said that if the argument is valid and the premises are true, then the conclusion must be true. We have thus talked about one possibility that is marked in the following table:

		Premises	
		(All) True	(Some) False
Argument	Valid	The conclusion is guaranteed to be true	See (1), (2)
	Invalid	See (3), (4)	See (5), (6)

Let us consider the other three cases. Is the conclusion of a valid argument with some false premises true or false? Is the conclusion of an invalid argument with all true premises true or false? Is the conclusion of an invalid argument with some false premises true or false?

VALID ARGUMENTS WITH SOME FALSE PREMISES

An argument may be valid even if some of its premises are false. After all, we can reason correctly on the basis of false information. In such a case, however, the truth value of the conclusion is not determined: the conclusion may be false, but it may also be true.

Here is an example of a valid argument with a false premise and a false conclusion:

(1) All men are tall. (F)

Danny DeVito is a man. (T)
_____

So, Danny DeVito is tall. (F)

"F" is short for "false"; "T" is short for "true."

The argument is clearly valid, but one of its premises is equally clearly false since not all men are tall.

However, we can find a similar argument with a true conclusion:

(2) All men are tall. (F)

Arnold Schwarzenegger is a man. (T)
_____

So, Arnold Schwarzenegger is tall. (T)

In sum, if an argument is valid but at least one of its premises is false, the conclusion may be true or false.

INVALID ARGUMENTS WITH ALL TRUE PREMISES

A valid argument form is truth-preserving: it guarantees the truth of the conclusion if the premises are true. An invalid argument form is not truth-preserving, so there is no guarantee that the conclusion will be true if the premises are true.

Consider first the argument form we will use for illustration:

Some women are professional politicians.

[   ] is a woman.
_____

[   ] is a professional politician.

This argument form is invalid. From the fact that some women are professional politicians, it does not follow that any particular woman is a professional politician. The argument will have a true conclusion or a false conclusion depending on what woman we happen to pick.

If we pick Meghan Markle, the premises will be true but the conclusion false:

(3) Some women are professional politicians. (T)
Meghan Markle is a woman. (T)
_____

Meghan Markle is a professional politician. (F)

If we pick Kamala Harris, the argument will have true premises and a true conclusion:

(4)   Some women are professional politicians. (T)
       Kamala Harris is a woman. (T)

       Kamala Harris is a professional politician. (T)

In sum, if an argument exhibits an invalid argument form, even if all its premises are true, there is no guarantee that its conclusion will be true or that it will be false. What is guaranteed for an invalid argument form is that it has at least one argument instance with true premises and a false conclusion.

INVALID ARGUMENTS WITH SOME FALSE PREMISES

If an invalid argument has some false premises, its conclusion can be false but it also can be true. Here are two such examples (we use the same invalid argument form).

(5)   Some women are professional politicians. (T)
       Barack Obama is a woman. (F)

       Barack Obama is a professional politician. (T)

(6)   Some women are professional politicians. (T)
       Danny De Vito is a woman. (F)

       Danny De Vito is a professional politician. (F)

In sum, if some of the premises of an invalid argument are false, we have no guarantee as to the truth value of its conclusion: it may be false but it may also be true.

SUMMARY

We can thus complete our table:

		Premises	
		(All) True	(Some) False
Argument	Valid	**The conclusion is guaranteed to be true**	The conclusion may be true or false
	Invalid	The conclusion may be true or false	The conclusion may be true or false

As this table shows, **valid** arguments are **truth-preserving**. Given true premises, the conclusion is guaranteed to be true.

Awesome!

You plug in truth and you are guaranteed to get truth out.

You don't even need to double check whether the conclusion is true.

This is exactly what one would expect from a solid reasoning tool.

IS AN ARGUMENT WITH ALL TRUE PREMISES AND A TRUE CONCLUSION VALID? (OPTIONAL)

Surprising as it may seem, the answer to the title question is negative. This is not to say that a valid argument cannot have true premises and a true conclusion. It can. However, the truth of the premises and the conclusion does not guarantee the validity of the argument.

The following table shows the relation between the truth and falsehood of premises, on the one hand, and validity or invalidity, on the other.

		Premises	
		(All) True	(Some) False
Conclusion	True	The argument may be valid or invalid	The argument may be valid or invalid
Conclusion	False	**The argument is guaranteed to be invalid**	The argument may be valid or invalid

We have already seen most examples of arguments that illustrate the relations captured in this table. Let's start with the bottom right cell and work counterclockwise.

An argument with some false premises and a false conclusion can be valid (e.g., argument (1) above) or invalid (e.g., argument (6)).

An argument with some false premises and a true conclusion can be valid (see, e.g., argument (2)) or invalid (e.g., argument (5)).

An argument with all true premises and a true conclusion can be invalid (e.g., argument (4)) or valid as the following example demonstrates:

(7)   All men are human beings. (T)

    Danny DeVito is a man. (T)
___

    So, Danny DeVito is a human being. (T)

If an argument has all true premises and a false conclusion, it is bound to be invalid since it is not truth-preserving (see, e.g., argument (3)).

In sum, the table shows that no constellation of truth and falsehood among the premises and the conclusion of any given argument guarantees its validity. However, an argument is guaranteed to be invalid if all its premises are true and its conclusion is false. In fact, such an argument serves as a counterexample to the validity of an entire argument form.

E. Soundness of Arguments

We have seen that logically valid arguments need not have true premises. However, logicians have introduced a special term to capture those valid arguments that also have true premises. They call such arguments "sound."

> **Definition of soundness**
> An argument is sound if and only if (a) it is logically valid and (b) all of its premises are true.

When you reflect on the definitions of soundness and validity, you will realize that the conclusion of a sound argument must be true as well.

Exercise E Soundness

Use the definitions of validity and soundness to explain why the conclusion of a sound argument must be true.

F. Enthymematic Arguments (optional)

Ordinary discourse is often economical. We do not always explicitly say what is (or what we take to be) obvious to the hearer. This leads to another problem in the logical reconstruction of ordinary arguments. Sometimes we need to add something to what is actually said to make the full argument explicit.

Consider a relatively simple example:

Abortion is wrong since all killing of innocents is wrong.

The proposition "Abortion is wrong" is the conclusion of this argument. Moreover, the conclusion is said to follow from the premise that all killing of innocents is wrong. It is clear, however, that the conclusion will only follow if one also accepts the premise that abortion is the killing of an innocent. After all, if one did not believe that abortion is such a killing, one would have no reason to believe that abortion is wrong on the basis that all killing of innocents is wrong. Thus, the argument properly reconstructed would look like this:

All killing of innocents is wrong.
An abortion is the killing of an innocent.
So, abortion is wrong.

Arguments that contain hidden premises are also called "**enthymematic arguments**" or "enthymemes." The premise that is hidden is sometimes called the "**enthymematic premise**."

The identification of hidden premises often helps to make progress in a debate. Sometimes hidden premises are obvious neither to the hearer nor to the speaker. When one brings them to light and makes them explicit, they can become the object of a debate themselves. It may, then turn out that even the proponent of the argument will agree that the hidden premise is objectionable.

Exercise F Hidden Premises

Identify the conclusion and all the premises (including the hidden premises) in the following arguments.

(a) Capital punishment is wrong because it is a killing.

(b) Abortion is wrong because it is the killing of an innocent child.

(c) Alcohol and drugs taken by pregnant women may have a detrimental impact on the development of the fetus, so they should never drink alcohol or take drugs.

(d) Sally has never received a violation from the Federal Aviation Administration during her 16-year flying career. Sally must be a great pilot.

(LSAT, Sample)

(e) The government of Zunimagua has refused to schedule free elections, release political prisoners, or restore freedom of speech; therefore, no more financial aid from the United States should be provided to Zunimagua.

(LSAT, Sample)

G. Fallacies (optional)

In their study of arguments, logicians have also encountered some problematic arguments. Some of them are invalid, though oftentimes, they appear to be valid on their surface. In other cases, the problems are different. Here are just some examples of the most famous fallacies.

EQUIVOCATION

One of the most famous of the fallacies is the fallacy of equivocation. The name of the fallacy comes from the Latin "aequus" (equal) and "voco" (call). The fallacy consists in using one word to cover two different concepts (meanings).

Consider the following example.

Anyone with grass in their possession violates U.S. drug laws.
President Biden has grass growing all around the White House.
So, President Biden violates the U.S. drug laws.

This argument has the structure of a valid argument form, of which the following argument is also an instance: "Anyone who has a valid NY driver's license has the right to drive a car in the U.S.A.; John Smith has a valid NY driver's license; so, John Smith has the right to drive a car in the U.S.A." And we could go on to cite other valid arguments that have this form. In fact, the logical form in question "All As are B, c is A (individual c has the property A); so, c is B" is valid. So, what's the problem?

The problem is that the word "grass" has multiple meanings. And, as it turns out, it occurs in two different meanings in the first and second premise. If we make this explicit, we will see that the argument no longer appears valid:

Anyone with marijuana in their possession violates U.S. drug laws.
President Biden has carpetgrass growing all around the White House.
So, President Biden violates the U.S. drug laws.

This argument is invalid.

Indeed, one should never use the same term with different meanings in an argument.

QUESTION-BEGGING ARGUMENTS

An interesting form of fallacy is the fallacy of begging the question. Consider this example:

God exists. The Bible says so. What the Bible says is true because, after all, the Bible is the word of God.

The argument may be reconstructed as follows:

The Bible says that God exists.
The Bible is the word of God.
God always speaks the truth.
What the Bible says is true.
So, God exists.

When the argument is reconstructed in this manner, it is clear that it is logically valid (after all, if X says that p and if what X says is true, then p). Moreover, for all we know, it might be that the argument's premises are true and so that its conclusion is true. Certainly, many people believe that is the case. So, what is wrong here?

Well, the problem is that, in order to accept some of the premises, we must already accept the conclusion of the argument! To accept that the Bible is the word of God, we must accept that God exists. Likewise, to accept that God always speaks the truth, we must accept that God exists. But the argument was supposed to establish that God exists! This argument purports to show that God exists on the basis of our already having accepted that God exists. It is circular in a way. Nobody who does not already believe that God exists will accept the conclusion. The argument begs the question.

AD HOMINEM FALLACY

A very old fallacy, often employed in politics, is the so-called *ad hominem* fallacy. It is directed at a person rather than their views.

> John Smith purports to have shown that the climate has changed and that the consequences will be disastrous for humankind. John Smith is a notorious womanizer. He has been unfaithful to his wife more times than I can count. He changes his personal climate constantly. Its consequences will be disastrous for him. But it surely does not follow that the consequences of climate change will be disastrous for humanity.

This is a personal attack without any engagement with the argument he makes.

IRRELEVANT CONCLUSION

Another fallacy and rhetorical figure frequently used in politics is the argument for an irrelevant conclusion. Here is a nice illustration from the presidential debate between Dan Quayle and Al Gore:

Quayle: Bill Clinton can't be trusted to tell the truth. He's deceived the American people time after time.

Gore: Dan, once again you're mistaken. Let's not forget who said, "Read my lips; no new taxes."

The fact that one person deceived the American people does not undermine the fact that another did so as well.

HASTY GENERALIZATION

This is a fallacy that all of us fall prey to. We tend to generalize hastily. We forget that a general statement is an extremely powerful claim. Consider:

All Americans smile all the time.

All Germans are tidy and punctual.

These are just a sample of the "nicer" prejudices to which we fall prey. What is particularly troubling is that we fall prey to them just after sampling a couple of instances.

NON SEQUITUR

There are many more types of fallacies. I have not discussed all of them here. But there is one final term that bags many of the fallacies without classifying them: *non sequitur* ("it does not follow" in Latin). In a *non sequitur* argument, it might look like there are structural reasons for the argument to be valid, though the argument is not valid. Here are a couple of examples (but you should not try to decipher a common structure):

> Some people are bad drivers. So, some drivers are bad people.

> The teacher said that Bob is good at *math*. It follows that Bob is lousy at history, English, and all the other subjects.

Summary

You have learned an important distinction between propositions and sentences. Propositions can be true or false; they are expressed by unambiguous declarative sentences. You have also learned that an argument is a group of propositions where one proposition (the conclusion) is taken to *follow from* the others (the premises). An argument has at least one premise and exactly one conclusion. There are deductive and non-deductive arguments. In a good non-deductive argument, the truth of the premises makes it more probable that the conclusion is true. In a deductive logically valid argument, the truth of the premises guarantees that the conclusion is true. Arguments are valid (or invalid) in virtue of their logical form.

An argument form is **logically valid** if and only if it is impossible for its conclusion to be false while its premises are true.

An argument is **sound** if and only if it is logically valid and all of its premises are true.

Some arguments (called "enthymematic") have missing premises. You have also learned about some famous fallacies.

The following table summarizes the properties of arguments and propositions:

propositions	arguments
true / false	valid / invalid
	sound / unsound

Since the premises of an argument are propositions, they may be true or false. The conclusion of an argument is likewise a proposition, so it may be true or false.

However, arguments are neither true nor false. An argument involves an inference (a transition, so to speak) from the premises to the conclusion. When we evaluate an argument, we evaluate how good the inference is (how good the transition from the premises to the conclusion is).

It is logical nonsense to say that:	
a proposition is valid / invalid / sound / unsound	an argument is true / false

It isn't nonsense to say „Bob's made a valid claim," is it?

In ordinary language, we use these terms differently. In logic, they have a technical meaning.

Unit 1.2

The Basics of Propositional Logic

Overview

In this unit, we will learn the basics of an old logical theory, the so-called propositional (statement) logic. The key issue for any logical theory is to propose a way of thinking about complex propositions. In propositional logic, complex propositions are constructed using five basic connectives of negation, conjunction, disjunction, conditional, and biconditional.

In this unit, you will learn:
- five connectives (of negation, conjunction, disjunction, conditional, biconditional),
- basic truth tables for each connective.

In this unit, you will learn how to:
- distinguish simple and complex propositions,
- symbolize very basic English sentences (Units 1.3-1.5 will develop the skill)
- construct a symbolization key
- recognize negations, conjunctions, disjunctions, conditionals, and biconditionals in English
- paraphrase conditionals into the standard *if-then* form.

Time:	4-6 hours
Difficulty:	●●●○○○○
Status:	**Essential**/Recommended/Optional
Number of exercises:	32
Prerequisites:	Introduction, Unit 1.1

A. Propositional Logic as a Logical Theory

One of the goals of logic is to find out which arguments are valid. This is a very difficult task. Like scientists in general, logicians approach it step by step. First, they propose relatively simple theories based on idealizations and simplifications. Then, gradually, they propose more and more complex theories that are also better at capturing what we consider to be valid arguments.

The first and the simplest of such theories is propositional logic. It is also sometimes referred to as statement logic or sentential logic. It is a relatively simple theory (as far as logical theories are concerned), which is not to say that all the logical techniques it introduces are simple.

One of the basic assumptions of this theory concerns the question: **What is the logical structure of complex propositions?** According to propositional logic, complex propositions are made up of simpler propositions by means of the so-called **propositional connectives** (or connectives, for short), i.e., such expressions as *not, and, or, if...then*, and *if and only if.*

Propositional logic is quite impressive, especially in view of its simplicity. It is a simple theory, and it also has its problems. The problems are handled by other logical theories.

 While some of the concepts of propositional logic are extremely intuitive and obvious, others are not. I will stress the points at which the theory oversimplifies matters. Be prepared for that.

One of such better, but also more complex, theories is the so-called quantificational or quantifier logic (which includes predicate logic and the logic of relations; cf. Workbooks 4-7). It captures as valid all those arguments that turn out to be valid in propositional logic, but it also captures as valid some other arguments that propositional logic wrongly qualifies as invalid. This is because quantificational logic has a more refined way of analyzing the logical structure of complex and simple propositions. It treats complex propositions as not only composed of the five connectives but also as composed of the so-called quantifiers (expressions such as *all* and *some*).

But this is not the end of the story. It turns out that quantificational logic is not the ultimate theory, for it again does not capture as valid all the arguments that we would want it to capture as valid. And so modal logics have been proposed, which analyze the behavior of such operators as *necessarily* and *possibly*. Deontic logics analyze the behavior of operators *permissibly* and *obligatorily*. And so on and so forth.

The science of logic is open-ended. At the end of the Workbooks, you will have only gotten your feet wet.

B. Simple and Complex Propositions

In the last unit, we said that arguments are valid (or invalid) by virtue of their logical form. One of the main tasks of a logical theory is to provide tools to grasp the logical form of propositions. In particular, the theory will treat some propositions as simple and others as complex.

In propositional logic, complex propositions are composed out of other propositions by means of one of five connectives: *not* (negation), *and* (conjunction), *or* (disjunction), *if...then* (conditional), and *if and only if* (biconditional). Propositions that are not so composed are called simple propositions. In other words, a proposition is simple just in case it is neither a negation, a conjunction, a disjunction, a conditional, nor a biconditional.

> There are five propositional connectives and five corresponding types of complex propositions.

Propositional connective	Type of complex proposition
not...	negation
...and...	conjunction
...or...	disjunction
if...then...	conditional
...if and only if...	biconditional

Consider some examples of complex propositions first (the occurrences of the connectives have been marked):

Charlie did [not] ask what the time was.
Susan borrowed a book from Ann, [and] she did [not] return it.
[If] Alan keeps his room tidy for more than a week [then] he will get a cat [or] a dog.
Kerstin will go out with Tim [if and only if] he apologizes to her first.

The following propositions are simple (in propositional logic):

The Speaker of the House has confirmed the rumor that work on the health bill has stopped three weeks before Christmas.
Mary will feed the hamster.
All men are jealous.
Whoever lives around the corner of Elm Street has a horrible view.

Simple propositions need not be expressed by simple sentences. What accounts for logical simplicity is the lack of connectives in a proposition. More precisely, logically simple propositions neither contain any connectives nor is it possible to paraphrase them in terms of complex propositions.

Definition of complex and simple propositions

A **complex proposition** (in propositional logic) is a proposition constructed from other propositions by means of one of the propositional connectives.

A **simple proposition** (in propositional logic) is a proposition that is not constructed from other propositions by means of any propositional connective.

Exercise B. Simple vs. Complex Propositions

Identify simple and complex propositions.
Mark the connectives in complex propositions.

(a)   John is one of those extraordinarily nice men who hate all women that wear big hats.

(b)   John invited Susan out and she agreed.

(c)   If Susan does not come on time, John will be distraught.

(d)   Susan was quite punctual.

(e)   John did not believe his eyes.

(f)   Susan was wearing the biggest hat John has ever seen in his entire life.

(g)   John started pleading for Susan to take off what seemed to him to be one of the ugliest things ever produced by a human hand.

(h)   Susan agreed to take off the hat if and only if John takes off the bow tie and the cowboy boots.

(i)   Susan's ex-husband wore bow ties, and her ex-father-in-law wore cowboy boots.

C. The Symbolization Key (Legend)

We will learn to use the symbolic notation of propositional logic to represent propositions expressed by English sentences. In other words, we will learn to **symbolize** English sentences. Simple propositions will be represented by the so-called **propositional constants** (written as the capital letters of the alphabet: A, B, C, etc.). Complex propositions will be represented by complex formulas constructed from propositional constants, connectives, and parentheses.

First, we need to learn to construct the so-called **symbolization key** (legend).

> The **symbolization key** is a list of all simple propositions that occur in a proposition (a group of propositions) with their unique (one-to-one) letter assignments.

Consider, for example, the following proposition:

John is rich if and only if Susan is poor.

To construct the symbolization key, it is useful to mark all the connectives:

John is rich if and only if Susan is poor.

It is now clear what the simple propositions are. We need to list them and assign unique letters to them, for example:

R: John is **r**ich.
P: Susan is **p**oor.

Mark all the connectives.

You will see what the simple propositions are.

List them. Assign unique letters.

What letters stand for what simple proposition is almost completely arbitrary: you choose! It is useful to select a letter that will clearly remind us of the proposition it represents. Try not to use "T" or "F" because they play a special role. However, two rules must be obeyed:

> **"No Complexity" Rule:** No letter can represent a complex proposition.
> **"1-1" Rule:** Each simple proposition must have a unique letter assignment.

In constructing the symbolization key, it is useful to follow a 3-step procedure:
   a. Mark all connectives.
   b. List all simple propositions.
   c. Make one-to-one letter assignments.

Example 1

Let us construct a symbolization key for the following proposition:

> If John is rich then he is not handsome, and if John is handsome then he is not a rich man.

> Do it on your own:
> ☐ mark all connectives
> ☐ list all simple propositions
> ☐ make 1-to-1 letter assignments.

The first thing to do is to mark all connectives to see clearly what the simple propositions are:

> ⬚If⬚ John is rich ⬚then⬚ he is ⬚not⬚ handsome, ⬚and⬚ ⬚if⬚ John is handsome ⬚then⬚ he is ⬚not⬚ a rich man.

We list all simple propositions:

> John is rich
> John is handsome

> Don't forget to mark negations!

Note that "John is rich" and "He is a rich man" express the same proposition. The same proposition is also expressed by "John is handsome" and "he is handsome." (Go back to Unit 1.1 if you are puzzled.)

Finally, we need to do the one-to-one letter assignment for each proposition. We have two simple propositions, so we choose two capital letters. What two letters we choose does not matter. But it is useful to use letters that we can easily associate with the propositions. For example:

> **R**: John is **r**ich
> **H**: John is **h**andsome

Of course, we could have picked the letters *J* and *O* as well. Indeed, any two different letters would do.

Example 2

Let us construct a symbolization key for the following proposition:

> If Debbie is not a doctor then she is smart, and if Debbie is a doctor then she is smart and wealthy.

> Do it on your own:
> ☐ mark all connectives
> ☐ list all simple propositions
> ☐ make 1-to-1 letter assignments

We mark all connectives first so we can see what the simple propositions are:

> |If| Debbie is |not| a doctor |then| she is smart, |and| |if| she is a doctor |then| she is smart |and| wealthy.

We then list all simple propositions:

> Don't forget to mark negations!

> Debbie is a doctor
> Debbie is smart
> Debbie is wealthy

Once again, we need to get rid of the indexical *she*. The sentence "Debbie is smart and wealthy" expresses a conjunction of two simple propositions: "Debbie is smart" and "Debbie is wealthy."

Finally, we need to do the one-to-one letter assignment for each proposition. For example:

> **D**: Debbie is a **d**octor
> **S**: Debbie is **s**mart
> **W**: Debbie is **w**ealthy

Again, any three different letters would do.

Example 3

Let us construct a symbolization key for an argument (i.e., a group of propositions):

(1) John will get an A if and only if he works hard.
(2) If Susan stops partying then she will get an A.
(3) Susan and John did not get an A.
(4) So, Susan did not stop partying and John did not work hard.

> Do it on your own:
> ☐ mark all connectives
> ☐ list all simple propositions
> ☐ make 1-to-1 letter assignments

We proceed in the same way as above. However, it is crucial to treat the group of propositions as a whole. So we work with all four propositions at each step. We mark all connectives:

(1) John will get an A [if and only if] he works hard.

(2) [If] Susan stops partying [then] she will get an A.

(3) Susan [and] John did [not] get an A.

(4) So, Susan did [not] stop partying [and] John did [not] work hard.

Don't forget about negations!

If we were to list the simple propositions mechanically, we would obtain the list on the left (the numbers in parentheses refer to the proposition number where the proposition occurs). Some of these, however, differ only in the tenses. In propositional logic, we abstract from tenses.

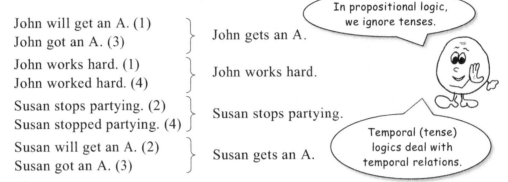

John will get an A. (1)
John got an A. (3)
} John gets an A.

John works hard. (1)
John worked hard. (4)
} John works hard.

Susan stops partying. (2)
Susan stopped partying. (4)
} Susan stops partying.

Susan will get an A. (2)
Susan got an A. (3)
} Susan gets an A.

In propositional logic, we ignore tenses.

Temporal (tense) logics deal with temporal relations.

In other words, we will treat sentences formulated in different tenses as expressing the same proposition. It does not matter in which of the tenses you phrase the propositions in the symbolization key. The important thing is not to distinguish between sentences merely based on their tenses. Above, I have rendered all sentences in the simple present. This is a useful strategy to follow, but it is not obligatory. However, it helps to control the temptation to add sentences that differ only in the tense to the list.

Finally, we assign four different letters to the propositions in the following way, for example:

J: John gets an A.
H: John works **h**ard.
P: Susan stops **p**artying.
S: **S**usan gets an A.

However, the following symbolization key is also fine.

J: John will get an A.
H: John works **h**ard.
P: Susan stops **p**artying.
S: **S**usan will get an A.

COMMON ERRORS

The construction of a symbolization key is sometimes tricky. You'll get better at it with practice. For now, let's look at some common errors.

Error 1: Failure to obey the "No Complexity" Rule

The symbolization key must not include any complex propositions. In particular, it must not include negations! They are easy to miss… Here are examples of how you can go wrong:

R: ~~If John is rich then he is not handsome~~
H: ~~If John is handsome then he is not a rich man~~

R: John is rich
N: ~~John is not rich~~
H: John is handsome
D: ~~John is not handsome~~

Error 2: One proposition cannot be represented by more than one letter

The symbolization key contains simple propositions. However, one proposition can be expressed by many sentences. Consider, for example, the following sentences:

R: ~~John is rich~~
M: ~~John is a rich man~~
S: ~~John is a rich person~~

Although different sentences are used, they all express the same proposition. They should thus be represented by a single letter. For all of these sentences, there should be only one entry in the symbolization key, e.g.:

R: John is rich

Error 3: One letter cannot represent more than one proposition

Here is another way in which one can fail to obey the "1-1" Rule. You might be tempted to keep letter assignments mnemonic but fail to assign different letters to different propositions:

J: John is rich
J: John is handsome

Error 4: Sentences with indexicals used

Bear in mind that sentences with indexicals do not uniquely represent propositions. They *must not* be used in a symbolization key.

J: John is rich
H: ~~He is handsome~~

Error 5: The symbolization key does not contain propositions

Symbolization keys in propositional logic contain propositions. Propositions should not be abbreviated in any other way than by assigning propositional letters to them.

R: ~~rich~~

H: ~~handsome~~

Error 6: Wrong letters are used

By convention, propositions are represented by capital letters. Do not use anything else. It is important to stick to conventions.

~~r:~~ John is rich

~~h:~~ John is handsome

~~Rich:~~   John is rich

~~Handsome:~~   John is handsome

Exercise C.1. Symbolization Key Errors

In Ex. C.1-3, identify errors committed in the construction of symbolization keys.

(a)   John invited Susan out and she agreed.

J: John invites Susan out
S: She agrees

(b)   John did not believe his eyes.

J: John did not believe his eyes

(c)   Susan's ex-husband wore bow ties and her ex-father-in-law wore cowboy boots.

B: bow ties
C: cowboy boots

(d)   Susan agreed to take off the hat if and only if John takes off the bow tie and the cowboy boots.

S: Susan agrees to take off the hat
J: John takes off the bow tie
J: John takes off the cowboy boots

Exercise C.2. Symbolization Key Errors

(a)   John will be distraught if and only if Susan does not come on time.
Susan was punctual.
So, John was not distraught.

J: John is distraught
S: Susan comes on time
P: Susan is quite punctual

(b)   John will be distraught if and only if Susan does not come on time.
      Susan was quite punctual.
      So, John was not distraught.

      J: John will be distraught
      S: Susan comes on time
      W: John was distraught

(c)   John will be distraught if and only if Susan does not come on time.
      Susan was quite punctual.
      So, John was not distraught.

      John: John will be distraught
      Susan: Susan comes on time

Exercise C.3. Symbolization Key Errors

(a)   John invited Susan out and she didn't agree to go out with him.
      If Susan agrees to go out with John then she will wear a big hat.
      Susan will wear a big hat if and only if she will want to teach John a lesson.
      If Susan wants to teach John a lesson, then he will not invite her out.

      J: John invited Susan out
      S: She didn't agree to go out with him
      A: Susan agrees to go out with John
      S: Susan will wear a big hat
      J: She will want to teach John a lesson
      W: Susan wants to teach John a lesson
      H: He will not invite her out

(b)   If Ben swims, then he will jog or he will diet.
      If Ben diets then she will not jog.
      If Ben does not jog, then he will not swim.
      If Ben is on a diet, then he will not swim and he will not jog.

      S: Ben swims
      J: Ben will jog
      D: Ben will diet
      B: Ben diets
      N: Ben does not jog
      A: Ben is on a diet
      H: He swims
      E: He jogs

Exercise C.4. Symbolization Key

Construct symbolization keys for each of the following propositions.

(a)   John invited Susan out and she agreed.

    +---+
    | |
    | |
    | |
    +---+

(b)   John did not believe his eyes.

    +---+
    | |
    | |
    | |
    +---+

(c)   Susan's ex-husband wore bow ties and her ex-father-in-law wore cowboy boots.

    +---+
    | |
    | |
    | |
    +---+

(d)   Susan agreed to take off the hat if and only if John takes off the bow tie and the
       cowboy boots.

    +---+
    | |
    | |
    | |
    +---+

Exercise C.5. Symbolization Key

Construct symbolization keys for each of the following groups of propositions.

(a)   John will be distraught if and only if Susan does not come on time.
       Susan was punctual.
       So, John was not distraught.

    +---+
    | |
    | |
    | |
    +---+

(b)   John invited Susan out and she didn't agree to go out with him.
       If Susan agrees to go out with John then she will wear a big hat.
       Susan will wear a big hat if and only if she wants to teach John a lesson.
       If Susan wants to teach John a lesson, then he will not invite her out.

    +---+
    | |
    | |
    | |
    | |
    | |
    +---+

D. Negation

We turn to the five types of complex propositions (negations, conjunctions, disjunctions, biconditionals, and conditionals), which are constructed from simpler propositions by means of the five connectives. Let us start with negation.

The following table summarizes the basic information about negation (note that any proposition can enter into the box ⌞_____⌟):

Connective:	It is not the case that
Symbol:	~
Symbol name:	tilde
Logical form:	~⌞_____⌟
	~p
Component:	negated proposition: p

Other symbols are sometimes used to represent negation, e.g., ¬, −.

Here is an example of a negation:

(1) It is not the case that the sun shines.

A **negation** is a complex proposition that is composed of the tilde and some proposition, which is called the **negated proposition**. In sentence (1), "The sun shines" is the negated proposition. The negated proposition can be either simple or complex. In (1), the negated proposition is simple. We will later consider examples where the negated proposition is complex. After we construct a symbolization key, we can symbolize (1) as:

[1] ~S   **S**: The **s**un shines.

The negation connective is a **one-place connective**: it forms a complex proposition out of *one* simpler proposition. The other four connectives are two-place connectives, i.e., they form a complex proposition out of two simpler propositions.

THE BASIC TRUTH TABLE FOR NEGATION

The meaning of the negation connective is given by the so-called basic truth table for negation. (Logicians say that the basic truth table specifies the semantic properties of the negation connective.) The basic truth table for negation tells us how the truth value of a negation depends on the truth value of the negated proposition.

In the case of negation, the basic truth table is exceedingly intuitive. The negated proposition can be either true or false. If the negated proposition p is true then the negation ~p will be false. If the negated proposition p is false then the negation ~p will be true. You can check that this is so in the following example (or skip to the bottom of next page).

Consider the proposition "The cup is full of coffee." Let us first consider a situation in which the proposition "The cup is full of coffee" is true. The capital letter "T" will indicate that the proposition is true, while the capital letter "F" will indicate that the proposition is false. This is why we should abstain from using these two letters in our symbolization keys.

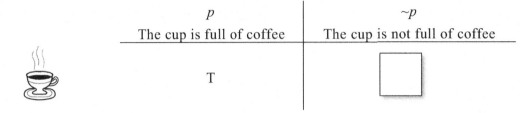

	p The cup is full of coffee	*~p* The cup is not full of coffee
	T	

Given the way things are (the cup is full of coffee), to say "The cup is *not* full of coffee" is to say something false. (Write "F" in the above space.)

Consider the situation depicted below, in which the proposition "The cup is full of coffee" is false.

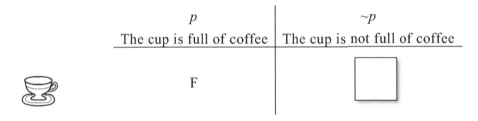

	p The cup is full of coffee	*~p* The cup is not full of coffee
	F	

Now to say "The cup is *not* full of coffee" is to say something true. (Write "T" in the above space.)

This relationship between the truth value of a negated proposition and the resulting truth value of the negation will always be preserved, no matter what propositions we consider. This is summarized in the basic truth table for negation.

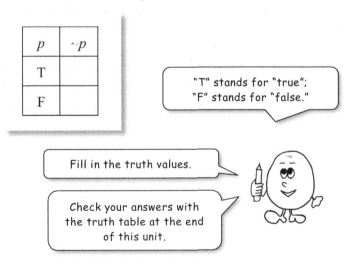

p	*~p*
T	
F	

"T" stands for "true"; "F" stands for "false."

Fill in the truth values.

Check your answers with the truth table at the end of this unit.

NEGATIONS IN ENGLISH

The expression *it is not the case that* is a paradigmatic reading of the negation connective. However, negations can be expressed in English using other phrases as well. The following sentences express the same proposition that is expressed by sentence (1):

(1a) The sun does |not| shine.
(1b) |It would be false to say that| the sun shines.
(1c) |The claim that| the sun shines |is a falsehood|.
(1d) The sun |failed| to shine.

While these sentences do differ in meaning, they all express the same proposition from the point of view of propositional logic. This is because their truth value depends on the truth value of the component proposition in the way characteristic of negation.

To symbolize (1a)-(1d), we need to construct a symbolization key:

[1a-1d] ~S   S: The sun shines

Example

Consider now an example where the negated proposition is complex, for example, a negation. Of course, other complex propositions, i.e., conjunctions, disjunctions, etc., can also be negated; cf. Unit 1.3.

(2) |It is not the case that| the sun does |not| shine.

Here, the negated proposition ("The sun does not shine") is itself a negation. (2) is thus a negation of a negation, which we can represent as follows:

[2] ~~S

Example

(3) |It would be a lie to claim that| |it is not the case that| the sun does |not| shine.

We can symbolize (3) as:

[3] ~~~S

Could we not drop the double negations?
(2) could be represented as S,
(3) as ~S...

Symbolizations ought to preserve the logical structure of the original propositions as closely as possible!

We will later learn that ~~S is logically equivalent to S, and ~~~S is logically equivalent to ~S. However, it is a good rule of thumb that symbolizations ought to preserve the logical structure of the original propositions. After all, we are often confused about what is logically equivalent to what. We need logic and its techniques to help us.

Exercise D.1. Match Negations

A: **A**nn makes dinner   B: **B**en makes lunch

~A ☐   1. It's not the case that Ben didn't make lunch.

~~A ☐   2. Ann didn't fail to make dinner.

~B ☐   3. Ben didn't make lunch.

~~B ☐   4. Ann failed to make dinner.

Symbolize the propositions. Match the symbolizations with the English sentences by writing the appropriate numbers in the boxes.

Exercise D.2. Match Negations

A: **A**nn makes dinner

~~A   ☐   1. Ann didn't fail to make dinner.

~~~A ☐   2. It's false that Ann didn't make dinner.

             3. It's a falsehood that Ann didn't fail to make dinner.

~~~~A ☐   4. It's not false that Ann didn't fail to make dinner.

             5. It's not true that Ann didn't fail to make dinner.

Exercise D.3. Match Negations

B: **B**en makes lunch

~~B   ☐   1. Ben didn't fail to make lunch.

~~~B ☐   2. It is false that Ben didn't fail to make lunch.

             3. It is false that Ben didn't make lunch.

~~~~B ☐   4. It isn't false that Ben didn't fail to make lunch.

             5. It isn't false that Ben didn't make lunch.

Exercise D.4. Match Negations

J: **J**ung's theory is true

~J   ☐   1. Jung's theory isn't false.

~~J   ☐   2. Jung's theory is false.

             3. It is not the case that Jung's theory isn't false.

~~~J ☐   4. It is not the case that it is false that Jung's theory isn't false.

~~~~J ☐

Exercise D.5. Match Negations

A: Adler's theory is true

~A ⬜

~~A ⬜

~~~A ⬜

~~~~A ⬜

1. It's not the case that Adler's theory isn't true.

2. It is false that it's not the case that Adler's theory isn't true.

3. Adler's theory isn't true.

4. It's wrong to think that it is false that it's not the case that Adler's theory isn't true.

5. It's not the case that Adler's theory isn't false.

Exercise D.6 Negations

A: **Abe** will make dinner   B: **Betty** will make dinner

(a)   Abe will not make dinner.

(b)   It would be false to say that Betty will make dinner.

(c)   It would be false to say that Betty will not make dinner.

(d)   It would be preposterous to think that Abe will make dinner.

(e)   It would be preposterous to think that it would not be the case that Betty will not make dinner.

(f)   Abe failed to make dinner.

E. Conjunction

The following table summarizes the basic information about conjunction (any propositions can enter into the boxes):

Connective: and

Symbol: •

Symbol name: dot

Logical form: [_____] • [_____]

$p \cdot q$

Components: conjuncts: p, q

Here is an example of a conjunction:

(1) Ann has an apple [and] Ann has a banana.

For stylistic reasons, we would rather say:

(1a) Ann has an apple [and] a banana.

(1a) expresses the very same proposition that (1) expresses. However, (1) makes it more clear that the dot is a connective that binds two propositions, i.e., it is a two-place connective.

The components of a conjunction are called conjuncts. In (1), the proposition "Ann has an apple" is the first conjunct, while "Ann has a banana" is the second conjunct.

THE BASIC TRUTH TABLE FOR CONJUNCTION

The basic truth table for conjunction is very intuitive as well. The truth table tells us how the truth value of a conjunction $p \bullet q$ depends on the truth values of the conjuncts p and q. Since we have two component propositions (p and q), we need to consider all possible truth value assignments for p and q. There are four different possibilities:

p is true, q is true;
p is true, q is false;
p is false, q is true;
p is false, q is false.

If you know how to fill out the truth table for conjunction, you may skip the more detailed explanation.

[What Ann has]	p Ann has an apple	q Ann has a banana	$p \bullet q$ Ann has an apple and a banana
🍎🍌	T	T	☐

If it is true that Ann has an apple and it is also true that Ann has a banana, then it will be true to say that Ann has an apple and a banana.

[What Ann has]	p Ann has an apple	q Ann has a banana	$p \bullet q$ Ann has an apple and a banana
🍎	T	F	☐

If it is true that Ann has an apple but it is not true that Ann has a banana, then it will be false to say that Ann has both an apple and a banana. Likewise:

[What Ann has]	p Ann has an apple	q Ann has a banana	$p \bullet q$ Ann has an apple and a banana
	F	T	

If it is not true that Ann has an apple but it is true that Ann has a banana, then it will be false to say that Ann has both an apple and a banana. Finally:

[What Ann has]	p Ann has an apple	q Ann has a banana	$p \bullet q$ Ann has an apple and a banana
	F	F	

If it is not true that Ann has an apple and it is not true that Ann has a banana, then it will be false to say that Ann has an apple and a banana.

> A conjunction is true if and only if both conjuncts are true.
>
> A conjunction is false if and only if at least one conjunct is false.

p	q	$p \bullet q$
T	T	
T	F	
F	T	
F	F	

Fill in the truth values.

Check your answers with the truth table at the end of this unit.

CONJUNCTIONS IN ENGLISH

There are many ways in which conjunctions may be expressed in English, among them:

... and ...	... although ...	... while …
both ... and ...	... even though ...	... despite the fact that ...
... as well as ...	... nevertheless …	... moreover …
... but ...	... still …	... in addition …
... however ...	... but still ...	...; ...
... though ...	... also ...	..., ...

The subtle meaning variations are disregarded by the theory of propositional logic. A conjunction is understood as any sentence whose truth value depends on the truth values of the conjuncts in the way specified by the basic truth table for conjunction.

Example

(2) John loves Mary even though she barely tolerates him.

[2] J • M

> **J**: John loves Mary
> **M**: Mary barely tolerates John

From the point of view of propositional logic, conjunction [2] also represents the following sentences:

(2a) John loves Mary despite the fact that she barely tolerates him.
(2b) John loves Mary and she barely tolerates him.
(2c) John loves Mary but she barely tolerates him.
(2d) John loves Mary while she barely tolerates him.
(2f) John loves Mary, however, she barely tolerates him.
(2g) John loves Mary; she barely tolerates him.
(2h) It is both true that John loves Mary as well as that she barely tolerates him.

Undoubtedly, sentences (2a)-(2h) differ in subtle shades of meaning. However, they are all true if and only if both components are true, which is why they are all represented as conjunction [2].

In the above examples, the components of the conjunctions were simple propositions. However, this need not be the case, as the following examples show.

Example

Here is an example where both conjuncts are negations.

(3) Andrew has no job; in addition, he can't cook.

[3] ~J • ~C

> **J**: Andrew has a job
> **C**: Andrew can cook

Example

If one of the conjuncts is a conjunction, we will need to enclose the conjunction component in parentheses:

(4) Ann has a dog while Betty has both a dog and a cat.

[4] A • (D • C)

> **A**: Ann has a dog
> **D**: Betty has a dog
> **C**: Betty has a cat

The parentheses are needed because the dot is a two-place connective, i.e., it binds two and *only two* propositions. If an English sentence suggests that there are more than two conjuncts, parentheses must be used.

Example

Consider the following example (we will discuss such cases in more detail in Unit 1.3):

    (5) Abe jogs, swims, and diets.

> **J**: Abe **j**ogs
> **S**: Abe **s**wims
> **D**: Abe **d**iets

    [5] (J • S) • D

This is one way in which the parentheses can be placed. But the following is equally good:

    [5′] J • (S • D)

We will later demonstrate that conjunction is associative; [5] and [5′] are in fact logically equivalent. It is crucial, however, that the parentheses be placed. The following formula is logical gibberish:

Symbolize the propositions. Match the symbolizations with the English sentences by writing in the appropriate numbers.

Exercise E.1. Match Conjunctions

A: Ann has a dog   **B**: Ben has a dog   **C**: Ann has a cat   **D**: Dan has a cat

A • B ☐	1. Ann and Ben both have a dog.
A • C ☐	2. Ann and Dan have a cat.
	3. Ann has a cat and, moreover, she has a dog.
B • D ☐	4. Ann has a dog, however, Ben also has a dog.
C • D ☐	5. Ann has both a dog and a cat.
D • C ☐	6. Ben has a dog but Dan has a cat.
	7. Dan has a cat even though Ann has a cat as well.
C • A ☐	8. Dan and Ann have a cat.

Exercise E.2. Match Conjunctions

A: **A**nn has a dog   **B**: **B**en has a dog   **C**: **A**nn has a **c**at   **D**: **D**an has a cat

A • ~B ☐

~B • A ☐

~D • C ☐

B • (A • C) ☐

~B • (A • C) ☐

(C • D) • (A • B) ☐

1. Dan doesn't have a cat despite the fact that Ann has a cat.

2. Ben has a dog but Ann has a dog and a cat.

3. Ben does not have a dog while Ann has both a dog and a cat.

4. Ben does not have a dog but Ann does.

5. Ann has a dog although Ben doesn't.

6. Ann and Dan both have a cat while Ann and Ben both have a dog.

7. Although Dan does not have a cat, Ann does.

Exercise E.3. Match Conjunctions

A: **A**dler's theory is true.   **J**: **J**ung's theory is true.   **R**: **F**reud's theory is true

A • ~J ☐

A • ~R ☐

~J • ~R ☐

A • (J • R) ☐

(A • J) • R ☐

1. While Adler's theory is true Freud's theory is false.

2. Jung's theory is false and so is Freud's.

3. Jung's theory and Freud's theory are both false.

4. Adler's theory, Jung's theory, and Freud's theory are true.

5. Adler's theory is true but Jung's theory is false.

6. Adler's theory is true but Freud's theory is not true.

Exercise E.4. Conjunctions

A: **A**be will make dinner   **B**: **B**etty will make dinner   **C**: **C**hris will make lunch

(a) Abe and Betty will both make dinner.

(b) Abe will make dinner but Betty will also make dinner.

(c) Abe will make dinner but Betty will not.

(d) Abe will not make dinner but Betty will.

(e) Abe will make dinner while Chris will make lunch.

(f) Chris will not make lunch even though Abe will make dinner.

(g) Despite the fact that Abe will not make dinner, Betty will make it.

(h) Abe will not make dinner despite the fact that Chris will make lunch.

F. Disjunction

The following table summarizes the basic information about disjunction (any propositions can enter into the boxes):

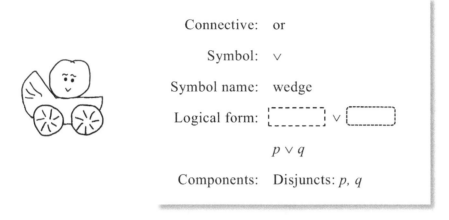

Connective:	or
Symbol:	∨
Symbol name:	wedge
Logical form:	[_ _ _ _ _] ∨ (_ _ _ _)
	$p \lor q$
Components:	Disjuncts: p, q

Here is an example of a disjunction:

(1) Ann has an apple or Ann has a banana.

Again, we would rather express (1) as (1a) or (1b).

(1a) Ann has an apple or a banana.
(1b) Ann has either an apple or a banana.

The components of a disjunction are called disjuncts. In (1), the proposition "Ann has an apple" is the first disjunct, while "Ann has a banana" is the second disjunct.

THE BASIC TRUTH TABLE FOR DISJUNCTION

Unlike the truth tables for negation and conjunction, the truth table for disjunction is not as intuitive. There is an intuitive problem with the first row of the truth table. Let us consider the unproblematic rows first.

[What Ann has]	p Ann has an apple	q Ann has a banana	$p \lor q$ Ann has an apple or a banana
🍎	T	F	☐

If it is true that Ann has an apple but not true that she has a banana, then it will be true to say that Ann has an apple or a banana.

[What Ann has]	p Ann has an apple	q Ann has a banana	$p \lor q$ Ann has an apple or a banana
🍌	F	T	☐

If Ann does not have an apple but she does have a banana, it will still be true to say that Ann has an apple or a banana.

[What Ann has]	p Ann has an apple	q Ann has a banana	$p \vee q$ Ann has an apple or a banana
	F	F	

If Ann has neither an apple nor a banana, then it will be false to say that Ann has an apple or a banana.

Now consider the first row of the truth table, where it is both true that Ann has an apple and that Ann has a banana. Imagine that I say, "Ann has an apple or a banana." Is what I have said true or false?

[What Ann has]	p Ann has an apple	q Ann has a banana	$p \vee q$ Ann has an apple or a banana
🍎🍌	T	T	

Well, when I ask this question of students in a logic class, about 50% say that the sentence is true, and another 50% say that the sentence is false. Some students change their minds in the middle. We sometimes use disjunctions in an *exclusive* manner and sometimes in an *inclusive* manner.

When a strict kitchen lady says, "You can have either chocolate cake or ice cream for dessert," while wagging her finger at you and raising her eyebrows as if to warn you, you will rather naturally understand that you can have either chocolate cake or ice cream but *not both of them*. The *exclusive disjunction* is false when both disjuncts are true.

In many other situations, however, we understand disjunctions in an inclusive manner. The sentence "John or Mary will work late" certainly leaves open the possibility that both John and Mary will work late. On the most natural reading, it represents an inclusive disjunction, which says that *at least one* of them will work late. The *inclusive disjunction* is true when both disjuncts are true.

So there are two types of disjunction: **inclusive disjunction** (true when both disjuncts are true) and **exclusive disjunction** (false when both disjuncts are true).

Logicians have decided to understand the wedge ($\vee$) as a symbol of *inclusive disjunction*, which is true when both disjuncts are true.

[What Ann has]	p Ann has an apple	q Ann has a banana	$p \vee q$ Ann has an apple or a banana
	T	T	T

Sometimes, though rarely, a different symbol (⊥) is used to represent exclusive disjunction. As you will see in Unit 1.4, there is a surefire way of representing any exclusive disjunction by means of inclusive disjunction, negation, and conjunction. So we will not lose anything if we do not add ⊥ to the repertoire of connectives.

A disjunction is true if and only if *at least one* disjunct is true.

A disjunction is false if and only if both disjuncts are false.

Fill in the truth values. (You should check at the end of this unit that you have done so correctly.)

p	q	$p \vee q$
T	T	
T	F	
F	T	
F	F	

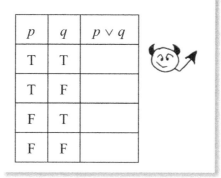

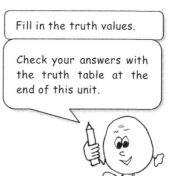

Fill in the truth values.

Check your answers with the truth table at the end of this unit.

DISJUNCTIONS IN ENGLISH

Disjunctions are expressed by such phrases as:

... or ...   ... or else ...

either ... or ...   at least one of ... is true

Example

(2) Ann will marry Burt or Chris.

[2] B ∨ C

B: Ann will marry **Burt**

C: Ann will marry **Chris**

You might point out that the most natural interpretation of sentence (2) would be as an exclusive disjunction. However, we will treat all disjunctions as inclusive disjunctions unless the exclusive disjunction is indicated by the addition of a phrase like *but not both*.

Isn't (2) an exclusive disjunction? Ann can't marry both Burt and Chris...

We will stick to the rule that all disjunctions are inclusive unless they contain an explicit mention of a phrase like "but not both." See Unit 1.4.

Why many disjunctive claims are inclusive…

It turns out that the inclusive understanding of "or" makes better sense of the inferential relations of many disjunctive claims. Imagine the following conversation:

> Jane says, "John was in Oxford or in Cambridge, I think."
> Jack replies, "No, that's not true. He was neither in Oxford nor in Cambridge."

Jack takes the claim "John was neither in Oxford nor in Cambridge" to be a negation of Jane's disjunctive claim. In doing so, he treats the disjunction that Jane has expressed as an inclusive disjunction. The negation of an inclusive interpretation of Jane's claim is "John was neither in Oxford nor in Cambridge." The negation of an exclusive interpretation of Jane's claim is "John was in Oxford if and only if he was in Cambridge."

When we deny disjunctions "*p* or *q*," we usually do so by appealing to claims of the form "neither *p* nor *q*" rather than biconditionals "*p* if and only if *q*." In doing so, we take disjunctions to be inclusive.

Further Examples

Disjuncts may be complex propositions. Consider a disjunction whose first disjunct is complex:

(3) Either Susan will get a dog and a parrot or
      she will get a cat.

[3] $(D \bullet P) \vee C$

C: Susan will get a **c**at
D: Susan will get a **d**og
P: Susan will get a **p**arrot

Here is a disjunction where the second disjunct is complex.

(4) Either Susan will get a dog or she will
      get a cat but not a parrot.

[4] $D \vee (C \bullet {\sim}P)$

Sometimes a comma may indicate a disjunction. Here is such an example.

(5) Susan will get a dog, a cat, or a parrot.

[5a] $D \vee (C \vee P)$
[5b] $(D \vee C) \vee P$

Proposition (5) can be symbolized either as [5a] or [5b]. However, the parentheses are critical because the wedge is a two-place connective.

We will study such and other complex symbolizations more systematically in Units 1.3-1.5.

Exercise F.1. Match Disjunctions

A: Ann diets   **B**: Ben diets   **E**: Ann exercises   **J**: Ann jogs   **S**: Ben swims

A ∨ B ☐

E ∨ J ☐

~A ∨ ~B ☐

~S ∨ ~B ☐

1. Ann either exercises or jogs

2. Ann exercises or jogs.

3. Ann or Ben diets.

4. Ben does not swim or does not diet.

5. Either Ann does not diet or Ben does not diet.

6. Either Ann or Ben diets.

Exercise F.2. Match Disjunctions

A: Ann diets   **B**: Ben diets   **E**: Ann exercises   **J**: Ann jogs   **S**: Ben swims

J ∨ (A • E) ☐

(A • E) ∨ (A • J) ☐

(J • S) ∨ (A • B) ☐

(A ∨ J) ∨ (B ∨ S) ☐

1. Ann either jogs or both diets and exercises.

2. Either Ann diets and exercises or she diets and jogs.

3. Either Ann diets or jogs or Ben diets or swims.

4. Either Ann jogs and Ben swims or they both diet.

Exercise F.3. Disjunctions

A: Abe will make dinner   **C**: Chris will make lunch
B: Betty will make dinner   **D**: Dan will make lunch

(a)   Abe or Betty will make dinner.

(b)   Either Betty or Abe will make dinner.

(c)   Either Chris will not make lunch or Abe will make dinner.

(d)   Either Chris will make lunch or Betty will not make dinner.

(e)   Either Chris will not make lunch or Dan will not make lunch.

(f)   Abe will make dinner or either Chris or Dan will make lunch.

(g)   Either Abe and Betty will make dinner or Chris and Dan will make lunch.

G. Material Biconditional

The following table summarizes the basic information about the material biconditional:

Connective:	if and only if
Symbol:	$\equiv$
Symbol name:	triple bar
Logical form:	$\boxed{} \equiv \boxed{}$
	$p \equiv q$
Components:	terms of the biconditional: p, q

The material biconditional is sometimes symbolized by means of variously shaped double arrows ($\leftrightarrow$ or $\Leftrightarrow$). Here is an example of a biconditional (we will talk only about material biconditionals, so we can skip the adjective *material* in most discussions):

(1) Ann will be elected if and only if Ben will be elected.

In other words, either both will be in the presidential offices or neither of them will. In (1), the first term of the biconditional is the proposition "Ann will be elected," while the proposition "Ben will be elected" is the second term.

THE BASIC TRUTH TABLE FOR THE BICONDITIONAL

The biconditional says, roughly, that one proposition is true if and only if another proposition is true. In other words, both are true or both are false. Let us consider the following example. Suppose that Ann goes to the store. We say:

Ann buys apples if and only if she buys bananas.

When will our claim be evidently false?

[What Ann buys]	p Ann buys apples	q Ann buys bananas	$p \equiv q$ Ann buys apples if and only if she buys bananas.
	T	F	$\boxed{}$

Our claim that she buys apples if *and only if* she buys bananas, was proven **false**: she bought apples but not bananas.

[What Ann buys]	p Ann buys apples	q Ann buys bananas	$p \equiv q$ Ann buys apples if and only if she buys bananas.
	F	T	

If Ann bought bananas but not apples then our claim is **false** again. We claimed, among other things, that *if* she bought bananas, she also bought apples, but she didn't.

[What Ann buys]	p Ann buys apples	q Ann buys bananas	$p \equiv q$ Ann buys apples if and only if she buys bananas.
	T	T	

On the other hand, if Ann has bought both apples and bananas then our prediction is confirmed; the biconditional is **true**.

[What Ann buys]	p Ann buys apples	q Ann buys bananas	$p \equiv q$ Ann buys apples if and only if she buys bananas.
	F	F	

Finally, if Ann bought neither apples nor bananas then our claim would still be confirmed. The biconditional is still **true**. We did not predict that she will actually buy both of them. Rather, we predicted that she would buy one if she buys the other.

> The biconditional is true if and only if its terms have the same truth values.
> The biconditional is false if and only if its terms have different truth values.

p	q	$p \equiv q$
T	T	
T	F	
F	T	
F	F	

Fill in the truth values.

Check your answers with the truth table at the end of this unit.

BICONDITIONALS IN ENGLISH

The biconditionals are expressed by such phrases as:

... if and only if ...   ... just in case ...
... if but only if...   ... iff ...
... when and only when ...   ... exactly if ...

> "iff" is an abbreviation of
> "if and only if."
> It's used frequently in definitions.

Examples

(2) There is thunder just in case there is lightning.
[2] R ≡ L

> **L:** There is lighting
> **R:** There is thunder

Here are other examples with more complex terms:

(3) Ann will get an A+ in logic just in case she gets 100% on all the quizzes and submits them all on time.
[3] A ≡ (Q • S)

> **A:** Ann gets an A+ in logic
> **Q:** Ann gets 100% on all quizzes
> **S:** Ann submits all quizzes on time

(4) Ben will be happy and rich if and only if he graduates from law school and does not fail.
[4] (H • R) ≡ (L • ~B)

> **B:** Ben fails
> **H:** Ben is happy
> **R:** Ben is rich
> **L:** Ben graduates from law school

Causal Relations in Logic

Many students who begin to study logic fall prey to the impression that biconditionals and conditionals express causal relations. The impression is wrong, however. In fact, there is no complex statement in propositional logic that could capture causal relations. Propositional logic is too weak to do so.

According to the so-called counterfactual theory of causality (proposed by David Lewis in 1973), causal relations can be captured by so-called counterfactuals. Simplifying a great deal, we can understand the claim

John's throwing the ball caused the window to break

in terms of the following counterfactual statement, among others:

If John had not thrown the ball, the window would not have broken.

Lewis uses the so-called possible-world semantics developed for modal logic to understand such claims.

Exercise G.1. Match Biconditionals

A: Ann diets   **B**: Ben diets   **E**: Ann exercises   **J**: Ann jogs   **S**: Ben swims

A ≡ B [   ]
E ≡ J [   ]
~E ≡ ~J [   ]
~B ≡ S [   ]

1. Ann diets if and only if Ben diets.

2. Ann exercises if and only if she jogs.

3. Ann diets exactly if Ben diets.

4. Ben does not diet when and only when he swims.

5. Ann does not exercise if and only if she does not jog.

Exercise G.2. Match Biconditionals

A: Ann diets   **B**: Ben diets   **E**: Ann exercises   **J**: Ann jogs   **S**: Ben swims

B ≡ (A ∨ E) [   ]
~S ≡ (~E • ~J) [   ]
J ≡ (A • ~E) [   ]

1. Ann jogs if and only if she diets but does not exercise.

2. Ben diets just in case Ann either diets or exercises.

3. Ben does not swim just in case Ann does not exercise and does not jog.

Exercise G.3. Match Biconditionals

A: Ann diets   **B**: Ben diets   **E**: Ann exercises   **J**: Ann jogs   **S**: Ben swims

(J • E) ≡ A [   ]
(A • B) ≡ (J • S) [   ]
(A ∨ J) ≡ (B ∨ S) [   ]

1. Ann both jogs and exercises just in case she diets.

2. Ann diets or jogs if but only if Ben diets or swims.

3. Ann and Ben both diet just in case Ann jogs and Ben swims.

Exercise G.4. Biconditionals

A: Abe will make dinner   **B**: Betty will make dinner   **C**: Chris will make lunch

(a)   Abe will make dinner if and only if Betty will.

(b)   Chris will make lunch just in case Betty makes dinner.

(c)   Abe makes dinner when and only when Betty does not.

(d)   Abe will not make dinner just in case Chris will not make lunch.

(e)   Chris will make lunch just in case Abe or Betty makes dinner.

(f)   Chris will not make lunch just in case Abe and Betty both make dinner.

H. Material Conditional

The following table summarizes the basic information about the material conditional:

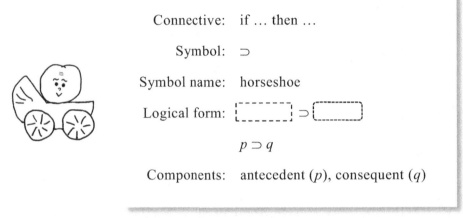

Connective:	if … then …
Symbol:	⊃
Symbol name:	horseshoe
Logical form:	$p \supset q$
Components:	antecedent (p), consequent (q)

The material conditional is sometimes symbolized by means of variously shaped arrows (→ or ⇒). The horseshoe is the most frequently used symbol for the material conditional in the English-speaking world. Again, I'll drop the adjective "material," since we will be concerned only with material conditionals.

The topic of the conditional is among the hardest for at least two reasons. First, conditionals are hard to symbolize. Second, it is hard to understand the truth table for the material conditional. However, the basic idea behind a conditional is simple. A conditional says that something (which is expressed in the consequent) is true on some condition (which is expressed in the antecedent).

> If *it rains* then John will get wet.
> If *Jane gets more than 90 points*, she will get an A.
> If *Mary puts on the new dress*, Newt will ask her out.

The italicized propositions are the antecedents. They express the condition for what the consequent expresses. The condition of John's getting wet is that it rains. The condition of Jane's getting an A is that she gets more than 90 points. The condition of Newt's asking Mary out is that she puts on a new dress.

CONDITIONALS IN ENGLISH

Let us consider the following conditional

(1) If *Mary puts on the new dress* then Newt will ask her out.

The antecedent is the proposition "Mary puts on the new dress." It expresses the condition on which the consequent ("Newt will ask Mary out") is true.

Numerous other phrases express conditionals in English, among them:

… provided that …	… in the event that …	… supposing that …
… given that …	… as long as …	… on the condition that …
… in case …	… assuming that …	… on the assumption that …

To symbolize a conditional, we must first determine exactly what propositions are the antecedent and the consequent. This is not always straightforward. There is no simple rule that would tell us, for example, that the first proposition is the antecedent while the second is the consequent. The following examples will serve as illustrations. Let us first formulate the proposition expressed by sentence (1) using some more connective phrases:

(1a) Assuming that *Mary puts on the new dress,* Newt will ask her out.
(1b) On the condition that *Mary puts on the new dress,* Newt will ask her out.
(1c) Provided that *Mary puts on the new dress,* Newt will ask her out.
(1d) Given that *Mary puts on the new dress,* Newt will ask her out.

We now have five different sentences that express one conditional. In all of them, the antecedent occurs first. We will now generate five more sentences that still express the same conditional but this time the consequent will occur first:

(1e) Newt will ask Mary out if *she puts on the new dress.*
(1f) Newt will ask Mary out assuming that *she puts on the new dress.*
(1g) Newt will ask Mary out on the condition that *she puts on the new dress.*
(1h) Newt will ask Mary out provided that *she puts on the new dress.*
(1i) Newt will ask Mary out given that *she puts on the new dress.*

In each case, the italicized proposition is the condition for the other (unitalicized) proposition. To make symbolization easier and to avoid mistakes, it is wise to paraphrase conditionals into the standard *if... then...* form before symbolizing them.

HOW TO PARAPHRASE A CONDITIONAL?

Paraphrase conditionals into the "if... then..." form before symbolizing them!

Let us take a different sentence:

(2) Ned will be happy provided that Susan goes out with him.

Now ask yourself, "How would I express this content as an if-then sentence?" Identify the condition first. Please fill in the missing fragments:

The key is to identify the antecedent (the condition) and the consequent (what depends on the condition)!

(2′) If ☐ ☐

(2′) is a good paraphrase of (2) when we understand both to mean the same thing (to have the same truth conditions).

(2′) If Susan goes out with Ned then he will be happy.

It is then clear that the symbolization is:

[2] S ⊃ N

N: Ned is happy
S: Susan goes out with Ned

Example

Kate says to Bob:

(3) Assuming that Bob manages to buy a suit, he will marry Kate.

The condition here is that Bob manages to buy a suit. It is the condition of their marrying. Let's paraphrase (3) into a standard *if... then...* form:

(3′) If ⎡   ⎤ then ⎡   ⎤

Make sure that (3′) and (3) both mean the same thing. We can symbolize (3) thus:

[3] S ⊃ M

S: Bob manages to buy a suit
M: Bob **m**arries Kate

Example

(4) Jane's cat Sim will stop scratching the furniture if she trains him well.

Identify the antecedent (the condition) and the consequent, then paraphrase:

(4′) If ⎡   ⎤ then ⎡   ⎤

[4] J ⊃ S

J: Jane trains Sim well
S: Sim stops scratching furniture

Example

(5) Edward will even move to Siberia on the condition that Susan and Jane go with him.

Paraphrase:

(5′) If ⎡   ⎤ then ⎡   ⎤

[5] (S • J) ⊃ E

E: Edward will move to Siberia
J: Jane goes with Edward
S: Susan goes with Edward

Example

(6) Edward will [not] move to Siberia [if] Susan does [not] go with him.

Paraphrase:

(6′) If [   ] then [   ]

[6] ~S ⊃ ~E

Example

(7) Ben will get a cat [and] a dog [provided that] Ann is [not] mad at him.

Paraphrase:

(7′) If [   ] then [   ]

[7] ~A ⊃ (C • D)

> **A**: **A**nn is mad with Ben
> **C**: Ben gets a **c**at
> **D**: Ben gets a **d**og

Example

(8) Ann will be mad at Ben [in case] he does[n't] get a cat.

Paraphrase:

(8′) If [   ] then [   ]

[8] ~C ⊃ A

> Symbolize the propositions. Match the symbolizations with the English sentences by writing in the appropriate numbers.

Exercise H.1. Match Conditionals

B: Ann goes out with **B**en   **H**: Ben invites Ann to the **t**heater   **M**: Ben invites Ann to the **m**ovies

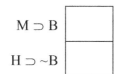

M ⊃ B [   ]

H ⊃ ~B [   ]

1. If Ben invites Ann to the movies, she will go out with him.
2. If Ben invites Ann to the theater then she will not go out with him.
3. Ann will not go out with Ben if he invites her to the theater.
4. Ann will go out with Ben if he invites her to the movies.

Exercise H.2. Match Conditionals

B: Ann goes out with **Ben**   **C:** Ann goes out with **Chris**   **H**: Ben invites Ann to the theater

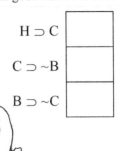

H ⊃ C
C ⊃ ~B
B ⊃ ~C

1. If Ben invites Ann to the theater, she will go out with Chris.

2. If Ann goes out with Chris, she will not go out with Ben.

3. If Ann goes out with Ben then she will not go out with Chris.

4. Ann will not go out with Chris if she goes out with Ben.

5. Ann will not go out with Ben if she goes out with Chris.

6. Ann will go out with Chris if Ben invites her to the theater.

Exercise H.3. Match Conditionals

A: Ann walks her dog   **B:** Ben walks his dog   **C:** Chris walks his dog   **D:** Deb walks her dog

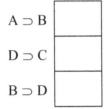

A ⊃ B
D ⊃ C
B ⊃ D

1. Assuming that Ann walks her dog, Ben will walk his dog.

2. Chris will walk his dog provided that Deb walks her dog.

3. Deb will walk her dog in case Ben walks his.

Exercise H.4. Match Conditionals

A: Ann walks her dog   **B:** Ben walks his dog   **C:** Chris walks his dog   **D:** Deb walks her dog

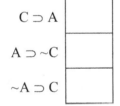

C ⊃ A
A ⊃ ~C
~A ⊃ C

1. If Ann walks her dog, then Chris will not walk his dog.

2. Ann will walk her dog given that Chris walks his dog.

3. Chris will walk his dog as long as Ann does not walk her dog.

Exercise H.5. Match Conditionals

A: Ann walks her dog   **B:** Ben walks his dog   **C:** Chris walks his dog   **D:** Deb walks her dog

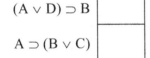

(A ∨ D) ⊃ B
A ⊃ (B ∨ C)

1. If Ann walks her dog, Ben or Chris will walk their dogs.

2. Ben will walk his dog when either Ann or Deb walks their dogs.

Exercise H.6. Match Conditionals

A: Ann walks her dog   **B:** Ben walks his dog   **C:** Chris walks his dog   **D:** Deb walks her dog

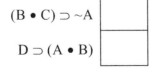

(B • C) ⊃ ~A
D ⊃ (A • B)

1. Ann and Ben will walk their dogs on the condition that Deb walks her dog.

2. Supposing that both Ben and Chris walk their dogs, Ann will not walk her dog.

In Ex. H.7-9, paraphrase the conditionals
into the if-then form
and then symbolize them.

Exercise H.7. Conditionals

A: **A**be will make dinner   **C**: **C**hris will make lunch
B: **B**etty will make dinner   **D**: **D**an will make lunch

(a) Betty will make dinner if Dan makes lunch.

If | Dan makes lunch | then | Betty will make dinner

(b) Chris will make lunch given that Abe makes dinner.

If | | then |

(c) Assuming that Chris makes lunch, Abe will make dinner.

If | | then |

(d) Given that Betty makes dinner, Chris makes lunch.

If | | then |

(e) On the supposition that Chris makes lunch, Abe makes dinner.

If | | then |

(f) Chris will make lunch provided that Betty will not make dinner.

If | | then |

(g) Provided that Dan makes lunch, Abe will not make dinner.

If | | then |

Exercise H.8. Conditionals

> **A**: **A**be will make dinner   **C**: **C**hris will make lunch
> **B**: **B**etty will make dinner   **D**: **D**an will make lunch

(a)   On the condition that Betty makes dinner, Chris will make lunch.

     If [_____] then [_____]   [_____]

(b)   Dan will not make lunch if Abe does not make dinner.

     If [_____] then [_____]   [_____]

(c)   Dan will make lunch if either Abe or Betty makes dinner.

     If [_____] then [_____]   [_____]

(d)   Abe will make dinner on the assumption that Betty does not.

     If [_____] then [_____]   [_____]

(e)   Abe will make dinner provided that either Chris or Dan make lunch.

     If [_____] then [_____]   [_____]

(f)   Given that either Chris or Dan make lunch, Abe or Betty will make dinner.

     If [_____] then [_____]   [_____]

(g)   Chris and Dan will both make lunch given that Abe and Betty both make dinner.

     If [_____] then [_____]   [_____]

Exercise H.9. Conditionals

D: Ann is on a **d**iet   **H**: Ann gets **h**ealthier   **I**: Bill is on a diet   **W**: Bill gains **w**eight
E: Ann **e**xercises regularly   **G**: Ann **g**ains weight   **J**: Bill **j**ogs regularly

(a)   Ann will get healthier if she goes on a diet and does not gain weight.

If [   ] then [   ]

(b)   Ann will go on a diet and will exercise regularly on the condition that Bill goes on a diet.

If [   ] then [   ]

(c)   Bill will go on a diet provided that Ann goes on a diet and does not gain weight.

If [   ] then [   ]

(d)   Given that Bill jogs regularly or is on a diet, he does not gain weight.

If [   ] then [   ]

(e)   Ann will exercise regularly provided that Bill jogs regularly and does not gain weight.

If [   ] then [   ]

(f)   Ann will exercise regularly given that she gets healthier or doesn't gain weight.

If [   ] then [   ]

(g)   Ann and Bill will not gain weight provided that they go on a diet.

If [   ] then [   ]

THE BASIC TRUTH TABLE FOR THE CONDITIONAL

 I should warn you that only half of the basic truth table for the conditional is intuitive. There is a theoretical explanation for the other half but you will be puzzled and unsatisfied (for good reasons). Let us begin with a row that *is* intuitive.

When is a conditional false?

Consider the following conditional:

(1) If Snow White eats the apple then she will die.

Let us try to think of the conditional "If Snow White eats the apple then she will die" as a kind of prediction. Suppose that we see that Snow White is about to eat an apple, and we think that if she does then she will die. When would we be wrong?

p Snow White eats the apple	q Snow White dies	$p \supset q$ If Snow White eats the apple then she will die
☐	☐	F

Our prediction would be false in case Snow White ate the apple but did not die, i.e., in case the antecedent is true and the consequent is false.

Consider another example.

(2) If you stir cornstarch into water, it will dissolve.

We know that prediction (2) is false. When you make the antecedent true (when you put cornstarch into water and stir it), you thereby make the consequent false (cornstarch will not dissolve).

When is a conditional true?

The short answer is: in all remaining cases, i.e., when it is not clearly false.

p	q	$p \supset q$
T	T	T
T	F	F
F	T	T
F	F	T

Well, we can understand why the conditional is true in the first row. Our prediction about Snow White will turn out to be true in case Snow White eats the apple and dies:

p Snow White eats the apple	q Snow White dies	$p \supset q$ If Snow White eats the apple then she will die
T	T	☐

This completes the intuitive part of the truth table for the conditional. If the antecedent is true and the consequent is true then the whole conditional is true. If the antecedent is true and the consequent is false then the whole conditional is false.

 However, there are no intuitive reasons why the conditional should be true in cases where the antecedent is false. It must seem absurd to you that it should be so. As mentioned earlier, propositional logic is a good theory but it has its limitations. In particular, it is too weak to capture our intuitions about conditionals.

However, there are **good theoretical** reasons why the truth table for the conditional must look the way it does in propositional logic. Given this choice of the truth table for the conditional, we can make sense of numerous logical relations between conditionals and other propositions. For example, we will be able to understand that a biconditional $p \equiv q$ is logically equivalent to a conjunction of conditionals $(p \supset q) \bullet (q \supset p)$. We will also be able to show that two symbolization schemata for *unless* are equivalent. Etc. The box on p. 68 conveys, in my view, the best explanation (due to Virginia Klenk).

> The conditional is false just in case its antecedent is true and its consequent is false.
>
> The conditional is true just in case either its antecedent is false or its consequent is true.

Fill in the truth values.

Check your answers with the truth table at the end of this unit.

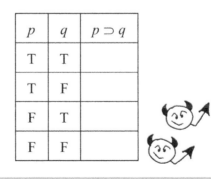

p	q	$p \supset q$
T	T	
T	F	
F	T	
F	F	

Why is the conditional true when the antecedent is false?

The truth table for the conditional is intuitive in its first "half":

p	q	$p \supset q$
T	T	T
T	F	F
F	T	
F	F	

The question to ask is what the truth values for the other "half" should be. There are exactly four possibilities of filling in the missing truth values in the last two rows.

p	q	p ❶ q
T	T	T
T	F	F
F	T	T
F	F	T

p	q	p ❷ q
T	T	T
T	F	F
F	T	T
F	F	F

p	q	p ❸ q
T	T	T
T	F	F
F	T	F
F	F	T

p	q	p ❹ q
T	T	T
T	F	F
F	T	F
F	F	F

It turns out that only the truth table for ❶ is not already "used up." Truth tables for ❷, ❸, and ❹ are already occupied.

The truth table for ❹ is nothing else but the truth table for conjunction. It is clear, however, that the truth conditions for conjunctions and conditionals differ. We accept as true the conditional "If you borrowed $1000 from me then you ought to pay me $1000." But we are not thereby committed to the conjunction "You borrowed $1000 from me and you ought to pay me $1000."

The truth table for ❸ is nothing but the truth table for biconditional. Again, however, conditionals and biconditionals differ. If we accept as true the conditional "You ought to pay me $1000 if you borrowed $1000 from me," we do not thereby accept as true the biconditional "You ought to pay me $1000 if *and only if* you borrowed $1000 from me." After all, there are other circumstances in which you ought to pay me $1000 (e.g., if you buy a coat from me for $1000).

The truth table for ❷ is just the truth table for the consequent q. But it would be quite disastrous to claim that the truth conditions for a conditional are the same as the truth conditions for the consequent of the conditional. Intuitively, the truth of the conditional depends not only on the consequent but also on the antecedent. If ❷ were accepted as the meaning of the conditional then the statement "If you borrowed $1000 from me then you ought to pay me $1000" would mean the same as "You ought to pay me $1000." But this would be absurd.

We are thus left with the truth table for ❶ as the only available way of representing conditionals in propositional logic.

Source: V. Klenk, *Understanding Symbolic Logic* (Upper Saddle River, NJ: Prentice Hall, 2002)

Summary

You have learned the distinction between simple and complex propositions.

A complex proposition (in propositional logic) is a proposition constructed from other propositions by means of one of the propositional connectives.

A simple proposition (in propositional logic) is a proposition that is not constructed from other propositions by means of any propositional connective.

Simple propositions are symbolized using the so-called propositional constants: A, B, C, etc. There are five types of complex propositions: negations (not, ~), conjunctions (and, •), disjunctions (or, ∨), conditionals (if-then, ⊃), and biconditionals (if and only if, ≡). There are many other connective phrases in English for each connective. The so-called basic truth tables determine the truth values of all complex propositions.

p	$\sim p$
T	**F**
F	**T**

p	q	$p \bullet q$
T	T	**T**
T	F	**F**
F	T	**F**
F	F	**F**

p	q	$p \vee q$
T	T	**T**
T	F	**T**
F	T	**T**
F	F	**F**

p	q	$p \equiv q$
T	T	**T**
T	F	**F**
F	T	**F**
F	F	**T**

p	q	$p \supset q$
T	T	**T**
T	F	**F**
F	T	**T**
F	F	**T**

You should understand the basic truth tables but then... memorize them!

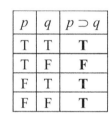

Try active memorization. It's the best way.

Close everything. Write out the basic truth tables on a piece of paper.

Check that you have done it correctly; if not, repeat the process.

You have also learned the basics of symbolization. You have acquired the important skill of constructing symbolization keys. A symbolization key is a list of all simple propositions that occur in a proposition (a group of propositions) with their unique (one-to-one) letter assignments. Two rules must be obeyed when constructing symbolization keys:

"No Complexity" Rule: No letter can represent a complex proposition.
"1-1" Rule: Each simple proposition must have a unique letter assignment.

Unit 1.3

The Basics of Symbolization

Overview

For logical techniques to be useful, we must be able to symbolize English sentences, i.e., represent them in logical notation. Symbolization is not always easy. It is a skill that you acquire in practice. There is no algorithm or surefire recipe you could learn and thereafter know how to symbolize.

We will proceed in steps. You will learn certain tricks or "keys" (like in guitar playing). You will learn what to look for in a sentence so that you can symbolize it effectively.

But in the end, it is all about practice. As before, there will be lots of exercises.

In this unit, you will learn:
- what the main connective is.

In this unit, you will learn how to:
- identify the main connective in a formula (parentheses-binding method),
- spot the main connective in English sentences,
- symbolize more complicated English sentences (Units 1.4-1.5 will develop the skill).

Time:	3-5 hours
Difficulty:	●●●○○○○
Status:	**Essential**/Recommended/Optional
Number of exercises:	23
Prerequisites:	Introduction, Unit 1.2

A. Main Connective

In this section, you will learn what the main connective is. Very roughly, the main connective is the *primary*, the *most important*, or the *dominant* connective in a proposition.

THE ROLE OF THE MAIN CONNECTIVE

To see why the main connective is important, consider two examples of English sentences where it is unclear what the main connective is. Such sentences are ambiguous: they can be read in different ways.

Example 1

Bob says to Kate:

I will show you my stamps or I will make you coffee and I will give you $1000.

Bob's utterance is ambiguous. It can be understood in two *radically* different ways:

> A: (I'll show you my stamps or I'll make you coffee) **and** I'll give you $1000.
>
> B: I'll show you my stamps **or** (I'll make you coffee and I'll give you $1000).

(Optimistic) Interpretation A

> [1A] $(S \lor C) \bullet B$

C: Bob will make Kate some coffee
S: Bob will show Kate stamps
B: **Bob** will give Kate $1000

In other words,

> (1A) Bob will show Kate stamps or make her coffee **but, in any event,** he will give her $1000.

The main connective in this proposition is the dot, which means that the whole proposition is a conjunction. Here is a way of representing what the proposition says:

The important point is that Kate will receive $1000 whether she is shown stamps or given coffee. You can see why, for Kate, this is a very optimistic interpretation of Bob's utterance.

(Realistic) Interpretation B

[1B] S ∨ (C • B)

In other words,

(1B) **Either** Bob will show Kate stamps **or** he will both make her coffee and give her $1000.

The main connective in this proposition is the wedge. The whole proposition is thus a disjunction. Here is a way of representing what the proposition says:

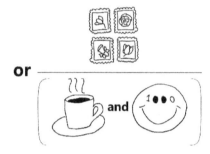

On this interpretation, Bob tells Kate that he will do one of two things: either he will show her stamps, or he will both make her coffee and give her $1000.

You can now appreciate the difference between [1] and [2]. If what Bob says is [1] then he is committed to giving Kate $1000. But if what he says is [2], then he does not commit himself to giving Kate $1000 since if he just shows her the stamps then he will still keep his promise.

From a semantic point of view (from the point of view of what the statements mean), the difference between them is enormous, as we have just seen. But from a syntactic point of view (from the point of view of their logical structure), the difference has to do with the way the parentheses are placed (fill in the blanks):

[1A] (S ∨ C) • B   main connective: ○dot ○wedge
[1B] S ∨ (C • B)   main connective: ○dot ○wedge

The way the parentheses are placed is usually crucial. For two-place connectives, the location of the parentheses determines what the main connective of a proposition is.

Example 2

Let's consider one more example of an ambiguous utterance. Bob says:

I will go to work and
I will drink coffee or
I will read a newspaper.

C: Bob will drink **c**offee
N: Bob will read a **n**ewspaper
W: Bob will go to **w**ork

Interpretation A

(I will go to work and I will drink coffee) or I will read a newspaper.

Either [   ] and [   ]

or [   ]

$(W \bullet C) \vee N$

main connective: ○ dot   ○ wedge

Interpretation B

I will go to work and (I will drink coffee or I will read a newspaper).

[   ] and either [   ]

or [   ]

$W \bullet (C \vee N)$

main connective: ○ dot   ○ wedge

In summary, the main connective is the dominant connective in a proposition. The main connective determines the type of a given proposition. When the main connective is a dot, the proposition is a conjunction (whether or not there are other connectives in the proposition); when the main connective is a wedge, the proposition is a disjunction; etc.

There are English sentences where it is unclear what the main connective is. Such sentences are ambiguous, however. They can sometimes be read in radically different ways. Such sentences do not represent propositions.

COMPLEX PROPOSITIONS WITH COMPLEX COMPONENTS

We have already seen five types of complex propositions: conjunctions, disjunctions, conditionals, biconditionals, and negations. So far, however, we have focused on complex propositions with simple components, such as the following conditional:

> **A**: **A**nn buys the ticket
> **B**: **B**en goes to the movie
> **C**: **C**arry goes to the movie
> **D**: **D**an buys the ticket

A ⊃ B $\boxed{\text{If}}$ Ann buys the ticket $\boxed{\text{then}}$ Ben will go to the movie.

However, the component propositions can also be complex. Consider conditionals with complex consequents:

A ⊃ (B ∨ C) $\boxed{\text{If}}$ Ann buys the ticket $\boxed{\text{then}}$ Ben $\boxed{\text{or}}$ Carry will go to the movie.

A ⊃ (B • C) $\boxed{\text{If}}$ Ann buys the ticket $\boxed{\text{then}}$ Ben $\boxed{\text{and}}$ Carry will go to the movie.

A ⊃ (B ⊃ C) $\boxed{\text{If}}$ Ann buys the ticket $\boxed{\text{then}}$ $\boxed{\text{if}}$ Ben goes to the movie $\boxed{\text{then}}$ Carry will go to the movie.

A ⊃ (B ≡ C) $\boxed{\text{If}}$ Ann buys the ticket $\boxed{\text{then}}$ Ben will go to the movie $\boxed{\text{if and only if}}$ Carry will go to the movie.

A ⊃ ~B   If Ann buys the ticket then Ben will $\boxed{\text{not}}$ go to the movie.

Of course, the antecedents can also be complex:

(A ∨ D) ⊃ B $\boxed{\text{If}}$ Ann $\boxed{\text{or}}$ Dan buys the ticket $\boxed{\text{then}}$ Ben will go to the movie.

(A • D) ⊃ B $\boxed{\text{If}}$ Ann $\boxed{\text{and}}$ Dan buy the ticket $\boxed{\text{then}}$ Ben will go to the movie.

(A ⊃ D) ⊃ B   Ben will go to the movie $\boxed{\text{on the condition that}}$ $\boxed{\text{if}}$ Ann buys the ticket $\boxed{\text{then}}$ Dan buys the ticket.*

(A ≡ D) ⊃ B $\boxed{\text{If}}$ Ann buys the ticket $\boxed{\text{if and only if}}$ Dan buys the ticket $\boxed{\text{then}}$ Ben will go to the movie.

~A ⊃ B $\boxed{\text{If}}$ Ann does $\boxed{\text{not}}$ buy the ticket $\boxed{\text{then}}$ Ben will go to the movie.

*Note that if we try to read off the formula using canonical "if then," we get a double "if": "**IF** if Ann buys the ticket then Dan buys the ticket **THEN** Ben will go to the movie." This sentence is hard to parse, so it is useful to try to use a different formulation of the conditional. Above, the main conditional is expressed using the consequent-first formulation; moreover, "on the condition that" is used rather than "if."

Of course, both components (here: consequent and antecedent) can be complex. I will not list all such propositions because there are 25 such possibilities. Here is one example:

(A ∨ D) ⊃ (B • C)   If Ann or Dan buys the ticket then Ben and Carrie will go to the movie.

Furthermore, the components of components can be complex as well. Indeed, there is no limit to how complex a proposition can be.

Symbolize the propositions. Match the symbolizations with the English sentences by writing in the appropriate numbers.

D: Ann **d**iets   **E**: Ann **e**xercises   **J**: Ann **j**ogs

Exercise A.1 Match Propositions

E ∨ (D • J) ☐   1   Ann will exercise or diet but, in either case, she will jog.

(E ∨ D) • J ☐   2   Either Ann will exercise or she will both diet and jog.

Exercise A.2 Match Propositions

(D ∨ E) • J ☐   1   Either Ann will diet or she will both exercise and jog.

(D ∨ E) ∨ J ☐   2   Ann will diet, exercise, or jog.

D ∨ (E • J) ☐   3   Ann will diet or exercise but, in any event, she will jog.

D ∨ (E ∨ J) ☐

Exercise A.3 Match Propositions

(D • E) • J ☐   1   Ann will diet and she will exercise or jog.

                  2   Ann will diet but she will either exercise or jog.

(D • E) ∨ J ☐

                  3   Ann will diet, exercise, and jog.

D • (E • J) ☐   4   Ann will either diet and exercise or jog.

D • (E ∨ J) ☐   5   Either Ann will both diet and exercise or she will jog.

| D: Ann diet | E: Ann exercises | H: Ann is healthy |

Exercise A.4 Match Propositions

D ⊃ H

~D ⊃ H

1   If Ann diets then she will be healthy.

2   Ann will be healthy if she does not diet.

3   Ann will be healthy if she diets.

4   If Ann does not diet then she will be healthy.

Exercise A.5 Match Propositions

D ⊃ ~H

~D ⊃ ~H

H ⊃ D

H ⊃ ~D

1   If Ann is healthy then she will not diet.

2   If Ann is healthy then she will diet.

3   If Ann does not diet then she will not be healthy.

4   If Ann diets then she will not be healthy.

Exercise A.6 Match Propositions

(D • E) ⊃ H

D • (E ⊃ H)

D ⊃ (E • H)

(D ⊃ E) • H

1   Ann diets and if she exercises then she will be healthy.

2   If Ann diets and exercises then she will be healthy.

3   If Ann diets then she will both exercise and be healthy.

4   If Ann diets then she will exercise but, in any event, she will be healthy.

Exercise A.7 Match Propositions

(D ∨ E) ⊃ H

D ∨ (E ⊃ H)

D ⊃ (E ⊃ H)

(D ⊃ E) ⊃ H

1   Ann will be healthy on the condition that if she diets then she will exercise.

2   Either Ann will diet or if she exercises then she will be healthy.

3   If Ann diets then if she exercises then she will be healthy.

4   If Ann either diets or exercises then she will be healthy.

B. How to Find the Main Connective: Stage 1 (Two-Place Connectives)

We will learn how to find the main connective in an arbitrarily complex proposition. We will use the method of binding parentheses. We will proceed in two stages. In stage 1, we will introduce the method for two-place connectives only (so we will skip negations). In stage 2, we will learn how to apply the method for all connectives (including negations).

MAIN CONNECTIVE IN PROPOSITION CONSTRUCTION

The main connective determines whether a given proposition is a negation, a conjunction, a disjunction, a biconditional, or a conditional.

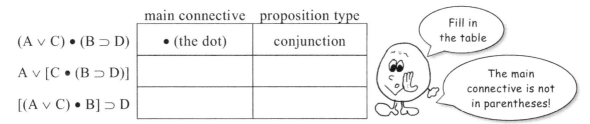

	main connective	proposition type
(A ∨ C) • (B ⊃ D)	• (the dot)	conjunction
A ∨ [C • (B ⊃ D)]		
[(A ∨ C) • B] ⊃ D		

A ∨ [C • (B ⊃ D)] is a disjunction; its main connective is the wedge. [(A ∨ C) • B] ⊃ D is a conditional; its main connective is the horseshoe.

If we were to imagine the process of constructing a complex proposition out of simple propositions then the main connective is the last connective used in constructing the proposition. We could imagine the construction of proposition (A ∨ C) • (B ⊃ D) in the following way:

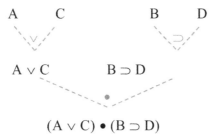

The proposition [(A ∨ C) • B] ⊃ D would be constructed in such a way that the conditional connective, the horseshoe, would be put last:

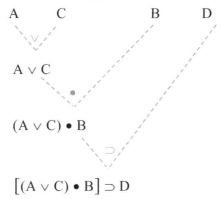

Reconstruct how proposition A ∨ [C • (B ⊃ D)] would be constructed:

A   C   B   D

Check your answer against the Solutions!

$$A \lor [C \bullet (B \supset D)]$$

THE METHOD OF BINDING PARENTHESES

You need to be able to determine what the main connective is in an arbitrarily complex proposition, even such as this:

$$(((A \lor B) \bullet (C \lor D)) \supset C) \equiv (A \supset ((C \supset D) \supset B))$$

Fortunately, there is a simple method that helps to make this task manageable. It consists in binding pairs of parentheses. Let us begin with a simpler example, however.

Example 1

What is the main connective of the following proposition?

$$(A \equiv E) \supset ((C \bullet D) \lor B)$$

We begin by binding (or pairing) the innermost parentheses that connect the simple propositions:

$$(A \equiv E) \supset ((C \bullet D) \lor B)$$

The propositions thus marked we treat (in thought) as wholes (whole propositions):

$$(A \equiv E) \supset ((C \bullet D) \lor B)$$

We repeat the process binding the next level of parentheses and treating the propositions thus marked as whole:

$$(A \equiv E) \supset ((C \bullet D) \lor B)$$

It becomes clear that the proposition is a conditional, the main connective is the horseshoe:

⊃

Example 2

What is the main connective of the following proposition? Try to do this on your own and check that you have done it correctly:

$$(((A \lor B) \bullet (C \lor D)) \supset C) \equiv (A \supset ((C \supset D) \supset B))$$

Work from inside out

We begin by binding the innermost parentheses that connect the simple propositions:

$$(((A \lor B) \bullet (C \lor D)) \supset C) \equiv (A \supset ((C \supset D) \supset B))$$

We repeat the process of binding the next level of parentheses:

$$(((A \lor B) \bullet (C \lor D)) \supset C) \equiv (A \supset ((C \supset D) \supset B))$$

And so on, until we have bound all the parentheses:

$$(((A \lor B) \bullet (C \lor D)) \supset C) \equiv (A \supset ((C \supset D) \supset B))$$

You can see now what the main connective is:

$$\equiv$$

The main connective is the triple bar, so the proposition is a biconditional.

Use the method of parentheses binding, to find the main connective in each proposition.

Exercise B.1 Main Connective

1. $(A \bullet B) \lor (C \supset D)$ 5. $(A \bullet (B \lor C)) \supset D$

2. $A \bullet (B \lor (C \supset D))$ 6. $(A \supset A) \supset (A \supset B)$

3. $((A \bullet B) \lor C) \supset D$ 7. $A \supset (A \supset (A \supset B))$

4. $A \bullet ((B \lor C) \supset D)$ 8. $((A \supset A) \supset A) \supset B$

Exercise B.2 Main Connective

1. (((A • B) • C) ≡ (A ∨ C)) ⊃ (A • (B ∨ C))

2. (((A ≡ B) ⊃ (B ≡ C)) • (C ⊃ D)) ∨ (B ⊃ ((A • B) ≡ C))

3. (((A ∨ B) • (C ∨ D)) ⊃ C) ≡ ((A ⊃ ((C ⊃ D) ⊃ B)) ⊃ D)

C. How to Find the Main Connective: Stage 2 (Including Negations)

So far, we have only considered two-place connectives. It is time to consider the one-place connective of negation.

Two Examples

Let us consider two propositions:

    [1] ~(V • L)   [2] ~V • L

Proposition [1] is a **negation** of a conjunction (V • L); the main connective of [1] is the tilde. Proposition [2] is a **conjunction** whose first conjunct is a negation (~V); the main connective of [2] is the dot.

      The difference between these propositions is enormous. Consider the following symbolization key:

> **V**: Adam will go to heaven
> **L**: Adam will go to hell

  (1) It is not the case that: Adam will   (2) Adam will not go to
        go both to heaven and to hell.   heaven but to hell.

What proposition (1) says is true: Adam cannot go both to heaven and hell. Note that proposition (1) does not tell us *where* Adam will go. Proposition (2), on the other hand, does tell us exactly where he will go, though he won't be happy about it.

Consider another pair of propositions of the same logical form:

[3] ~(A • C)   [4] ~A • C

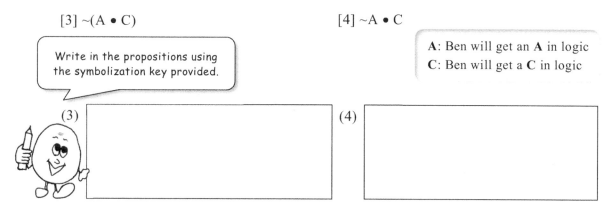

Write in the propositions using the symbolization key provided.

A: Ben will get an **A** in logic
C: Ben will get a **C** in logic

(3)   (4)

Proposition (3) again says something true: Ben will not get both an A and a C in logic, but it does not tell us what he will get. Proposition (4) tells us exactly what Ben will get: not an A but a C.

MAIN CONNECTIVE IN PROPOSITION CONSTRUCTION

If we were to imagine the process of constructing the propositions we were just talking about, it would consist in combining negation and conjunction but in reverse order.

In proposition ~(V • L), the tilde is put in last, which makes the tilde the main connective. In proposition ~V • L, the dot is put in last, which makes the dot the main connective.

A   B   C   A   B   C

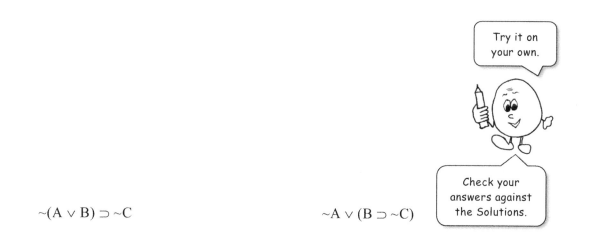

Try it on your own.

Check your answers against the Solutions.

~(A ∨ B) ⊃ ~C   ~A ∨ (B ⊃ ~C)

Of course, we can construct more complex propositions. Here is how we can represent the construction of proposition ~~(V • L) ⊃ ~~~(~V • L):

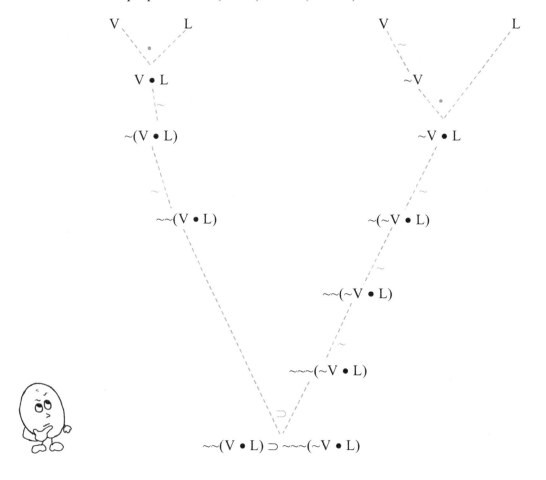

There are at least two conventions. According to one ("They"), all complex propositions (including negations) are enclosed in parentheses. According to the other ("We"), negations are not enclosed in parentheses. Here are some examples:

"They"	"We"
~(~B)	~~B
~(~(~C))	~~~C
(~A) ∨ (~B)	~A ∨ ~B
~(~(~C)) ∨ (~B)	~~~C ∨ ~B
(~(~B) • ~(~(~A))) ⊃ (~D)	(~~B • ~~~A) ⊃ ~D
~(~(A • B))	~~(A • B)
(~A) • B	~A • B
~(A • B)	~(A • B)

I hope that you agree that our convention is more perspicuous.

THE METHOD OF BINDING PARENTHESES (INCLUDING NEGATION)

The connective of negation differs from the other connectives since it is a one-place connective. According to the convention we adopted, we do not mark complex negations with parentheses, though we could do so (see the box on p. 82).

The negation operator always binds what immediately follows it. Let's consider what is negated depending on whether the tilde is followed by a letter, a parenthesis, or another tilde.

1) "~" is followed by a letter

What is negated? Answer: the simple proposition symbolized by the letter. For example, in the following cases:

$$\underset{\smile}{\sim}A \vee B \qquad\qquad (B \supset \underset{\smile}{\sim}A) \equiv C \qquad\qquad (\underset{\smile}{\sim}A \bullet B) \supset C$$

"~" negates proposition A.

2) "~" is followed by an open parenthesis "("

What is negated? Answer: the proposition that is enclosed by this parenthesis and its closing "partner" parenthesis. In the following three cases, for example, "~" negates the disjunction A ∨ B.

$$\underset{\smile}{\sim}(A \vee B) \qquad\qquad \underset{\smile}{\sim}(A \vee B) \supset C \qquad\qquad B \bullet (\underset{\smile}{\sim}(A \vee B) \vee C)$$

The formulas in the parentheses can be more complex. In the following cases, the shaded area marks the formula that is negated:

$$\underset{\smile}{\sim}((A \vee B) \bullet (C \vee A)) \qquad \underset{\smile}{\sim}((A \vee B) \bullet C) \vee A \qquad \underset{\smile}{\sim}((A \vee B) \bullet C) \vee A)$$

In the first case, the conjunction of A ∨ B and C ∨ A is negated. In the second case, the conjunction of A ∨ B and C is negated. In the third case, the disjunction of ((A ∨ B) • C) and A is negated.

3) "~" is followed by another "~"

What is negated? Answer: another negation. For example:

$$\underset{\smile}{\sim}\sim A \vee B \qquad\qquad \underset{\smile}{\sim}\sim(\sim A \vee B) \qquad\qquad \underset{\smile}{\sim}\sim\sim(A \vee B)$$

The first tilde negates the second tilde. The second tilde can negate either a simple proposition (case 1), a complex proposition within parentheses (case 2), or another negation (case 3):

$$\sim\underset{\smile}{\sim}A \vee B \qquad\qquad \sim\underset{\smile}{\sim}(\sim A \vee B) \qquad\qquad \sim\sim\underset{\smile}{\sim}(A \vee B)$$

Examples 1 and 2

Let us apply the method to two examples in parallel. Try it on your own. Then check out the explanations.

> Work from inside out!

$$\sim(\sim A \vee \sim\sim B) \bullet \sim C \qquad\qquad \sim(\sim A \vee \sim(\sim B \bullet \sim C))$$

We proceed from within. First, we bind all tildes to letters:

$$\sim(\sim A \vee \sim B) \bullet \sim C \qquad\qquad \sim(\sim A \vee \sim(\sim B \bullet \sim C))$$

Then, we bind the next level of propositions (we think of propositions that are already bound as wholes):

$$\sim(\sim A \vee \sim B) \bullet \sim C \qquad\qquad \sim(\sim A \vee \sim(\sim B \bullet \sim C))$$

We repeat this for the next level of propositions (again, think of propositions already bound as wholes):

$$\sim(\sim A \vee \sim B) \bullet \sim C \qquad\qquad \sim(\sim A \vee \sim(\sim B \bullet \sim C))$$

One final step is required:

$$\sim(\sim A \vee \sim B) \bullet \sim C \qquad\qquad \sim(\sim A \vee \sim(\sim B \bullet \sim C))$$

We can now see that the first proposition is a conjunction while the second is a negation.

Use the method of parentheses binding, to find the main connective in each proposition.

Exercise C.1 Main Connective

1. ~A ⊃ (B ∨ A)   5. ~(~A ∨ B) ⊃ C

2. ~(A ⊃ B) ∨ A   6. ~(~A ∨ (B ⊃ C))

3. ~((A ⊃ B) ∨ A)   7. ~~(A ∨ (B ⊃ C))

4. ~~A ∨ (B ⊃ C)   8. ~~(A ∨ B) ⊃ C

Exercise C.2 Main Connective

1.   ~(~(~A ∨ ~B) ⊃ ~(A • B)) ⊃ ~(~A ∨ ~A)

2.   ~(~(A ⊃ (B • A)) ≡ ~~~(~B ⊃ ~A))

3.   ~~(~A ∨ ~(B • ~C)) ⊃ ~((~C ∨ B) ≡ A)

D. Symbolization as an Art and as a Skill

Symbolization is very difficult but also very useful. It allows us to bridge the gap between logical theory and its applications to real arguments. If the logical methods we will learn later are to have any relevance to real life, you need to learn how to symbolize. We will consider more and more complex examples. They will alert you to factors you need to watch for.

As already mentioned, unfortunately, there is no algorithm for symbolizations. But there are some rules of thumb that you should keep in mind:

Paraphrase	Rephrase the statement in such a way as to make its logical structure more perspicuous.
Mark connectives	Mark all of the connectives
Key	Construct the symbolization key; choose letters that are easy to remember
Main Connective	Decide what the main connective is; insert parentheses
Partial Symbolization	In very complicated statements, proceed step-by-step, replacing simple statements with letters.

FIVE EXAMPLES

Let us start with some examples. Before we work through them step by step, it is a good idea
for you to try to symbolize them now:

D: Susie wears a new **d**ress   **A**: Jack asks Ann out
H: Susie wears a new **h**at   **J**: Jack asks Susie out
R: Susie frets
S: Susie goes out with Jack   **N**: Ned asks Susie out
U: Susie goes out with Ned   **E**: Ned asks Ann out

If you have your pencil ready... ready, steady, go...

(1) If Susie wears a new dress then either Jack or Ned will ask her out.

(2) If Susie wears a new dress and a new hat then either Jack or Ned will ask her out.

(3) If Susie wears a new dress and will no longer fret then either Jack or Ned will ask her
out.

(4) Either Susie will go out with both Jack and Ned or they will both ask Ann out.

(5) If Susie goes out with Jack or Ned then either Jack or Ned will not ask Ann out.

Example 1

(1) If Susie wears a new dress then either Jack or Ned will ask her out.

The proposition has a relatively clear logical structure. It will be evident when you mark all of the connectives:

If Susie wears a new dress then either Jack or Ned will ask her out.

We need to decide what the main connective is and place the parentheses accordingly. In our case, it seems relatively clear that "if-then" is the main connective. Think about what (1) says. It says roughly, "If blah-blah-blah then bleh-bleh-bleh." We should put in the parentheses thus:

If Susie wears a new dress then (either Jack will ask her out or Ned will ask her out).

We can now substitute letters from the symbolization key into the proposition:

If D then (either J or N)

Finally, we substitute appropriate symbols for the connectives:

$D \supset (J \vee N)$

As a rule of thumb, it is good to read out the symbolized proposition using the symbolization key. In this way, you can check whether your symbolization and the original statement say the same thing. (This is particularly important for more complicated symbolizations.).

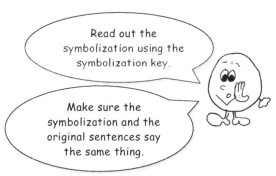

Read out the symbolization using the symbolization key.

Make sure the symbolization and the original sentences say the same thing.

What could go wrong? You could take the wedge to be the main connective:

$(D \supset J) \vee N$

However, this formula is a symbolization of a different English sentence.

$(D \supset J) \vee N$ Either if Susie wears a new dress then Jack will ask her out or Ned will ask her out.

Note the relative position of "either" and "if-then."

What else could go wrong? You could forget to place the parentheses:

D ⊃ J ∨ N

This is not a proper symbolization. In the system we have adopted, it is not a well-formed formula since it is not clear what the main connective is. The parentheses are needed to identify the main connective.

In the system at hand, this is gibberish.

Example 2

Let us consider a variation on the proposition we have just symbolized.

> (2) If Susie wears a new dress and a new hat then either Jack or Ned will ask her out.

Again, the crucial thing is to decide what the main connective is and place the parentheses accordingly. The proposition is a conditional. It says, "If blah-blah-blah then bleh-bleh-bleh." So the parentheses should be put thus:

> [If] (Susie wears a new dress [and] Susie wears a new hat) [then] ([either] Jack will ask her out [or] Ned will ask her out).

Substitute simple propositions with letters from the symbolization key:

> If (D and H) then (either J or N)

Substitute connective phrases with respective symbols:

> (D • H) ⊃ (J ∨ N)

What could go wrong? Again, you might misidentify the main connective as "and" or "or." Once again consider such possibilities and contrast them with the above proposition.

D • (H ⊃ (J ∨ N))   Susie will wear a new dress [but] [if] she wears a new hat [then] [either] Jack [or] Ned will ask her out.

((D • H) ⊃ J) ∨ N   [Either] [if] Susie wears a new dress [and] a new hat [then] Jack will ask her out [or] Ned will ask her out.

What else could go wrong? Here too, both sets of parentheses are necessary to disambiguate the proposition. All of the following are not well-formed formulas:

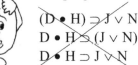

(D • H) ⊃ J ∨ N
D • H ⊃ (J ∨ N)
D • H ⊃ J ∨ N

All of these formulas are logical gibberish.

Example 3

Let us consider another variation:

> (3) If Susie wears a new dress and will no longer fret then either Jack or Ned will ask her out.

The proposition is once again a conditional of the form "If Susie blah-blah-blah then bleh-bleh-bleh." So the parentheses should be put thus:

> [If] (Susie wears a new dress [and] Susie will [no longer] fret) [then] ([either] Jack will ask her out [or] Ned will ask her out).

It is crucial to identify the negation (the phrase "no longer") inside the first set of parentheses. Substitute simple propositions with letters from the symbolization key:

> If (D and not R) then (either J or N)

Substitute connective phrases with respective symbols:

> (D • ~R) ⊃ (J ∨ N)

Of course, here also you may have made the same sorts of mistakes as in the above two examples.

Example 4

> (4) Either Susie will go out with both Jack and Ned or they will both ask Ann out.

Let us begin by marking all of the connective phrases:

> Either Susie will go out with both Jack and Ned or they will both ask Ann out.

The proposition is a disjunction; it says, "Either blah-blah-blah or bleh-bleh-bleh."
The first disjunct is a conjunction. What is perhaps not obvious at first is that so is the second disjunct. It is also a conjunction but it needs to be spelled more fully. Here is the paraphrased proposition with parentheses in place:

> Either (Susie will go out with both Jack and Ned) or (they will both ask Ann out).

We turn to the parentheses. Let us expand both conjunctions so it is quite clear what simple propositions are being conjoined.

> Either (both Susie will go out with Jack and Susie will go out with Ned) or (both Jack will ask Ann out and Ned will ask Ann out).

We are now ready to do the partial symbolization:

> Either (both S and U) or (both A and E)

We complete the symbolization by adding the connectives:

> (S • U) ∨ (A • E)

What could go wrong? As before, you may have misidentified the main connective. Once again, consider the possibilities and contrast them with the current proposition:

S • (U ∨ (A • E))   Susie will go out with Jack and either she will go out with Ned or both Jack and Ned will ask Ann out.

((S • U) ∨ A) • E   Either Susie will go out with both Jack and Ned or Jack will ask Ann out but, in any event, Ned will ask Ann out.

Example 5

> (5) If Susie goes out with Jack or Ned then either Jack will not ask Ann out or Ned will not ask Ann out.

Let's go step-by-step. First, mark all occurrences of the connective phrases:

If Susie goes out with Jack or Ned then either Jack will not ask Ann out or Ned will not ask Ann out.

It is clear now that the proposition is a conditional: "If blah-blah-blah then bleh-bleh-bleh." We place the parentheses accordingly.

If (Susie goes out with Jack or Ned) then (either Jack will not ask Ann out or Ned will not ask Ann out).

The disjunction in the antecedent of the conditional is relatively straightforward, we can symbolize it partially:

(S ∨ U) ⊃ (either Jack will not ask Ann out or Ned will not ask Ann out)

In the second set of parentheses, there is a disjunction of two negations. We can complete the symbolization thus:

(S ∨ U) ⊃ (~A ∨ ~E)

What could go wrong? As before, you may have taken misidentified the main connective. Contrast the following possibilities with proposition (5):

S ∨ (U ⊃ (~A ∨ ~E))   Either Susie goes out with Jack or if she goes out with Ned then either Jack will not ask Ann out or Ned will not ask Ann out.

((S ∨ U) ⊃ ~A) ∨ ~E   Either if Susie goes out with Jack or Ned then Jack will not ask Ann out, or Ned will not ask Ann out.

What else can go wrong? In addition to the other mistakes mentioned above, here you might be tempted to "pull out" the negation in front of the parentheses.

(S ∨ U) ⊃ ~(A ∨ E)

This a serious mistake. You will be able to appreciate it as a mistake only in Unit 1.4 in which we will learn about alternative ways to symbolize "neither-nor" and "not-both" phrases. For now, don't be tempted to transform the formulas. In your symbolization, stay as close to the original structure of the symbolized proposition as you possibly can.

(S ∨ U) ⊃ ~(A ∨ E)   If Susie goes out with Jack or Ned then it is not the case that either Jack or Ned will ask Ann out.

In other words: If Susie goes out with Jack or Ned then neither Jack nor Ned will ask Ann out.

Don't be tempted to pull out negations in front of parentheses!

In logic, the following pairs DO NOT say the same:
~(p • q)   ~p • ~q
~(p ∨ q)   ~p ∨ ~q
~(p ⊃ q)   ~p ⊃ ~q

Stay as close to the original structure of the symbolized proposition as you possibly can.

D: Ann **d**iets   G: Ann **g**ains weight   I: Billy d**i**ets
E: Ann **e**xercises   H: Ann is **h**ealthy   O: Billy j**o**gs
J: Ann **j**ogs   W: Billy gains **w**eight
S: Ann **s**wims

Exercise D.1 Symbolization

(a)   If Ann exercises then she will not gain weight.

(b)   If Ann does not exercise then she will gain weight.

(c)   If Ann either diets or exercises then she will be healthy.

(d)   If Ann diets and swims then she will be healthy.

(e)   If Ann diets and jogs then she will not gain weight.

Exercise D.2 Symbolization

(a)   If Ann swims then she will not jog.

(b)   If Billy diets then he will not jog

(c)   If Billy diets or jogs then he will not gain weight.

(d)   If Billy and Ann are on a diet, they will both jog.

(e)   If Billy either jogs or is on a diet then Ann will either swim or jog.

Exercise D.3 Symbolization

(a)   If either Ann or Billy gains weight then if Ann does not diet then Billy will not diet.

(b)   If Ann and Billy are both on a diet then Ann will jog if and only if Billy jogs.

(c)   Either Ann and Billy will diet or they will both jog.

(d)   Either Ann will diet or she will both swim and jog.

THE DISAMBIGUATING FORCE OF "EITHER ... OR...," "BOTH ... AND ...," "IF ... THEN..."

Several connectives can be phrased using one word (e.g., "or," "and," "if") or two words ("either-or," "both-and," "if-then"). Here are simple examples:

It rains or it snows   Either it rains or it snows

It's cloudy and it's windy   Both it's cloudy and it's windy

It's cloudy if it rains   If it rains then it's cloudy

When the structure of the propositions is uncomplicated, it does not matter whether one-word or two-word phrases are used. But when the structure of propositions becomes complicated, the two-word phrases help tremendously; they help decide what is said and what the main connective is.

Example 1

The following sentence is ambiguous.

(1) Susie will go out with Ned or Ann will go out with Jack and it will rain.

> **S:** Susie will go out with Ned
> **A:** Ann will go out with Jack
> **R:** It will rain

It can be disambiguated by the following propositions:

(1a) Either Susie will go out with Ned or both Ann will go out with Jack and it will rain.

[1a] $S \lor (A \bullet R)$

(1b) It is both the case that either Susie will go out with Ned or Ann will go out with Jack and that it will rain.

[1b] $(S \lor A) \bullet R$

Note that we have used the two-word connectives "both-and" and "either-or" to disambiguate the original sentence.

Example 2

The following sentence is also ambiguous:

(2) Susie will go out with Ned or Ann will go out with Jack if it rains.

If "or" is the main connective, we obtain the following proposition:

(2a) Either Susie will go out with Ned or if it rains then Ann will go out with Jack.

[2a] $S \lor (R \supset A)$

Alternatively, the proposition can be a conditional:

(2b) If it rains then either Susie will go out with Ned or Ann will go out with Jack.
[2b] $R \supset (S \lor A)$

In either case, one has to be careful about what the antecedent is.

Disambiguate the following
ambiguous sentences.
Then symbolize the propositions.

Exercise D.4 Disambiguation

(a)   Abe will read a couple of textbooks or listen to some lectures and solve some problems.

1:	
2:	

L: Abe will **l**isten to some lectures	[1]
R: Abe will **r**ead some textbooks	
S: Abe will **s**olve some problems	[2]

(b)   If Ann finishes her graduate studies then she will work as a scientist or she will become a teacher.

1:	
2:	

G: Ann finishes her **g**raduate studies	[1]
S: Ann will work as a **s**cientist	
R: Ann will become a teache**r**	[2]

(c)   Claire will go to Hawaii and Ben will go to Florida if Ann will go to the Bahamas

1:	
2:	

A: **A**nn will go to the Bahamas	[1]
B: **B**en will go to Florida	
C: **C**laire will go to Hawaii	[2]

(d)   Ann will finish her graduate studies and she will work as a scientist or she will become a teacher if she can live with little pay.

1:

2:

3:

4:

5:

G: Ann finishes her graduate studies
L: Ann can live with little pay
S: Ann will work as a scientist
R: Ann will become a teacher

[1]

[2]

[3]

[4]

[5]

THE MAIN CONNECTIVE DETERMINED BY MEANING

We now turn to some more complicated examples where the main connective is determined by meaning rather than by some syntactic feature.

Do the examples yourself first. Then check the step-by-step explanation that follows.

Example 1

(1)   If Susie goes out with Jack then Ned will ask Ann out but if Susie goes out with Ned then Jack will ask Ann out.

J: Jack will ask Ann out
N: Ned will ask Ann out
S: Susie will go out with Jack
U: Susie will go out with Ned

We begin by marking all occurrences of the connective phrases:

> [If] Susie goes out with Jack [then] Ned will ask Ann out [but] [if] Susie goes out with Ned [then] Jack will ask Ann out.

Here we cannot determine what the main connective is in any mechanical way. There are at least two candidates: the first conditional or the conjunction. However, it is clear to anyone who hears the statement that "but" is the main connective. What is said has the following shape: "blah-blah-blah **but** bleh-bleh-bleh." In fact, when you read the statement out loud, you *will* emphasize "but." Otherwise, you will not have expressed the intention behind the statement.

> ([If] Susie goes out with Jack [then] Ned will ask Ann out) [but] ([if] Susie goes out with Ned [then] Jack will ask Ann out)

Perhaps to emphasize the point that "but" is the main connective, you can reformulate the statement in this fashion to convince yourself that this is indeed what is said:

> [It is both the case that] ([if] Susie goes out with Jack [then] Ned will ask Ann out) [and that] ([if] Susie goes out with Ned [then] Jack will ask Ann out)

In this case, once we decide what the main connective is, the rest is easy:

> (if S then N) and (if U then J)
>
> [1] $(S \supset N) \bullet (U \supset J)$

What could go wrong?

Suppose someone thought that the conditional is the main connective:

> [If] Susie goes out with Jack [then] (Ned will ask Ann out [but] ([if] Susie goes out with Ned [then] Jack will ask Ann out))
>
> [*] $S \supset (N \bullet (U \supset J))$

Perhaps you sense that [*] is problematic. It makes little sense (not because of logic but because of the meaning). To see this, we will first look at an example of a sensible proposition with that structure. It will help us better understand the logical structure of such propositions. We will then be able to see that our proposition (1) does not fit such a structure at all.

First, let's consider a reasonable proposition with the same structure as [*]:

> [If] the polygon has 4 right angles [then] (it is a rectangle [and] ([if], in addition, its sides are equal [then] it is a square)).

Note that the insertion of "in addition" is very natural. It also indicates that the second "if" provides an additional condition (equal sides), which supplements the condition provided by the first "if" (4 right angles). This example illustrates the general structure of a statement like [*]. We can capture it schematically in the following way:

> If [condition1] then ([what depends on condition1] and (if [condition2] then [what depends on both condition 1 and condition2]).

Crucially, if a conditional has another conditional as a consequent, then the consequent of the second conditional depends on the antecedents of both conditionals.

Now let's see whether we can understand (1) in this fashion:

<u>If</u> Susie goes out with Jack <u>then</u> (Ned will ask Ann out <u>but</u> (<u>if</u> Susie goes out with Ned <u>then</u> Jack will ask Ann out))

According to this claim, Jack will ask Ann out on the condition that, among other things, Susie goes out both with Jack and Ned. By our (to date) dating standards, this would be unusual. While there is a possibility that a girl will go out with two boys (or vice versa), given the rarity of such an event, one would at least expect some additional hints that this is the way that we should understand the sentence. One such hint could be the insertion of "in addition," which is perspicuously missing.

Example 2

In this example, the main connective is also determined by the meaning of the statement.

(2) Susie is responsible for her action just in case she committed the act and she either intended or desired to commit it.

Try to do the symbolization yourself using the following symbolization key. (Those of you who already know a little about predicate logic will realize that the symbolization key that is available in propositional logic does not and cannot capture the full sense of the statement; the following key is a simplification.)

C: Susie **c**ommitted the act
D: Susie **d**esired to commit the act
I: Susie **i**ntended to commit the act
R: Susie is **r**esponsible for the act

Let's mark all occurrences of the connective phrases:

Susie is responsible for her action <u>just in case</u> she committed the act <u>and</u> she <u>either</u> intended <u>or</u> desired to commit it.

As before, if you think about what is said, you will have no problem deciding that the statement is a biconditional rather than a conjunction. When you read the statement, you will emphasize "just in case." This is a good, though not surefire, guide to what the main connective is. We naturally interpret such a statement as providing necessary and sufficient conditions for Susie's responsibility for the action.

Once you decided on the main connective, the rest is relatively simple:

Susie is responsible for her action <u>just in case</u> (she committed the act <u>and</u> she <u>either</u> intended <u>or</u> desired to commit it)

There is a complex statement within the parentheses; the main connective in the parentheses is "and" (the occurrence of "either" as well as the merged sentence structure are good indicators).

Susie is responsible for her action <u>just in case</u> (she committed the act <u>and</u> (she <u>either</u> intended <u>or</u> desired to commit it))

The rest is straightforward:

R just in case (C and (I or D))
[2] $R \equiv (C \bullet (I \vee D))$

What could go wrong?

Suppose someone thought that (2) is a conjunction:

(R just in case C) and (I or D)

[*]   (R ≡ C) • (I ∨ D)

(Susie is responsible for her action [just in case] she committed the act) [and] (she [either] intended [or] desired to commit it)

From a logical point of view, [*] is as good a proposition as any. However, [*] differs dramatically from [2]. According to [2], there are two necessary and (jointly) sufficient conditions for Susan's responsibility: to be responsible, Susan must have committed the act and she also must have had an appropriate mental state (either intention or desire). According to [*], on the other hand, there is *only one* necessary and sufficient condition for Susan's responsibility. In particular, it is sufficient for Susan to have committed the act to be responsible, i.e. no mental conditions are required at all. In addition, [*] says that it so happens that Susie is also in a certain mental state (either intention or desire). However, [*] does not treat this mental state as a condition of responsibility. In other words, what follows from [*] is that Susie is responsible for her action just in case she committed the act period; no further conditions are necessary.

Since we do not usually accept such a strict notion of responsibility, it is more natural to interpret (2) as [2] rather than [*]. If we wanted to express [*], we might do so in the following way:

Susie is responsible for her action just in case she committed the act and, incidentally, it so happens that she also either intended or desired to commit it.

Exercise D.5 Symbolization (Main Connective Determined by Meaning)

D: Ann **d**iets	G: Ann **g**ains weight	I: B**i**lly diets
E: Ann **e**xercises	H: Ann is **h**ealthy	O: Billy j**o**gs
J: Ann **j**ogs		W: Billy gains **w**eight
S: Ann **s**wims		

(a)   If Ann swims then she will not jog and if she jogs then she will not swim.

(b)   If Ann jogs then Billy jogs and if she swims then Billy diets.

(c)   If Ann jogs then Billy jogs and if, in addition, she swims then Billy diets.

(d)   Ann will jog just in case Billy jogs and Billy will go on a diet just in case Ann goes on a diet.

(e)   Billy does not gain weight just in case he diets and he also jogs.

(f)   Billy does not gain weight just in case he diets and, incidentally, it so happens that he also jogs.

Exercise D.6 Symbolization (Main Connective Determined by Meaning)

D: Ann **d**iets   **G**: Ann **g**ains weight   **I**: Billy d**i**ets
E: Ann **e**xercises   **H**: Ann is **h**ealthy   **O**: Billy j**o**gs
J: Ann **j**ogs   **W**: Billy **w**ains weight
S: Ann **s**wims

(a)   If Ann diets then so does Billy but if she does not diet
       then Billy gains weight.

(b)   Billy will gain weight just in case Ann gains weight and
       Billy will jog just in case Ann swims, jogs, or exercises.

(c)   If Billy diets then Ann also diets and if he jogs then she
       also jogs.

(d)   If Billy diets then Ann also diets and if, in addition, he
       jogs then she also jogs.

(e)   Ann will be healthy just in case she diets and either
       jogs, swims, or exercises.

(f)   Ann will be healthy just in case she diets and,
       incidentally, it so happens that she either jogs, swims,
       or exercises.

THE MAIN CONNECTIVE DETERMINED BY COMMA PLACEMENT

In some cases, the main connective is determined by the presence or absence of a comma. Consider the following two statements:

(1) If Jung's theory is false then Freud's theory is true, on the condition that Adler's theory is false.

(2) If Jung's theory is false, then Freud's theory is true on the condition that Adler's theory is false.

These two statements differ only in the way in which the comma is placed. In English, the placement of the comma is often indicative of what the main connective is. Let's place the parentheses as indicated by the commas:

(1) (If Jung's theory is false then Freud's theory is true) on the condition that Adler's theory is false

(2) If Jung's theory is false then (Freud's theory is true on the condition that Adler's theory is false)

Try to do the symbolization yourself, given the following symbolization key:

A: **A**dler's theory is true
J: **J**ung's theory is true
R: F**r**eud's theory is true

Let's mark all occurrences of the connective phrases:

(1) ([If] Jung's theory is [false] [then] Freud's theory is true) [on the condition that] Adler's theory is [false]

(2) [If] Jung's theory is [false] [then] (Freud's theory is true [on the condition that] Adler's theory is [false])

Let's do a partial symbolization. We will replace simple propositions with letters and symbolize negations. You should note that the proposition "The theory is false" can be paraphrased in terms of the negation "The theory is not true."

(1) (If ~J then R) on the condition that ~A

(2) If ~J then (R on the condition that ~A)

Now let's turn to the connective "on the condition that." Recall (from Unit 1.2) that whenever we say "*p* on the condition that *q*," *q* is the condition for *p*. In other words, "*p* on the condition that *q*" means the same as "if *q* then *p*." We should render the propositions in their standard *if-then* form thus:

(1) If ~A then (if ~J then R)

(2) If ~J then (if ~A then R)

All that remains is to substitute the symbols:

[1] ~A ⊃ (~J ⊃ R)

[2] ~J ⊃ (~A ⊃ R)

Exercise D.7 Symbolization (Comma Placement)

D: Ann **d**iets	**G**: Ann **g**ains weight	**I**: Billy diets
E: Ann exercises	**H**: Ann is **h**ealthy	**O**: Billy jogs
J: Ann **j**ogs		**W**: Billy gains weight
S: Ann **s**wims		

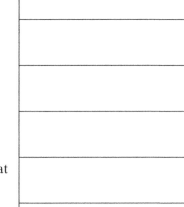

(a) If Ann swims, then she will not jog though she will diet.

(b) If Ann swims then she will not jog, but she will diet.

(c) If Ann is on a diet then Billy will be on a diet, but he will not jog.

(d) If Ann is on a diet, then Billy will be on a diet but he will not jog.

(e) If Ann jogs, then she will not gain weight provided that she goes on a diet.

(f) If Ann jogs then she will not gain weight, provided that she goes on a diet.

Exercise D.8 Symbolization (Comma Placement)

D: Ann **d**iets	**G**: Ann **g**ains weight	**I**: Billy d**i**ets
E: Ann **e**xercises	**H**: Ann is **h**ealthy	**O**: Billy j**o**gs
J: Ann **j**ogs		**W**: Billy gains **w**eight
S: Ann **s**wims		

(a)   If Ann diets then she will not gain weight, assuming that she is healthy.

(b)   If Ann diets, then she will not gain weight assuming that she is healthy.

(c)   If Billy and Ann diet, then they will jog provided that Ann is healthy.

(d)   If Billy and Ann diet then they will jog, provided that Ann is healthy.

(e)   Ann and Bill will jog or they will diet, provided that Ann is healthy.

(f)   Ann and Bill will jog, or they will diet provided that Ann is healthy.

About the Polish Notation

$\sim p$	Np
$p \bullet q$	Kpq
$p \vee q$	Apq
$p \supset q$	Cpq
$p \equiv q$	Epq

Did you know that we could be spared the trouble of using parentheses, detecting the main connective, etc.? We could use the Polish (prefix) notation introduced by Jan Łukasiewicz.

The key idea is that connectives are written first, as indicated in the table. When the terms of a formula are complex, the connective of that formula will stay in front (as the main connective), its terms will be made complex. For example,

$p \supset (p \vee q)$ would be represented as CpApq

$(p \bullet q) \supset q$ would be represented as CKpqq

$(p \vee q) \bullet \sim q$ would be represented as KApqNq.

The main connective is thus always first.

The notation has been extensively used in such devices as calculators, for example. The downside is that, for humans, it is rather difficult to scrutinize the logical structure of formulas written in Polish notation.

ECpCqrCqCpr

CCKApqrNAqrNNp

EAKpqrKAprAqr

Exercise D.9 Symbolization

> **A**: Ann is on a diet   **L:** Larry is getting fat
>
> **B**: Betty is on a diet.   **M:** Martin is getting fat
>
> **C**: Charlie is on a diet   **N:** Newt is getting fat

(a)   Either Ann is on a diet or Betty and Charlie are both on a diet.

(b)   It is both the case that either Ann or Betty is on a diet and that Charlie is on a diet.

(c)   Either Ann or Betty is on a diet and, in any event, Charlie is on a diet.

(d)   Either Larry and Martin are getting fat or Martin and Newt are getting fat

(e)   Either Ann or Betty is on a diet; however, it is also the case that either Betty or Charlie is on a diet.

(f)   Either both Larry and Martin are getting fat or Newt is not getting fat.

> **D**: Ann **d**iets   **G**: Ann **g**ains weight   **I**: Billy **d**iets
>
> **E**: Ann **e**xercises   **H**: Ann is **h**ealthy   **O**: Billy **j**ogs
>
> **J**: Ann **j**ogs   **W**: Billy **g**ains weight
>
> **S**: Ann **s**wims

Exercise D.10 Symbolization

(a)   If Ann does not exercise then she will both gain weight and lose health.

(b)   If Ann swims or jogs then Billy diets or jogs.

(c)   Either Ann will diet and swim or Billy will diet and jog.

(d)   Ann will either diet and swim or she will diet and jog.

(e)   If Ann swims or Billy jogs then both Ann and Billy will be on a diet.

D: Ann **d**iets   **G**: Ann **g**ains weight   **I**: **B**illy diets
E: Ann **e**xercises   **H**: Ann is **h**ealthy   **O**: Billy j**o**gs
J: Ann **j**ogs   **W**: Billy gains **w**eight
S: Ann **s**wims

Exercise D.11 Symbolization

(a)   Ann will be healthy just in case both she and Billy will jog.

(b)   Billy will jog if but only if either Ann jogs or exercises.

(c)   If Ann is on a diet but Billy is not, they will both be jogging.

(d)   Ann will either swim or jog if Billy either jogs or is on a diet.

(e)   If either Ann or Billy gains weight then if Ann does not diet then Billy will not diet.

Exercise D.12 Symbolization

(a)   If Ann and Billy are both on a diet then Ann will jog if and only if Billy jogs.

(b)   Either Ann and Billy will diet or they will both jog.

(c)   If Ann both diets and either swims or jogs then she will be healthy.

(d)   If either Ann and Billy both diet or they both jog then if Ann does not gain weight then Billy will not gain weight.

Summary

The main connective of a complex proposition determines what kind of proposition it is: a negation, a conjunction, a disjunction, a conditional, or a biconditional. You have learned to use the parentheses-binding method to identify the main connective of an arbitrarily complex proposition. You have also learned to identify the main connective in English sentences, which can be tricky sometimes. You have worked on enhancing your skill of symbolizing complicated English sentences.

Unit 1.4

"Neither Nor" and "Not Both" in Symbolizations

Overview

Now that you've acquired basic symbolization skills, it is time for you to learn some of the symbolization tricks. In this unit, we will take a closer look at conjunctions and disjunctions. We will learn how to handle multiple conjunctions and disjunctions. We will also learn to symbolize propositions with connective phrases such as "neither... nor..." and "not both... and ...," which are governed by de Morgan's laws.

      The symbolizations of "neither nor" and "not both" are intuitive. However, it is easy to get confused unless you do the exercises. As before, you need to do the exercises right after you read a section. Check your answers against the *Solutions*. If you have made a mistake, be sure that you understand what you misunderstood. Retake the exercise until your answers are 100% correct.

In this unit, you will learn:
- de Morgan's laws.

In this unit, you will learn how to:
- symbolize multiple conjunctions and disjunctions,
- symbolize "neither nor" and "not both,"
- symbolize exclusive disjunctions,
- symbolize more complicated English sentences (Unit 1.5 will develop the skill).

Time:	3-5 hours
Difficulty:	●●●●●○○
Status:	**Essential**/Recommended/Optional
Number of exercises:	24+1
Prerequisites:	Introduction, Unit 1.2, Unit 1.3

A. Multiple Conjunctions and Disjunctions

We have introduced both the connectives of conjunction and disjunction as two-place connectives. This means that "and" and "or" can only bind two propositions. In ordinary language, however, we often let "or" and "and" bind more than two propositions. In such cases, we often use a comma. Consider the following proposition:

(1) Ann, Betty, and Charlie are on a diet.

To symbolize (1), we need to render it as one of the following propositions:

> **A**: **A**nn is on a diet
> **B**: **B**etty is on a diet
> **C**: **C**harlie is on a diet
> **D**: **D**an is on a diet

[1a] $(A \bullet B) \bullet C$

[1b] $A \bullet (B \bullet C)$

Parentheses must be used though it does not matter whether we do it like in [1a] or [1b].

If the lists are longer, there will be more choices on how to put the parentheses. Consider a disjunction.

(2) Either Ann, Betty, Charlie, or Dan is on a diet.

We can capture the proposition but we need to render it as one of the following five propositions [2a]-[2e]:

[2a] $(A \vee B) \vee (C \vee D)$

[2b] $((A \vee B) \vee C) \vee D$

[2c] $(A \vee (B \vee C)) \vee D$

[2d] $A \vee (B \vee (C \vee D))$

[2e] $A \vee ((B \vee C) \vee D)$

Aren't there more possibilities? What about:
$(B \vee A) \vee (C \vee D)$?
$(A \vee D) \vee (C \vee B)$?
$D \vee (A \vee (B \vee C))$?

We stick to the rule that symbolizations ought to represent the symbolized propositions as closely as possible.

In (2), propositions A, B, C, D occur in this order.

B. "Neither ... Nor ..." and "Not Both ... and ..." (Take 1)

In this section, we will learn how to symbolize the very common connective phrases "neither ... nor ..." and "not both ... and ..." by means of negation and conjunction. In the next section, we will learn an alternative way of symbolizing them in terms of negation and disjunction. The availability of this alternative way is licensed by the so-called de Morgan's laws. We begin with the more intuitive symbolization.

"NOT BOTH ... AND ..." AS A NEGATION OF A CONJUNCTION

Suppose that a nice kitchen lady says to Ann:

> You can have both the banana and the cake.

What the nice kitchen lady says can be symbolized as:

> B • C

B: Ann can have the **b**anana
C: Ann can have the **c**ake

Imagine further that the nice kitchen lady's nasty superior storms in, grabs Ann's arm, and thunders:

> (1) You can*not* have both the banana and the cake.

What the nasty kitchen lady says is simply a denial (negation) of what the nice one said:

> [1] ~(B • C)

This provides a general recipe for symbolizing all propositions that have the "not both ... and ..." form:

> | Not both p and r | $\sim(p \bullet r)$ |

Consider the following examples:

> (2) John will ~~not both~~ become a doctor ~~and~~ a lawyer.
>
> [2] ~(D • L)

D: John is a **d**octor
L: John is a **l**awyer

> (3) Ann will not marry both Jim and Ned.
>
> [3] ~(J • N)

J: Ann marries **J**im
N: Ann marries **N**ed

> (4) Not both Donald and Joe will win the election.
>
> [4] ~(D • J)

D: **D**onald wins the election
J: **J**oe wins the election

> (5) Kate cannot both have the cake and eat it too.
>
> [5] ~(H • E)

H: Kate can **h**ave the cake
E: Kate can **e**at the cake

Mark all connectives

"NEITHER ... NOR ..." AS A CONJUNCTION OF NEGATIONS

Suppose that John's mother-in-law says to him:

(1) You are neither a doctor nor a lawyer.

What has she said?

Has she said that John is a doctor?   ○yes   ○no
Has she said that John is a lawyer?   ○yes   ○no

She's said that John is *not* a doctor *and* she's said that he is *not* a lawyer. In other words, what she's said can be captured in terms of a conjunction of two negations thus: John is *not* a doctor *and* John is *not* a lawyer.

[1] ~D • ~L

> **D**: John is a **d**octor
> **L**: John is a **l**awyer

Suppose that Jen looks into the fridge and sees a black banana shape. She thinks to herself:

(2) Yuck, I will *neither* eat this banana raw *nor* make a cake with it.

What has Jen said?

Will Jen eat this banana raw?   ○yes   ○no
Will she make a cake with this banana?   ○yes   ○no

Again, Jen has said *both* that she will *not* eat the banana raw *and* that she will *not* make a banana cake with it.

[2] ~R • ~C

> **C**: Jen makes a **c**ake with the banana
> **R**: Jen eats the banana **r**aw

In general,

| Neither *p* nor *r*   ~p • ~r |

Consider the following examples:

(3) It turned out that Ann will marry ⬚neither⬚ Jim ⬚nor⬚ Ned.

[3] ~J • ~N

> **J**: Ann marries **J**im
> **N**: Ann marries **N**ed

(4) Neither Donald nor Joe will win the election.

[4] ~D • ~J

> **D**: **D**onald wins the election
> **J**: **J**oe wins the election

(5) Kate can neither have the cake nor eat it.

[5] ~C • ~E

> **H**: Kate can **h**ave the cake
> **E**: Kate can **e**at the cake

Mark all connectives

Neither p nor r	$\sim p \bullet \sim r$
Not both p and r	$\sim(p \bullet r)$

A: **A**nn is on a diet   **D**: **D**irk is on a diet
B: **B**etty is on a diet   **E**: **E**velyn is on a diet
C: **C**harlie is on a diet   **G**: **G**arry is on a diet

Exercise B.1 Neither nor, Not both

(a)   Ann and Betty are not both on a diet.

(b)

(c)

$\sim A \bullet \sim B$

$\sim(B \bullet D)$

(d)   Neither Evelyn nor Betty is on a diet.

(e)   Ann and Dirk are not both on a diet.

Exercise B.1+ Neither nor, Not both

(a)   Neither Evelyn nor Garry is on a diet.

(b)   Dirk and Evelyn are not both on a diet.

(c)   Neither Garry nor Charlie is on a diet.

(d)   Neither Dirk nor Garry is on a diet.

(e)   Dirk and Garry are not both on a diet.

Exercise B.2 Neither nor, Not both

(a)   Neither Dirk nor Charlie is on a diet.

(b)   Betty and Dirk are not both on a diet.

(c)   Neither Garry nor Evelyn is on a diet.

(d)   Ann is on a diet but neither Betty nor Charlie is on a diet.

(e)   If Ann is on a diet then Betty and Garry are not both on a diet.

"BOTH NOT" AS A CONJUNCTION OF NEGATIONS

Instead of the connective phrase "neither... nor...," we can sometimes use "both not ... and not ... "; consider the following example:

(1) Ann and Betty both don't have a cat.

What have we said?

Does Ann have a cat?   ○yes   ○no
Does Betty have a cat?   ○yes   ○no

What we've said in (1) can be captured thus:

Ann does not have a cat and Betty does not have a cat.

[1] ~A • ~B

> **A:** Ann has a cat
> **B:** Betty has a cat

This looks like a symbolization pattern for "neither...nor...." Indeed, we can rephrase (1) as "Neither Ann nor Betty has a cat."

Both not *p* and not *r*	~*p* • ~*r*

Be careful!
"**both not** p and **not** r"
is NOT equivalent to
"**not both** p and r"!

> **A:** Ann is on a diet   **D:** Dirk is on a diet
> **B:** Betty is on a diet   **E:** Evelyn is on a diet
> **C:** Charlie is on a diet   **G:** Garry is on a diet

Exercise B.3 Both-Not, Not both

(a) Ann and Betty are both not on a diet.

(b) Charlie and Ann are not both on a diet.

(c) Evelyn and Ann are both not on a diet.

(d) Charlie and Betty are both not on a diet.

(e) Charlie and Dirk aren't both on a diet.

"NEITHER ... NOR ... NOR ..."

Suppose that there are three suitors for Ann: Jim, Ned, and Blake. However, none of them stands a chance. Ann's desperate mother exclaims:

(1) Ann will marry ⟨neither⟩ Jim ⟨nor⟩ Ned ⟨nor⟩ Blake.

What has Ann's mum said?

Has she said that Ann will marry Jim?	○yes	○no
Has she said that Ann will marry Ned?	○yes	○no
Has she said that Ann will marry Blake?	○yes	○no

The answers to all of these questions are negative. Proposition (1) can be symbolized as a conjunction of negations. However, since the dot is a two-place connective, we need to add parentheses (in either of two ways):

[1a]   (~J • ~N) • ~B

[1b]   ~J • (~N • ~B)

> **B**: Ann marries **B**lake
> **J**: Ann marries **J**im
> **N**: Ann marries **N**ed

What if Ann had four or five such suitors?

You'll see in section F.

> **A**: **A**nn is on a diet   **D**: **D**irk is on a diet
> **B**: **B**etty is on a diet   **E**: **E**velyn is on a diet
> **C**: **C**harlie is on a diet   **G**: **G**arry is on a diet

Exercise B.4 Neither nor-Nor

(a) Neither Ann nor Betty nor Evelyn is on a diet.	
(b) Neither Charlie, Dirk, nor Garry is on a diet.	
(c) Neither Garry nor Betty nor Evelyn is on a diet.	
(d) Charlie, Dirk, and Garry are all not on a diet.	
(e) Charlie, Dirk, and Garry are not all on a diet.	

"NEITHER ... NOR ..." AND "NOT BOTH ... AND ..." IN COMPLEX PROPOSITIONS

We have already seen in the exercises that "neither nor" and "not both" phrases can be components in complex propositions (see examples 1 and 2 below). It is also possible for *neither-nor* and *not-both* propositions to have complex terms (see examples 3 and 4 below).

Example 1

(1) John will not be happy if he is neither a doctor nor a lawyer.

Let's mark the connective phrases:

John will ⌷not⌷ be happy ⌷if⌷ he is ⌷neither⌷ a doctor ⌷nor⌷ a lawyer.

The main connective is clearly "if." We need to paraphrase the proposition into the canonical if-then form. We can also insert the parentheses:

⌷If⌷ **(**John is ⌷neither⌷ a doctor ⌷nor⌷ a lawyer**)** ⌷then⌷ he will ⌷not⌷ be happy

We are ready to do a partial symbolization:

(neither D nor L) ⊃ ~H

> **D**: John is a **d**octor
> **H**: John is **h**appy
> **L**: John is a **l**awyer

All that remains is to substitute the neither nor phrase:

[1] (~D • ~L) ⊃ ~H

Example 2

(2) John is not both a doctor and a lawyer; moreover, he is neither a doctor nor a lawyer.

Let's mark the connective phrases:

John is ⌷not⌷ ⌷both⌷ a doctor ⌷and⌷ a lawyer⌷; moreover,⌷ he is ⌷neither⌷ a doctor ⌷nor⌷ a lawyer.

The main connective is indicated by the semicolon and "moreover." This is a conjunction. Let's insert the parentheses:

(John is ⌷not⌷ ⌷both⌷ a doctor ⌷and⌷ lawyer**)**⌷; moreover,⌷ **(**he is ⌷neither⌷ a doctor ⌷nor⌷ a lawyer**)**

We are ready to do a partial symbolization:

(not both D • L) • (neither D nor L)

All that remains is to substitute the neither nor and not both phrases:

[2] ~(D • L) • (~D • ~L)

> Could we not **pull the negation out** of the second set of parentheses:
> ~(D • L) • ~(D • L) ?
>
> ...or **distribute the negation** in the first set of parentheses:
> (~D • ~L) • (~D • ~L)?

> Don't be tempted to transform propositions before you learn proofs!

> In particular, the following pairs DO NOT say the same thing:
> ~(p • q)   ~p • ~q
> ~(p ∨ q)   ~p ∨ ~q
> ~(p ⊃ q)   ~p ⊃ ~q

Example 3

So far, we have seen examples where the terms of "neither nor" were simple propositions. Here is an example where its terms are complex.

(3) Neither is it the case that Ned or Jim will get an A in logic nor is it the case that Jim or Betty will get an A in logic.

We proceed as usual. Let's mark the connectives:

Neither is it the case that Ned or Jim will get an A in logic nor is it the case that Jim or Betty will get an A in logic.

Note that "is it the case that" is part of the connective phrase "neither nor." It is a phrase that is useful in disambiguating complex propositions. Sentence (3) says "neither something nor something else," where the "somethings" are themselves complex. Indeed, "neither nor" is the main connective. Let's insert the parentheses accordingly:

Neither is it the case that (Ned or Jim will get an A in logic) nor is it the case that (either Jim or Betty will get an A in logic)

We can abbreviate simple propositions with letters:

Neither (N or J) nor (J or B)

B: Betty gets an A in logic
J: Jim gets an A in logic
N: Ned gets an A in logic

Let's do a partial symbolization of the parentheses:

Neither (N ∨ J) nor (J ∨ B)

We can treat the propositions in the parentheses as wholes. Make sure that they have parentheses around them!

Finally, we symbolize "neither nor." It is useful to think about the symbolization schema:

$$\text{Neither } p \text{ nor } r \qquad \sim p \bullet \sim r$$

in terms of a template:

$$\text{neither } (N \vee J) \text{ nor } (J \vee B)$$

$$\sim (N \vee J) \bullet \sim (J \vee B)$$

When we enter the complex propositions into the template, we obtain the following symbolization:

[3] ~(N ∨ J) • ~(J ∨ B)

Always double-check that there is a sufficient number of parentheses!

Example 4

(4)   Neither Freud's nor Jung's theory is false.

This proposition looks simpler than it is. It is a *neither-nor* proposition. But its terms are complex. This is because the proposition "Freud's theory is false" is in fact a negation of the proposition "Freud's theory is true." Let us make this explicit. We will also mark all the connectives:

Neither Freud's theory is not true nor Jung's theory is not true.

"Neither nor" is the main connective. Let's put the parentheses in so that the complex components are visible (some of you may already realize that we will ultimately drop the parentheses):

Neither (Freud's theory is not true) nor (Jung's theory is not true)

We can proceed with a partial symbolization:

Neither (not R) nor (not J)

Neither (~R) nor (~J)

> **R**: Freud's theory is true
> **J**: Jung's theory is true

At this point, it becomes clear that the parentheses are not necessary as they embrace negations.

We can use the above template to arrive at the symbolization:

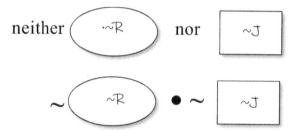

We thus arrive at:

[4]   ~~R • ~~J

The symbolization of (4) is a conjunction of two double negations.

Should we cancel the double negations? Well, ~~p is indeed logically equivalent to p. However, until you know what logical equivalence is and, more importantly, until you are able to determine whether two propositions are logically equivalent, it is a good rule of thumb not to make any simplifications. Try to stay as close to the complexity of the original sentence as possible. It is easy to make mistakes otherwise. In particular, there are contexts where two negations are not cancellable. For example, ~(~p • r) is not logically equivalent to p • r.

In the following exercises, symbolize the propositions. In Ex. B.5, provide an interpretation in English.

Don't make any simplifications or transformations until you've mastered proofs!

Exercise B.5. Neither nor – Complex Terms

> **A**: Ann is sick   **B**: Betty is sick   **C**: Charlie is sick   **D**: Dirk is sick

(a)   Neither A nor B

Neither Ann nor Betty is sick.	~A • ~B

(b)   Neither ~A nor ~B

(c)   Neither (A • B) nor (C • D)

(d)   Neither (A ∨ B) nor (A • B)

(e)   Neither (A ⊃ B) nor (B ⊃ A)

(f)   Neither (A ≡ B) nor (B ≡ A)

Exercise B.6 Neither nor – Complex Terms

(a)   Neither is it the case that both Ann and Betty are sick nor is it the case that Dirk is while Chris is not sick.

(b)   Neither is it so that either Dirk or Charlie are sick nor is it so that Charlie is not sick if and only if Dirk is not sick.

(c)   Neither Charlie is not sick nor Betty and Ann are both sick.

(d)   Neither is it true that if Charlie is sick then Betty or Dirk is sick nor is it true that if Betty or Dirk is sick then so is Charlie.

(e)   Either neither Ann nor Betty is not sick or neither Betty nor Charlie is not sick.

Example 5

Components of not both propositions can also be complex.

> (5) Ned will not both make A in logic or calculus and fulfill his duties as husband or boyfriend.

Let's begin by rephrasing the sentence in such a way that it is clear that it is a negation of a conjunction.

> It is not the case that both Ned will make A in logic or calculus and Ned will fulfill his duties as husband or boyfriend.

Let's mark all the connective phrases:

> [It is not the case that] [both] Ned will make A in logic [or] calculus [and] Ned will fulfill his duties as husband [or] boyfriend.

The proposition is complex – there is a negation, a conjunction, and two disjunctions. However, it is clear that the disjunctions fall into parentheses:

> [It is not the case that] [both] (Ned will make A in logic [or] calculus) [and] (Ned will fulfill his duties as husband [or] boyfriend)

It will be helpful to do a partial symbolization:

> Not both (L ∨ C) and (H ∨ B)

Again it is useful to think about the schema:

> **B**: Ned fulfills duties as **B**oyfriend
> **C**: Ned gets an A in **C**alculus
> **H**: Ned fulfills duties as **H**usband
> **L**: Ned gets an A in **L**ogic

> Not both p and r $\sim(p \bullet r)$

in terms of a template:

> not both $(L \vee C)$ and $(H \vee B)$
>
> $\sim \big((L \vee C) \bullet (H \vee B) \big)$

After writing in the components, we obtain:

> [5] $\sim\big((L \vee C) \bullet (H \vee B)\big)$

In the following exercises, symbolize the propositions. In Ex. B.7, provide an interpretation in English.

Exercise B.7 Not both – Complex Terms

> **A**: Ann is rich   **B**: Betty is rich   **C**: Charlie is rich   **D**: Dirk is rich

(a)   Not both A and B

Not both Ann and Betty are rich.	~(A • B)

(b)   Not both ~A and ~B

(c)   Not both (A • B) and (C • D)

(d)   Not both (A ∨ B) and (A • B)

(e)   Not both (A ⊃ B) and (B ⊃ A)

(f)   Not both (A ≡ B) and (A ≡ B)

Exercise B.8 Not both – Complex Terms

(a)	It is not both the case that Ann and Betty are both rich and that Dirk and Chris are not rich.	
(b)	It is not both true that Ann is rich if and only if Chris is rich and that Betty is rich if and only if Dirk isn't.	
(c)	If it is not both so that Ann is rich if and only if Betty is and that Betty is rich if and only if Charlie is, then neither Ann nor Betty is rich.	
(d)	If neither Ann nor Betty is rich then it's not both the case that either Ann or Charlie is rich and that either Betty or Dirk is rich.	
(e)	It is not both the case that Ann and Betty are not both rich and that Chris and Dirk are not both rich.	

> **A**: **A**nn is happy **D**: **D**irk is happy
> **B**: **B**etty is happy **E**: **E**velyn is happy
> **C**: **C**harlie is happy **G**: **G**arry is happy

Exercise B.9 Neither nor, Not both

(a) Either Ann is not happy or Betty and Charlie are not both happy.

(b) It is not the case that neither Ann nor Betty is happy.

(c) It is not the case that Charlie and Dirk are not both happy.

(d) It would be a lie to say that Evelyn and Ann are both not happy.

(e) It is neither the case that Ann is not happy nor that Betty is not happy.

Exercise B.10 Neither nor, Not both

(a) Ann is happy but Betty and Evelyn are not both happy.

(b) If neither Betty nor Evelyn is happy then Charlie and Garry are not both happy.

(c) If Betty and Evelyn are not both happy then neither Charlie nor Garry is happy.

(d) Neither Ann nor Betty nor Evelyn is happy.

(e) Neither Garry nor Betty nor Evelyn is happy.

C. The Exclusive Disjunction "Either ... or ... but Not Both"

 When we introduced disjunction in Unit 1.2, we said that our intuitions are divided. Sometimes we take disjunctions to be inclusive but other times we take disjunctions to be exclusive. In logic, disjunction (represented by "∨") is inclusive. However, there is a way of expressing the exclusive disjunction by means of inclusive disjunction. We can now see how.

Suppose Billy's mother says to him:

(1)   You can have either a cat or a dog but you can't have both.

This is a way of making explicit that an exclusive disjunction is intended. We can paraphrase proposition (1) to make its structure clearer:

> Billy can have either a cat or a dog but he cannot have both a cat and a dog.

When we mark all the connectives, it will become clear that "but" is the main connective:

(Billy can have either a cat or a dog) but (he cannot have both a cat and a dog)

(C or D) • (not both C and D)

[1] $(C \vee D) • \sim(C • D)$

> **C**: Billy can have a **c**at
> **D**: Billy can have a **d**og

In general, exclusive disjunction is symbolized as a conjunction of inclusive disjunction and a negation of a conjunction:

Either p or r but not both	$(p \vee r) • \sim(p • r)$

Did you know...

...that exclusive disjunction has played an important role in the development of artificial intelligence (AI) and, in particular, neural networks.

The first neural networks (so-called perceptrons) appeared in the 1950s. Researchers working on perceptrons worked in parallel with researchers in the so-called classical AI program until the late 1960s. The turning point was a sustained critique of perceptron research by Minsky and Papert. It turned out that perceptrons had serious limitations. One of them was the fact that they could not master the truth table for exclusive disjunction (the XOR problem). Minsky and Papert's critique has virtually stopped neural network research for over a decade.

In the mid-1980s, David Rumelhart and James McClelland published the results of their research on neural networks. Their networks had a more complex architecture (with so-called hidden layers). Moreover, they used a non-linear activation function. Such networks could master exclusive disjunction. They turned out to have many advantages and are widely used nowadays.

Exercise C. Exclusive-Disjunction

		A: Ann is happy	B: Betty is happy	C: Charlie is happy	D: Dirk is happy

(a)	Either Ann or Betty is happy but not both.	
(b)	Either Betty or Charlie is happy but they aren't both happy.	
(c)	Either Charlie or Dirk is happy but not both.	
(d)	If either Ann or Charlie is happy though not both, then Betty or Dirk is happy.	
(e)	Either Betty is not happy or Dirk is not happy but not both.	

D. De Morgan's Laws

De Morgan's laws express equivalences between negated conjunctions and disjunctions, on the one hand, and conjunctions of negations and disjunctions of negations, on the other. I will state de Morgan's laws first. We will then look at some intuitive examples that illustrate the laws. Finally, we will look at the mistakes we sometimes make.

The first de Morgan's law says that a negation of a disjunction is equivalent to a conjunction of negations. The second law says that a negation of a conjunction is equivalent to a disjunction of negations.

De Morgan's laws
$\sim(p \lor r)$ is logically equivalent to $\sim p \bullet \sim r$
$\sim(p \bullet r)$ is logically equivalent to $\sim p \lor \sim r$

Example 1

Tom comes late for lunch. Jane, the kitchen lady, says to him, "You will not have the spaghetti or the pizza, love":

(1) It is not the case that Tom will have either spaghetti or pizza.

[1] $\sim(S \lor P)$

> **P**: Tom has **p**izza
> **S**: Tom has **s**paghetti

What has she said?

Has she said that Tom will have spaghetti?   ○yes ○no

Has she said that Tom will have pizza?   ○yes ○no

Clearly, she's said that Tom will have neither spaghetti nor pizza:

[1′] $\sim S \bullet \sim P$

(1′) Tom will |not| have spaghetti |and| he will |not| have pizza.

According to de Morgan's first law, $\sim(S \lor P)$ is logically equivalent to $\sim S \bullet \sim P$.

Example 2

Consider another example to illustrate the second law. Jane, the kitchen lady, says to Tom, "You will not have both the ice cream and the cake":

(2) It is not the case that Tom will have both the ice cream and the cake.

[2] ~(I • C)

> **I**: Tom has the **ice cream**
> **C**: Tom has the **cake**

What has she said?

Here, we need to be careful. She has made a negative claim: something will not be the case. There are four theoretical possibilities:

(i) Tom eats the ice cream and the cake.

(ii) Tom eats the ice cream but not the cake.

(iii) Tom eats the cake but not the ice cream.

(iv) Tom eats neither the ice cream nor the cake.

Proposition (2) excludes the first of these possibilities (i). This means that Jane allows for three remaining options:

(ii) Tom eats the ice cream but not the cake.

(iii) Tom eats the cake but not the ice cream.

(iv) Tom eats neither the ice cream nor the cake.

The three possible situations (ii)-(iv) can be expressed by a shorter disjunction (recall that disjunction is inclusive):

(2′) Either Tom does not have the ice cream or he does not have the cake.

[2′] ~I ∨ ~C

According to de Morgan's second law, ~(I • C) is logically equivalent to ~I ∨ ~C.

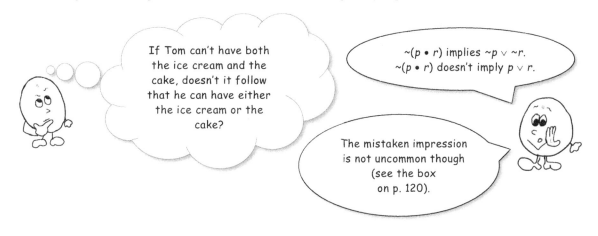

Example 3

Consider yet another illustration of the second law.

> S: Skinner's theory is true
> W: Watson's theory is true

    (3) It is not the case that both Skinner's and Watson's theories are true.

    [3] ~(S • W)

(3) denies one possibility (that both theories are true) but leaves three possibilities in play: either (a) Skinner's theory is false and Watson's theory is true, or (b) Skinner's theory is true and Watson's theory is false, or (c) Skinner's theory is false and Watson's theory is false. In other words, (3) means that at least one of the two theories is false:

    (3′) Either Skinner's or Watson's theory is false.

In other words:

    (3′) Either Skinner's theory is not true or Watson's theory is not true.

    [3′] ~S ∨ ~W

Indeed, according to de Morgan's second law, ~(S • W) is logically equivalent to ~S ∨ ~W.

Does "not both p and r" imply "either p or r"?

Does the claim "Skinner's and Watson's theories are not both true" imply that one of the theories is true? Does the fact that Tom will not have both the ice cream and the cake imply that he will have either the ice cream or the cake?

No. Yet, it is not uncommon to think otherwise. There are at least two explanations why we might have such a mistaken impression.

First, in some situations, the third possibility (neither p nor r) might actually be excluded. In such cases, to deny both p and r is to allow either (a) that ~p and r, or (b) that p and ~r. In such cases, it will be true that either p or r because the possibility that neither p nor r is excluded. However, in such cases, it is also true that either ~p or ~r. For example, suppose that in a dining hall, every student must take a salad (whether they want to or not, they will get some salad). Jane says to Tom, "We have a Greek salad and a Caesar salad but you cannot have both." Given the dining hall rule, Tom will get one of them (either the Greek salad or the Caesar salad). Note, however, that in this case, it is also true that either Tom won't get the Greek salad or he won't get the Caesar salad (~p ∨ ~r). The latter follows no matter what additional restrictions are in play: it is logically implied by ~(p • r).

Another reason why we might think that "not both p and r" implies "either p or r" is that we might associate "not both p and r" with "either p or r" since the phrases frequently occur together. For example, both phrases are used when we express an exclusive disjunction. For example, we may often hear "You can have either the pastrami or the salmon sandwich but not both." It might then be natural for us to interpret the instruction "You cannot have both the pastrami and the salmon sandwich" by silently adding to it "You can have either the pastrami or the salmon sandwich." But this is not a logical implication. It is merely a situational association.

Fill in the missing symbolizations.
Use de Morgan's laws to match
logically equivalent propositions.

A: **A**nn is happy   C: Ann is **c**heerful.
B: **B**etty is happy   S: Betty is **s**incere.

Exercise D de Morgan's Laws

Ann is not happy and she is not cheerful.

Ann is not happy or she is not cheerful.

It is not the
case that Ann is happy and cheerful.

It is not the
case that Ann is happy or cheerful.

Ann and Betty are both not happy.

It is not the case that Ann or Betty is happy.

Ann and Betty are not both happy.

Either Ann or Betty is not happy.

Betty is either not happy or not sincere.

It is not the case that Betty is either happy or sincere.

Betty is both
not happy and not sincere.

It isn't the case
that Betty is both happy and sincere.

E. "Neither ... Nor ..." and "Not Both ... and ..." (Take 2)

De Morgan's laws offer two alternative symbolizations of "neither nor" and "not both" propositions. So far, we have learned to symbolize them in terms of negations and conjunctions. We will now learn to do the symbolizations in terms of negations and disjunctions.

"NEITHER ... NOR ..." AS A NEGATION OF A DISJUNCTION

De Morgan's first law shows us that we can symbolize any *neither-nor* proposition either as a conjunction of negations, as we have done so far, or equivalently as a negation of a disjunction.

Neither p nor r	$\sim p \bullet \sim r$	$\sim(p \vee r)$

This is quite intuitive as you can see on the examples we have looked at.

Example 1

John's mother-in-law said to him:

(1) You will be neither a doctor nor a lawyer.

[1] $\sim D \bullet \sim L$

[1'] $\sim(D \vee L)$

D: John is a **d**octor
L: John is a **l**awyer

She could just as well have said:

(1') You won't become either a doctor or a lawyer.

Example 2

Recall what Jen thought to herself when she found a black banana in the fridge:

(2) Yuck, I will neither eat this banana raw nor make a cake with it

[2] $\sim R \bullet \sim C$

C: Jen makes a **c**ake with the banana
R: Jen eats the banana **r**aw

She could have had an equivalent thought:

(2') I won't either eat this banana raw or make a cake with it.

[2'] $\sim(R \vee C)$

Example 3

Similarly, the claim:

(3) Ann will marry neither Jim nor Ned

[3] $\sim J \bullet \sim N$

J: Ann marries **J**im
N: Ann marries **N**ed

can be expressed equivalently as :

(3') Ann won't marry either Jim or Ned.

[3'] $\sim(J \vee N)$

"NOT BOTH ... AND ..." AS A DISJUNCTION OF NEGATIONS

The second *de Morgan's law* helps in the symbolization of "not both" propositions.

Not both p and r	$\sim(p \bullet r)$	$\sim p \lor \sim r$

Example 1

Consider a case where the equivalence is intuitive. Consider the claim:

(1) Adler's and Jung's theories are not both true.

[1] $\sim(A \bullet J)$

A: Adler's theory is true
J: Jung's theory is true

According to de Morgan's second law, we can also represent the proposition thus:

[1′] $\sim A \lor \sim J$

(1′) Either Adler's or Jung's theory is false.

If you think about it, this is indeed all that someone who makes claim (1) commits herself to. To say that Adler's and Jung's theories are not both true is to say that at least one of them is false: either Adler's theory or Jung's theory is false.

Claim (1) can be made by someone who does not believe that either of the theories is true. Most contemporary psychologists believe that neither Adler's nor Jung's theories are true, but they can make a claim like (1) and fully believe it. To make a claim like (1) is merely to say that the theories are incompatible with one another. In other words, the theories cannot be both true, i.e., at least one of them (or possibly both) is false.

Example 2

(1) It won't both snow and rain at the same time.

[1] $\sim(S \bullet R)$

S: It snows
R: It rains

[1′] $\sim S \lor \sim R$

(1′) Either it won't snow or it won't rain.

Neither p nor r	$\sim p \bullet \sim r$	$\sim(p \lor r)$
Not both p and r	$\sim(p \bullet r)$	$\sim p \lor \sim r$

In Ex. E.1-E.6, provide at least two different equivalent symbolizations.

A: **A**nn is depressed   D: **D**irk is depressed
B: **B**etty is depressed   E: **E**velyn is depressed
C: **C**harlie is depressed   G: **G**arry is depressed

Exercise E.1 Neither nor, Not both

(a)   Charlie and Ann are not both depressed.

(b)   Neither Ann nor Betty is depressed.

(c)   Ann and Betty are not both depressed.

(d)   Neither Betty nor Evelyn is depressed.

(e)   Charlie and Garry are both not depressed.

Exercise E.2 Neither nor, Not both

(a)   Neither Ann nor Betty is depressed.

(b)   Both Charlie and Garry are not depressed.

(c)   Betty and Evelyn are not both depressed.

(d)   Neither Betty nor Evelyn is depressed, though Ann is.

(e)   If Ann is depressed then Betty and Charlie are not both depressed.

Exercise E.3 Neither nor, Not both

(a)   Either Ann is not depressed or Betty and Charlie are not both depressed.

(b)   It is not the case that neither Ann nor Betty is depressed.

(c)   It is not the case that Charlie and Dirk are not both depressed.

(d)   It would be a lie to say that Evelyn and Ann are both not depressed.

(e)   It is neither the case that Ann is not depressed nor that Betty is not depressed.

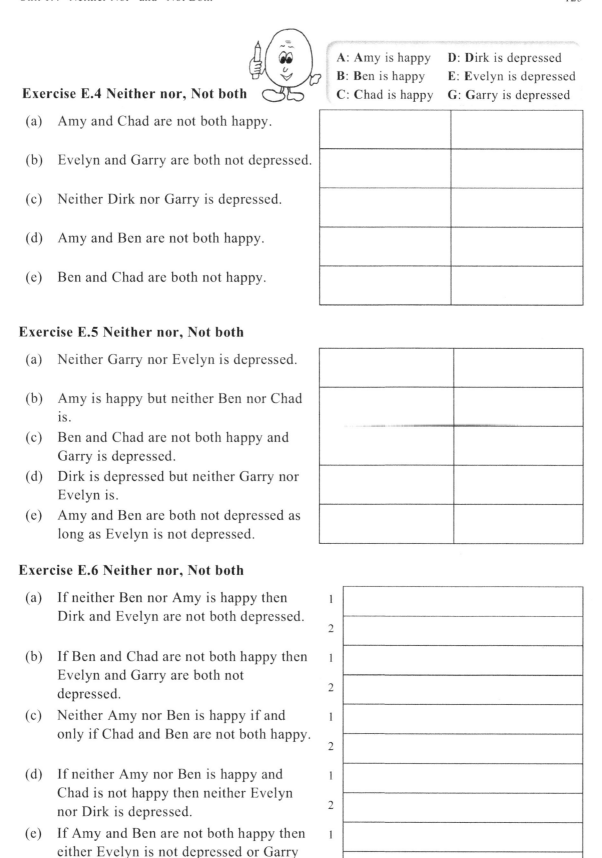

A: Amy is happy	D: Dirk is depressed
B: Ben is happy	E: Evelyn is depressed
C: Chad is happy	G: Garry is depressed

Exercise E.4 Neither nor, Not both

(a)   Amy and Chad are not both happy.

(b)   Evelyn and Garry are both not depressed.

(c)   Neither Dirk nor Garry is depressed.

(d)   Amy and Ben are not both happy.

(e)   Ben and Chad are both not happy.

Exercise E.5 Neither nor, Not both

(a)   Neither Garry nor Evelyn is depressed.

(b)   Amy is happy but neither Ben nor Chad is.

(c)   Ben and Chad are not both happy and Garry is depressed.

(d)   Dirk is depressed but neither Garry nor Evelyn is.

(e)   Amy and Ben are both not depressed as long as Evelyn is not depressed.

Exercise E.6 Neither nor, Not both

(a)   If neither Ben nor Amy is happy then Dirk and Evelyn are not both depressed.

(b)   If Ben and Chad are not both happy then Evelyn and Garry are both not depressed.

(c)   Neither Amy nor Ben is happy if and only if Chad and Ben are not both happy.

(d)   If neither Amy nor Ben is happy and Chad is not happy then neither Evelyn nor Dirk is depressed.

(e)   If Amy and Ben are not both happy then either Evelyn is not depressed or Garry and Dirk are not both depressed.

F. "All," "Some," "Not All," "None"

The words "all," "some," but also "not all" and "none," are so-called quantificational operators. They appear in all their glory in quantifier logic. Indeed, most of the occurrences of "all" and "some" and related expressions cannot be expressed in terms of propositional logic. However, some of those occurrences can be paraphrased in propositional logic, e.g., when they concern a finite group of people or objects.

"ALL"

Consider a group of four people: Ann, Betty, Charlie, and Dirk. When we say about them:

> (1) All of them are on a diet

we mean the same as:

> (1′) Ann, Betty, Charlie, and Dirk are on a diet

which we can symbolize as any of the following:

> [1a] $(A \bullet B) \bullet (C \bullet D)$
>
> [1b] $A \bullet ((B \bullet C) \bullet D)$
>
> [1c] $A \bullet (B \bullet (C \bullet D))$
>
> [1d] $((A \bullet B) \bullet C) \bullet D$
>
> [1e] $(A \bullet (B \bullet C)) \bullet D$

A: **A**nn is on a diet
B: **B**etty is on a diet
C: **C**harlie is on a diet
D: **D**irk is on a diet

"SOME"

Similarly, we can understand a proposition such as:

> (2) At least one of them is on a diet.

or equivalently:

> (2′) Some of them are on a diet.

Since we are talking about Ann, Betty, Charlie, and Dirk, (2) means:

> (2″) Ann, Betty, Charlie, or Dirk is on a diet.

It can be symbolized as any of the following:

> [2a] $(A \vee B) \vee (C \vee D)$
>
> [2b] $A \vee ((B \vee C) \vee D)$
>
> [2c] $A \vee (B \vee (C \vee D))$
>
> [2d] $((A \vee B) \vee C) \vee D$
>
> [2e] $(A \vee (B \vee C)) \vee D$

"NONE"

"Negative" quantificational expressions can also be paraphrased in propositional logic provided that we restrict their range to a specified group of people.

      Consider the following proposition about Ann, Betty, Charlie, and Dirk:

    (3) None of them is on a diet.

In this context, (3) means:

    (3′) Neither Ann, Betty, Charlie, nor Dirk is on a diet

which can be represented, for example (let's skip parentheses permutations), as:

    [3a] (~A • ~B) • (~C • ~D)

Equivalently, we can represent (3) as:

    [3b] ~[(A ∨ B) ∨ (C ∨ D)]

"NOT ALL"

We can also find a way of representing a proposition like:

    (4) Not all of them are on a diet.

Since we are concerned with the same group of people, (4) means:

    (4′) Ann, Betty, Charlie, and Dirk are not all on a diet.

It is best understood as a negation of the claim that they are all on a diet, i.e., as:

    [4a] ~[(A • B) • (C • D)]

or equivalently as, for example:

    [4b] (~A ∨ ~B) ∨ (~C ∨ ~D)

Aside from the different ways of placing parentheses, we can also combine the two different ways of symbolizing "not both" or "not-all" phrases. For example:

    [4c] ~(A • B) ∨ ~(C • D)

> In the following exercises, symbolize the propositions. In Ex. F.1 and F.2, quantificational expressions pertain to groups of 4 and 6 persons, respectively.

Exercise F.1 All-Some-None-Not-All

> **A**: **A**nn is on a diet   **C**: **C**harlie is on a diet
> **B**: **B**etty is on a diet.   **D**: **D**irk is on a diet

(a)   All four are on a diet.

(b)   At least one of the four is on a diet.

(c)   Someone from the group is on a diet.

(d)   Not all are on a diet.

(e)   Nobody in the group is on a diet.

Exercise F.2 All-Some-None-Not-All

> **A**: **A**my is busy   **J**: **J**ohn is busy
> **B**: **B**etty is busy   **K**: **K**en is busy
> **C**: **C**lara is busy   **L**: **L**arry is busy

(a)   All the boys in this group are busy.

(b)   There is a girl in this group who is busy.

(c)   Not all girls are busy.

(d)   Nobody in this group is busy.

(e)   Not everybody in this group is busy.

Exercise F.3 All-Some-None-Not-All

(a)   Some, but not all, of the boys in this
       group are busy.

(b)   Not all girls in this group are not busy
       but at least one girl is not busy.

(c)   Neither all girls nor all boys in this
       group are busy.

G. Complicated Symbolizations

The material that you have now covered should give you enough preparation to face up to many symbolization tasks in propositional logic. In the complicated symbolizations, you will be required to apply all the "tricks" you have learned at once, which is what makes those symbolizations complicated. Bear in mind that there will often be more than one correct way of symbolizing a proposition.

Example 1

   (1) Jane will not go out with Bill if he neither smokes nor drinks heavily.

Let's mark the connectives and place the parentheses; there is only one way to do so:

Jane will │not│ go out with Bill │if│ (he │neither│ smokes │nor│ drinks heavily)

Since this is a conditional, it is best to paraphrase it into the canonical "if-then" form:

│If│ (Bill │neither│ smokes │nor│ drinks heavily) │then│ Jane will │not│ go out with him.

We can now do a partial symbolization. We will first substitute propositional letters for simple propositions and then symbolize the "easy" connectives:

If (neither S nor D) then not J

(neither S nor D) ⊃ ~J

> D: Bill drinks heavily
> J: Jane goes out with Bill
> S: Bill smokes

We are left with "neither ... nor ...," which we can symbolize in two ways:

   [1a] (~S • ~D) ⊃ ~J

   [1b] ~(S ∨ D) ⊃ ~J

Example 2

   (2) Either both Ned and Jim will get an A in logic or neither of them will.

We must rephrase (2) to make its full content explicit:

> Either both Ned and Jim will get an A in logic or neither Ned nor Jim will get an A in logic.

"Either-or" provides a good indication of where to put the parentheses:

│Either│ (│both│ Ned │and│ Jim will get an A in logic) │or│ (│neither│ Ned │nor│ Jim will get an A in logic).

We do a partial symbolization:

Either (N and J) or (neither N nor J)

(N • J) ∨ (neither N nor J)

> N: Ned will get an A in logic
> J: Jim will get an A in logic

Finally, we symbolize "neither nor":

   [2a] (N • J) ∨ (~N • ~J)

   [2b] (N • J) ∨ ~(N ∨ J)

Example 3

(3) It isn't both the case that neither Ann nor Ben will get an A in logic and that neither Will nor Jill will get an A in logic.

Whew... This sounds complicated... Let's mark the connectives:

It is ⊠not⊠ ⊠both⊠ the case that ⊠neither⊠ Ann ⊠nor⊠ Ben will get an A in logic ⊠and⊠ that ⊠neither⊠ Will ⊠nor⊠ Jill will get an A in logic.

We have one occurrence of "not both" and two occurrences of "neither nor." Clearly, the *neither-nor* propositions are components of a more complex proposition. We can indicate that by placing parentheses around them:

It is ⊠not⊠ ⊠both⊠ the case that (⊠neither⊠ Ann ⊠nor⊠ Ben will get an A in logic) ⊠and⊠ that (⊠neither⊠ Will ⊠nor⊠ Jill will get an A in logic)

I hope you agree that once we've put parentheses in, the proposition looks simpler than what we started with. It's a *not-both* proposition with quite complicated components.

Let's abbreviate simple propositions with propositional letters:

not both (neither A nor B) and (neither W nor J)

We are left with "not both ... and ..." and "neither... nor... ." We can symbolize the *neither nor* propositions either (a) as conjunctions of negations or (b) as negations of disjunctions:

aa:	not both ($\sim$A $\bullet$ $\sim$B) and ($\sim$W $\bullet$ $\sim$J)
bb:	not both $\sim$(A $\vee$ B) and $\sim$(W $\vee$ J)

A: **A**nn gets an A in logic
B: **B**en gets an A in logic
J: **J**ill gets an A in logic
W: **W**ill gets an A in logic

Of course, we could also mix the symbolizations but let's ignore that possibility for simplicity's sake. We can then complete the process by symbolizing "not both." It's useful to use the symbolization templates. Here are the results of plugging (aa) formulas into the two possible not both symbolizations:

[3caa] $\sim$(($\sim$A $\bullet$ $\sim$B) $\bullet$ ($\sim$W $\bullet$ $\sim$J))

[3daa] $\sim$($\sim$A $\bullet$ $\sim$B) $\vee$ $\sim$($\sim$W $\bullet$ $\sim$J)

Plug in (bb) formulas (check with Solutions):

[3cbb]

[3dbb]

$\sim$ (◯ $\bullet$ ☐)

Not both ◯ and ☐

$\sim$ ◯ $\vee$ $\sim$ ☐

Example 4

(4) It is neither the case that Ann and Ben will both get an A in logic nor that neither Will nor Jill will not get an A in logic.

Let's mark the connectives:

It is ⌐neither¬ the case that Ann ⌐and¬ Ben will ⌐both¬ get an A in logic ⌐nor¬ that ⌐neither¬ Will ⌐nor¬ Jill will ⌐not¬ get an A in logic.

There are two occurrences of the "neither nor" but the first one is the main connective. Let us indicate that by placing parentheses accordingly:

It is ⌐neither¬ the case that (Ann ⌐and¬ Ben will ⌐both¬ get an A in logic) ⌐nor¬ that (⌐neither¬ Will ⌐nor¬ Jill will ⌐not¬ get an A in logic).

Let's abbreviate and partially symbolize:

neither (both A and B) nor (⌐neither¬ Will ⌐nor¬ Jill will ⌐not¬ get an A in logic)

Note that there is an additional negation within the scope of "neither nor" in the second parentheses.

neither (A • B) nor (neither ~W nor ~J)

It is useful to use the template to symbolize "neither nor"; let's do it for the parentheses first:

(a)   neither (A • B) nor (~~W • ~~J)

(b)   neither (A • B) nor ~(~W ∨ ~J)

> **A**: **A**nn gets an A in logic
> **B**: **B**en gets an A in logic
> **J**: **J**ill gets an A in logic
> **W**: **W**ill gets an A in logic

We can then plug in the propositions in the parentheses into our template.

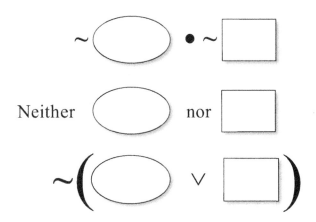

We thus obtain:

[4aa]   ~(A • B) • ~(~~W • ~~J)

[4bb]   ~((A • B) ∨ ~(~W ∨ ~J))

Of course, there are other possibilities:

[4ab]   ~(A • B) • ~~(~W ∨ ~J)

[4ba]   ~((A • B) ∨ (~~W • ~~J))

A: Ann is on a diet   **L**: Larry is getting fat
B: Betty is on a diet   **M**: Martin is getting fat
C: Charlie is on a diet   **N**: Newt is getting fat

Exercise G.1 Symbolizations

(a) Either both Ann and Betty are on a diet, or neither of them is.

(b) Either both Ann and Betty are on a diet, or not both of them are.

(c) Not both Larry and Martin are getting fat, though both Martin and Newt are getting fat.

(d) It is both the case that neither Ann is on a diet nor Larry is getting fat and that neither Betty nor Charlie is on a diet.

(e) It is not the case that neither Ann nor Charlie is on a diet.

Exercise G.2 Symbolizations

(a) Either neither Ann nor Charlie is on a diet or neither Betty nor Charlie is on a diet.

(b) It is not the case that not both Martin and Newt are getting fat.

(c) Neither is it the case that if Larry is getting fat then Ann is on a diet nor that if Martin is getting fat then Betty is on a diet.

(d) Neither is it the case that Ann or Betty is on a diet nor that Betty or Charlie is on a diet.

(e) It is not both the case that neither Ann nor Betty is on a diet and that neither Betty nor Charlie is on a diet.

Exercise G.3 Symbolizations

(a) Neither Ann nor Charlie nor Betty is on a diet if Martin and Newt are not both getting fat.

(b) It is not both the case that Ann and Betty are not both on a diet and that Betty and Charlie are not both on a diet.

(c) Neither is it the case that neither Larry nor Martin is getting fat nor is it the case that neither Martin nor Newt is getting fat.

A: **A**my is nice   **D**: **D**onna is nice   **K**: **K**atrina is nice   **M**: **M**ary is nice
B: **B**etty is nice   **J**: **J**ennifer is nice **L**: **L**ucy is nice   **S**: **S**usan is nice

Exercise G.4 Symbolizations

(a)   Katrina and Mary are never both nice.

(b)   Katrina and Susan are never both nice, either.

(c)   Either Jennifer is nice or Mary is nice, but never both.

(d)   Both Jennifer and Katrina are nice but neither Susan nor Donna is nice.

(e)   Amy and Susan aren't both nice, but it's not the case that neither of them is nice.

Exercise G.5 Symbolizations

(a)   If Jennifer is nice, then Lucy is nice provided that Donna is nice.

(b)   Lucy is nice if Jennifer is nice, provided that Donna is nice.

(c)   If neither Amy nor Betty is nice, then neither Mary nor Susan is nice provided that Lucy isn't nice.

(d)   Lucy isn't nice if neither Mary nor Betty is nice, provided that Amy and Susan aren't both nice.

(e)   Jennifer and Lucy aren't both nice just in case either neither Mary nor Jennifer is nice or neither Katrina nor Lucy is nice.

Exercise G.6 Symbolizations

(a)   Jennifer, Katrina, Mary, and Lucy are all nice.

(b)   At least one of these four girls is nice.

(c)   At least one of these four girls is not nice.

(d)   Not all four girls are nice.

(e)   None of these four girls is nice.

Summary

You have learned how to symbolize "neither nor" and "not both" phrases. De Morgan's laws are the basis for the two equivalent symbolizations for each of them.

De Morgan's laws
~$(p \lor r)$ is logically equivalent to ~$p \bullet$ ~r ~$(p \bullet r)$ is logically equivalent to ~$p \lor$ ~r

You have learned to symbolize exclusive disjunction by means of inclusive disjunction and an appropriate *not-both* condition. You have learned to symbolize many-place conjunctions and disjunctions. You have also learned to paraphrase quantified phrases ("all," "some," "none," "not all") as long as they concern a finite group of subjects. You have also enhanced your skill of symbolizing some more complicated English sentences.

For many complex symbolizations, it is useful to use the templates.

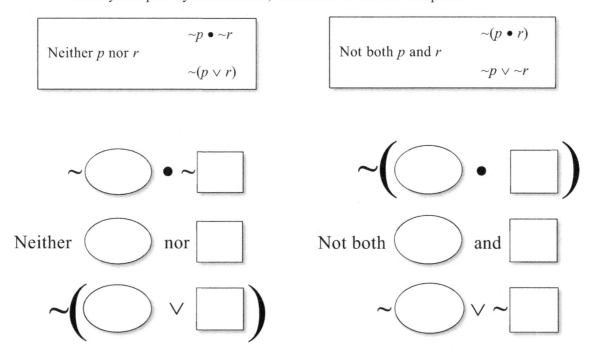

Unit 1.5

"... Only If ..." in Symbolizations

Overview

In this unit, you will learn about "only if." You will also learn to apply the distinction between necessary and sufficient conditions.

This is a hard unit. The connective phrase "only if" is perhaps the most confusing of all. But you can do it. Just remember to do all the exercises!

In this unit, you will learn:
- the distinction between necessary and sufficient conditions.

In this unit, you will learn how to:
- symbolize "only if,"
- symbolize more complicated English sentences.

Time:	4-6 hours
Difficulty:	●●●●●●●
Status:	Essential/**Recommended**/Optional
Number of exercises:	22
Prerequisites:	Introduction, Unit 1.2, Unit 1.3

A. Your worst nightmare: "Only if"

 Few phrases are as confusing as "only if." You should read what is said below with understanding and then learn the symbolization schema *by heart*. It's a good idea to do something to refresh your mind before doing the unit. Take your dog for a walk… Go jogging… Do your pilates… Take a nap…

"IF" – A REMINDER

To appreciate how confusing "only if" is, let us remind ourselves how we would symbolize a proposition of the form "*r* if *p*." Consider an example.

  (1) Jane will go out with Ken if *he asks her politely*.

Since Ken's asking Jane politely (italicized) is the condition for her going out with him, it belongs in the antecedent of a conditional. We put (1) into a standard form as follows:

> If *Ken asks Jane politely* then she will go out with him.

  J if K

  If K then J

  [1] K ⊃ J

> **K**: Ken asks Jane politely
> **J**: Jane will go out with Ken

This is the way to symbolize "if" propositions in general. What follows "if" belongs in the antecedent of the conditional.

r if *p*	*p* ⊃ *r*

"ONLY IF"

No one is ever ready for "only if" (except perhaps for the fraction of a percentile of the population who are graced with a formal mind).

Let us consider some intuitive "only if" propositions.

(1)   Jane will win the lottery only if *she buys the ticket.*

(2)   Gabby is a mother only if *Gabby is a woman.*

(3)   It rains only if *it is cloudy.*

Example 1

Let us start with the first example:

B: Jane **b**uys the lottery ticket
W: Jane **w**ins the lottery

(1)   Jane will win the lottery only if *she buys the ticket.*

Proposition (1) is true: you can win a lottery only if you buy the ticket. Without a ticket, you won't win the lottery.

It is a natural mistake to think that what follows "only if" is an antecedent of the conditional (after all, this is how we thought of "*r* if *p*" propositions). *Let's make this mistake* and see what happens! Let's treat the proposition that follows "only if" (i.e., "Jane buys the ticket") as the antecedent of a conditional. We obtain the proposition:

If *Jane buys the ticket* then she'll win the lottery.

B ⊃ W

This proposition is evidently false! Buying the ticket is certainly not sufficient for winning the lottery (we all wish it were, but it isn't). But our original proposition (1) was true!

So how can we say
what (1) says?

There are two equivalent ways of saying what (1) means:

(1a)   If *Jane* does not *buy the ticket* then she will not win the lottery;

(1b)   If Jane won the lottery then [this must mean that] *she bought the ticket.*

After all, only if Jane buys the ticket can she win the lottery!

[1a]   ~B ⊃ ~W

[1b]   W ⊃ B

In general:

p only if *r*	if *p* then [this must mean that] *r*	*p* ⊃ *r*
	if not *r* then not *p*	~*r* ⊃ ~*p*

Example 2

   (2) Gabby is a mother $\boxed{\text{only if}}$ *Gabby is a woman*.

This proposition is once again true (after all, only women are mothers). However, the sentence resulting from the natural mistake of assuming that the italicized sentence belongs in the antecedent is again evidently false:

   If *Gabby is a woman* then Gabby is a mother.
   W ⊃ M

M: Gabby is a **m**other
W: Gabby is a **w**oman

From the fact that Gabby is a woman, it does not follow that she is a mother, though, from the fact that Gabby is a mother, it *does* follow that she is a woman.

   Here are two equivalent ways of paraphrasing proposition (2):

   [2b] M ⊃ W

   (2b) $\boxed{\text{If}}$ Gabby is a mother $\boxed{\text{then [this must mean that]}}$ *Gabby is a woman*

since only women can be mothers! Here is another way to express the same proposition:

   (2a) $\boxed{\text{If}}$ *Gabby is* $\boxed{\text{not}}$ *a woman* $\boxed{\text{then}}$ Gabby is $\boxed{\text{not}}$ a mother.

   [2a] ~W ⊃ ~M

Again, both [2a] and [2b] are correct symbolizations of (2).

Example 3

   (3) It rains $\boxed{\text{only if}}$ *it is cloudy*.

Proposition (3) is once again true (the rain falls from some cloud or other). However, if we make the natural mistake of assuming that the italicized sentence belongs in the antecedent, we will obtain a false sentence:

   If *it is cloudy* then it rains.
   C ⊃ R

C: It is **c**loudy
R: It **r**ains

After all, it can be cloudy and it can snow rather than rain. It can be just plain cloudy with no precipitation at all. However, if it rains then there must be some cloud or other in the sky:

   (3b) $\boxed{\text{If}}$ it rains $\boxed{\text{then [this must mean that]}}$ *it is cloudy*.

   [3b] R ⊃ C

since only if it is cloudy can it rain! Another way of expressing the same proposition:

   (3a) $\boxed{\text{If}}$ *it is* $\boxed{\text{not}}$ *cloudy* $\boxed{\text{then}}$ it does $\boxed{\text{not}}$ rain.

   [3a] ~C ⊃ ~R

Again, both [3a] and [3b] are permissible symbolizations of (3).

The "natural mistake" in symbolizing "only if"

 To learn to symbolize "only if" propositions, you must recognize the fact that you will be inclined to commit the "natural mistake." The "natural mistake" consists in following our natural tendency to treat what follows "only if" as the antecedent of a conditional.

Here are two ways to overcome the mistake.

(A) *Do the exact opposite* of what you are naturally inclined to do: rather than putting what follows "only if" in the antecedent, put it in the consequent of the conditional. **Symbolize "*p* only if *r*" as "*p* ⊃ *r*"** (if *p* then [this means that] *r*).

(B) Alternatively, *follow your natural inclination* to put what follows "only if" into the antecedent but then remember that *both the antecedent and the consequent must be negated.* Symbolize "*p* only if *r*" **as "~*r* ⊃ ~*p*."**

You should be able to do both symbolizations.

The symbolization schema mentioned in (A) is particularly useful for very complex propositions.

	if *p* then [this must mean that] *r*	*p* ⊃ *r*
p only if *r*		
	if not *r* then not *p*	~*r* ⊃ ~*p*

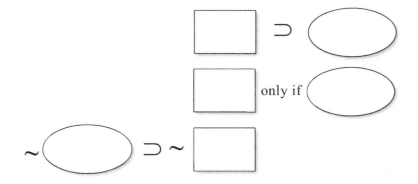

Paraphrase and symbolize only-if conditionals
in two equivalent ways.

Exercise A.1 "Only If"

(a)   Trippy is a cat only if Trippy can meow.

$$\boxed{} \supset \bigcirc$$

$$\boxed{\text{Trippy is a cat}} \text{ only if } \bigodot{\text{Trippy can meow}}$$

$$\sim \bigcirc \supset \sim \boxed{}$$

1:	
2:	

C: Trippy is a **c**at   [1]
M: Trippy can **m**eow   [2]

(b)   Tramp is a dog only if Tramp can bark.

$$\boxed{} \supset \bigcirc$$

$$\boxed{} \text{ only if } \bigcirc$$

$$\sim \bigcirc \supset \sim \boxed{}$$

1:	
2:	

B: Tramp can **b**ark   [1]
D: Tramp is a **d**og   [2]

Exercise A.2 "Only If"

(a)   Truppy is a fish only if Truppy can swim.

1:	
2:	

H: Truppy is a fish
S: Truppy can swim

[1]	
[2]	

(b)   It rains only if it is cloudy.

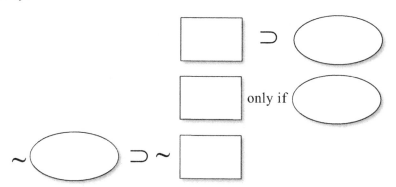

1:	
2:	

C: It is cloudy
R: It rains

[1]	
[2]	

Exercise A.3 "Only If"

(a)   It snows only if it is cloudy.

1:

2:

     C: It is **c**loudy   [1]

     S: It **s**nows   [2]

(b)   It snows only if it is very cold.

1:

2:

     V: It is **v**ery cold   [1]

     S: It **s**nows   [2]

(c)

1:   If Ken passed logic [this means that] he worked very hard.

2:

     P: Ken **p**asses logic   [1]

     W: Ken **w**orks very hard [2]

(e)   Ken will like logic only if he grasps "only if."

1:

2:

     L: Ken **l**ikes logic   [1]

     G: Ken **g**rasps "only if" [2]

Symbolize only-if conditionals
in two equivalent ways.

A: Adam is on a diet   E: Ben exercises
B: Ben is on a diet.   H: Adam is healthy
C: Charlie is on a diet L: Ben is healthy

Exercise A.4 "Only If"

(a) Adam will be healthy only if he goes on a diet.

(b) Ben will be healthy only if he exercises regularly.

(c) Adam will go on a diet only if Ben goes on a diet.

(d) Ben will go on a diet only if Charlie goes on a diet.

Exercise A.5 "Only If"

(a) Charlie will go on a diet only if Ben goes on a diet.

(b) Ben will exercise only if he goes on a diet.

(c) Ben will be healthy only if he goes on a diet.

(d) Only if Adam goes on a diet will Charlie go on a diet.

Exercise A.6 "Only If"

Suppose that a logic teacher says: "You must work hard to get an A in this course. Even if you work hard, you are not guaranteed to get an A. To get an A, you must get at least 90% on all quizzes." Ascertain the truth or falsehood of the following claims:

(a) You will get an A for this course *if* you get 95% on all your quizzes.   ○ true
                                                                                   ○ false

(b) You will get an A for this course *only if* you get 95% on all your quizzes. ○ true
                                                                                   ○ false

(c) You will get an A for this course *if* you work hard.   ○ true
                                                                                   ○ false

(d) You will get an A for this course *only if* you work hard.   ○ true
                                                                                   ○ false

MORE COMPLEX EXAMPLES

When symbolizing more complex propositions, we should use the same procedures as before.

Example 1

(1) It rains or snows only if it is cloudy, but it is not the case that if it is cloudy then it rains or snows.

The first thing to do is to mark all connective phrases:

It rains │or│ snows │only if│ it is cloudy, │but│ │it is not the case that│ │if│ it is cloudy │then│ it rains │or│ snows.

We then need to decide what the main connective is and how to place parentheses. It seems rather clear that the main connective is "but" (note the comma!). Moreover, the proposition has the general structure: blah-blah, but it is not the case that bleh-bleh:

((It rains │or│ snows) │only if│ it is cloudy) │but│ │it is not the case that│ (│if│ it is cloudy │then│ (it rains │or│ snows))

Let's do a partial symbolization but leave "only if" not symbolized:

((R ∨ S) only if C) • ~(C ⊃ (R ∨ S))

C: It is **c**loudy
R: It **r**ains
S: It **s**nows

The final step is to symbolize "only if" in the first conjunct. We can do it in one of two ways:

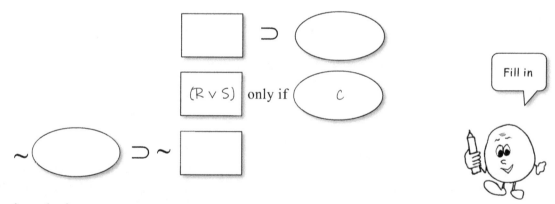

We thus obtain:

[1a] ((R ∨ S) ⊃ C) • ~(C ⊃ (R ∨ S))

[1b] (~C ⊃ ~(R ∨ S)) • ~(C ⊃ (R ∨ S))

Example 2

(2) Only if it is cloudy and not sunny does it hail.

Let's begin by paraphrasing (2) into the more canonical "*p* only if *r*" form:

It hails only if it is cloudy and not sunny.

It is clear that "only if" is the main connective. We can do a partial symbolization:

It hails only if (it is cloudy and not sunny).

H only if (C • ~N)

C: It is **c**loudy
H: It **h**ails
N: It is su**n**ny

Again, we can use one of two symbolizations of only-if:

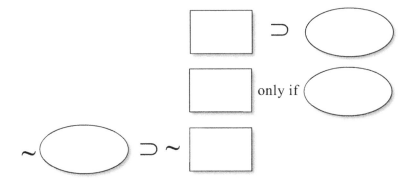

[2a]   H ⊃ (C • ~N)

[2b]   ~(C • ~N) ⊃ ~H

Example 3

(3)   Ann will go out with Ben only if he stops smoking or drinking, but Ben will stop drinking only if Ann goes out with him and stops drinking herself, and he will stop smoking only if he gets a good job.

The first thing to do is to find the main connective:

Ann will go out with Ben |only if| he stops smoking |or| drinking|, but| Ben will stop drinking |only if| Ann goes out with him |and| stops drinking herself|, and| he will stop smoking |only if| he gets a good job.

The main connective here is "but," which is partially indicated by the comma and partially by the meaning of what is said. Note also that within the second conjunct "Ben will stop drinking |only if| Ann goes out with him |and| stops drinking herself|, and| he will stop smoking |only if| he gets a good job," the second occurrence of "and" is the main connective. There are no syntactic indications that this is so except for the meaning of what is said. We can thus place the parentheses.

(Ann will go out with Ben |only if| (he stops smoking |or| drinking)) |but| ((Ben will stop drinking |only if| (Ann goes out with him |and| stops drinking herself)) |and| (he will stop smoking |only if| he gets a good job))

We can do a partial symbolization:

(A only if (S ∨ R)) • ((R only if (A • D)) • (S only if J))

A: **A**nn goes out with Ben
D: Ann stops **d**rinking
J: Ben gets a good **j**ob
S: Ben stops **s**moking
R: Ben stops **d**rinking

Again, we can use one of two symbolizations of "only if" (they can be mixed, of course) for each of the three "only if" components (be careful about the parentheses!):

(A only if (S ∨ R)) • ((R only if (A • D)) • (S only if J))

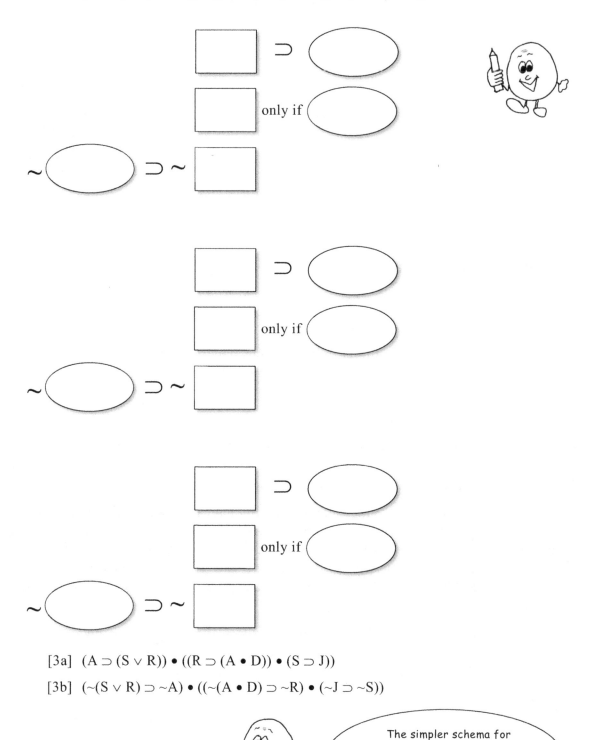

[3a] (A ⊃ (S ∨ R)) • ((R ⊃ (A • D)) • (S ⊃ J))

[3b] (~(S ∨ R) ⊃ ~A) • ((~(A • D) ⊃ ~R) • (~J ⊃ ~S))

The simpler schema for "p only if r," i.e. p ⊃ r, is especially helpful in complex symbolizations.

Exercise A.7 "Only If" – Complex Terms

A: **A**nn is sick   **C**: **C**harlie is sick
B: **B**etty is sick   **D**: **D**irk is sick

Formulate the proposition in English. Symbolize.

(a)   A only if B

Ann is sick only if Betty is sick	A ⊃ B ~B ⊃ ~A

(b)   ~A only if ~B

(c)   (A • B) only if (C • D)

(d)   (A ∨ B) only if (C ∨ D)

(e)   (A ⊃ B) only if (B ⊃ A)

(f)   (A ≡ B) only if (C ≡ D)

(g)   ~(A • B) only if ~(C • D)

(h)   (~A • ~B) only if (~C • ~D)

Exercise A.8 "Only If" – Complex Terms

A: Ann is on a diet	**E**: Betty exercises
B: Betty is on a diet.	**H**: Ann is healthy
C: Charlie is on a diet	**L**: Betty is healthy

(a)   Ann will go on a diet only if she isn't healthy.

(b)   Betty will be healthy only if either she goes on a diet or starts exercising regularly.

(c)   Ann will go on a diet only if both Betty and Charlie go on a diet.

(d)   Betty will either go on a diet or start exercising regularly only if Ann goes on a diet.

(e)   Charlie will go on a diet only if Betty goes on a diet but Ann does not.

Exercise A.9 "Only If" – Complex Terms

(a)   Betty will exercise only if she does not go on a diet.

(b)   Only if Charlie and Betty are on a diet will Ann go on a diet.

Paraphrase:

(c)   Only if Betty either is healthy or starts exercising will Charlie go on a diet.

Paraphrase:

(d)   Ann and Betty will be healthy only if they both go on a diet.

(e)   Neither Ann nor Betty will go on a diet only if neither of them will be healthy.

IF, ONLY IF, IF AND ONLY IF

The following table and templates juxtapose the symbolizations of *if* propositions and *only if* propositions:

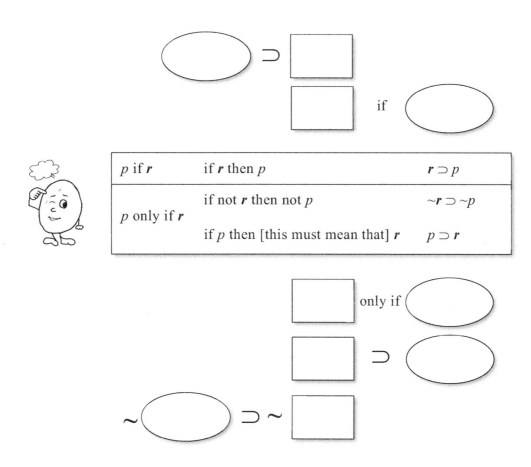

p if *r*	if *r* then *p*	*r* ⊃ *p*
p only if *r*	if not *r* then not *p*	~*r* ⊃ ~*p*
	if *p* then [this must mean that] *r*	*p* ⊃ *r*

In addition, of course, there are biconditionals, symbolized as follows:

p if and only if *r*	*p* ≡ *r*

We will later see that $p \equiv r$ is logically equivalent to the conjunction $(p \supset r) \bullet (r \supset p)$.

B. Complicated Symbolizations

Example 1

    (1) Jane will go out with Bill only if he doesn't smoke or drink heavily.

Let's underline the connectives:

    Jane will go out with Bill only if he doesn't smoke or drink heavily.

The main connective is "only if." It takes a little thought to see that "he doesn't smoke or drink heavily" is a negation: it is a negation of disjunction. We can thus paraphrase (1):

    Jane will go out with Bill only if it isn't the case that (he smokes or drinks heavily)

> **D**: Bill **d**rinks heavily
> **J**: **J**ane goes out with Bill
> **S**: Bill **s**mokes

After partial symbolization, we obtain:

    J only if ~(S ∨ D)

And now you need to search your memory for how "*p* only if *r*" is symbolized. There are two ways to do so. Since one of the terms is complex, let's use the diagram:

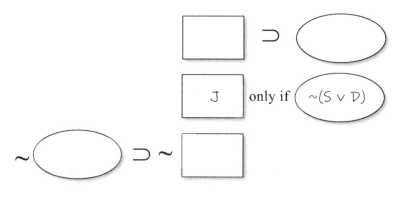

There are thus two ways to symbolize (1):

    [1a] J ⊃ ~(S ∨ D)

    [1b] ~~(S ∨ D) ⊃ ~J

Note that the second symbolization [1b] has a double negation in the antecedent. This is because the second symbolization schema has a negated antecedent, and we had to put an already negated proposition into it. Could we drop the double negation? As a matter of fact, [1b] is logically equivalent to (S ∨ D) ⊃ ~J. However, I urge you not to try to "simplify" propositions until you learn about methods that will allow you to check that you are transforming a proposition into a logically equivalent proposition.

> Could we not drop
> the double negations?

> Don't transform
> propositions before
> you learn proofs!

Example 2

Consider the following proposition:

> (2) Ann will pass logic and economics only if she both works hard and does not
> watch TV; moreover, Ann will work hard if and only if she does not watch TV,
> and Ann will not watch TV only if Ben watches TV or plays computer games.

Again, let's mark the connectives:

> Ann will pass logic |and| economics |only if| she |both| works hard |and| does |not|
> watch TV; |moreover|, Ann will work hard |if and only if| she does |not| watch TV,
> |and| Ann will |not| watch TV |only if| Ben watches TV |or| plays computer games.

It is relatively easy to find the main connective. The big indication of a "break" in the
sentence is provided by the semicolon and the word "moreover": (2) is a conjunction. (If you
read the sentence out loud, this is where you will pause.)

> (Ann will pass logic |and| economics |only if| she |both| works hard |and| does |not|
> watch TV) |moreover| (Ann will work hard |if and only if| she does |not| watch TV,
> |and| Ann will |not| watch TV |only if| Ben watches TV |or| plays computer games)

Since the conjuncts are quite complex, let's work on them separately to see what their inner
structure is. Consider the first conjunct:

> Ann will pass logic |and| economics |only if| she |both| works hard |and| does |not|
> watch TV

It is clear that "only if" is the main connective, so we can place the parentheses thus:

> (Ann will pass logic |and| economics) |only if| (she |both| works hard |and| does |not|
> watch TV)

Consider the second conjunct:

> Ann will work hard |if and only if| she does |not| watch TV, |and| Ann will |not|
> watch TV |only if| Ben watches TV |or| plays computer games

Here, the comma indicates that "and" is the main connective. The second conjunct is thus a
conjunction of a biconditional and a conditional:

> (Ann will work hard |if and only if| she does |not| watch TV) |and| (Ann will |not|
> watch TV |only if| (Ben watches TV |or| plays computer games))

After we put it all together, we have:

> ((Ann will pass logic |and| economics) |only if| (she |both| works hard |and| does |not|
> watch TV)) |moreover| ((Ann will work hard |if and only if| she does |not| watch
> TV) |and| (Ann will |not| watch TV |only if| (Ben watches TV |or| plays computer
> games)))

After partial symbolization, we obtain:

((L • E) only if (H • ~V)) • ((H ≡ ~V) • (~V only if (B ∨ G)))

> **L**: Ann passes logic
> **E**: Ann passes economics
> **H**: Ann works hard
> **V**: Ann watches TV
> **B**: Ben watches TV
> **G**: Ben plays comp. games

((L • E) only if (H • ~V)) • ((H ≡ ~V) • (~V only if (B ∨ G)))

The rest is easy. Remember that there are two ways to symbolize "only if."

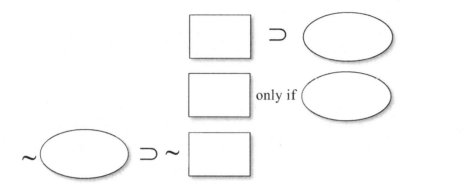

There are thus at least two possible ways of completing the symbolization:

[2a] ((L • E) ⊃ (H • ~V)) • ((H ≡ ~V) • (~V ⊃ (B ∨ G)))

[2b] (~(H • ~V) ⊃ ~(L • E)) • ((H ≡ ~V) • (~(B ∨ G) ⊃ ~~V))

Exercise B.1 Symbolization

A: Amy is nice	**E**: Betty will go out with Chris
B: Betty is nice	**K**: Betty will go out with Dirk
C: Chris is nice	**M**: Amy will go out with Chris
D: Dirk is nice	**Y**: Amy will go out with Dirk

(a)   Amy will go out with Chris only if Chris is nice and does not go out with Betty.

(b)   Amy will go out with Dirk only if Betty goes out with him, provided, however, that Dirk is nice.

(c)   Chris will be nice only if either Amy or Betty goes out with him.

(d)   Amy will go out with Chris or Dirk only if the boys are both nice.

(e)   Amy or Betty will go out with Dirk only if, first, neither goes out with Chris, and, second, Dirk is nice.

Exercise B.2 Symbolization

A: Amy is nice   E: Betty will go out with Chris
B: Betty is nice   K: Betty will go out with Dirk
C: Chris is nice   M: Amy will go out with Chris
D: Dirk is nice   Y: Amy will go out with Dirk

(a) Either Amy or Betty will go out with Chris; however, Amy will go out with Chris only if she does not go out with Dirk, and Betty will go out with Chris if she does not go out with Dirk.

(b) Either if Chris is nice then Amy will go out with him only if Betty doesn't or if Dirk is nice then Betty will go out with him only if Amy doesn't.

(c) Dirk will be nice only if, first, Amy is nice and goes out with him and, second, Betty is nice but goes out with Chris.

(d) Neither Amy nor Betty will go out with Chris if Dirk is nice, but if Dirk is not nice then Amy or Betty will go out with Chris only if he is nice.

Exercise B.3 Symbolization

(a) Neither Amy nor Betty is nice, but Chris will go out with at least one of them only if Dirk will go out with at least one of them.

(b) Neither Chris nor Dirk is nice; however, Amy will go out with at least one of them and Betty will also go out with at least one of them.

(c) Neither Chris nor Dirk is nice; however, Amy will go out with one of them and Betty will go with the other.

C. Necessary and Sufficient Conditions (optional)

To grasp the difference between "if" and "only if" is in effect to grasp the difference between sufficient and necessary conditions, respectively. We usually express sufficient conditions by means of "if" and necessary conditions by means of "only if."

SUFFICIENT (BUT NOT NECESSARY) CONDITIONS

Consider some examples of **sufficient** (though **not necessary**) conditions.

    (1) *Logi's being a hamster* is a sufficient condition for Logi's being a mammal.

    (2) *Stan's forgetting about the anniversary* is sufficient for Ann's getting angry.

    (3) *John's being 28 years old* is a sufficient condition for his being an adult.

We can paraphrase these sentences as conditionals, where the italicized condition is in the antecedent.

    (1′) If *Logi is a hamster* then Logi is a mammal.

    (1″) Logi is a mammal if *Logi is a hamster*.

Logi's being a hamster is sufficient (guarantees) that Logi is a mammal. But being a hamster is not necessary for being a mammal. Some mammals are not hamsters.

    (2′) If *Stan forgets about their anniversary* then Ann will be angry.

    (2″) Ann will be angry if *Stan forgets about their anniversary*.

Stan's forgetting about their anniversary suffices to make Ann angry. However, Stan's forgetfulness is not necessary for Ann's anger; she might get angry for other reasons.

    (3′) If *John is 28 years old* then he is an adult.

    (3″) John is an adult if *he is 28 years old*.

John's being 28 years old guarantees that he is an adult (legally speaking). Being 28 years old is not a necessary condition for being an adult. A 30-year-old person is an adult, too.

NECESSARY (BUT NOT SUFFICIENT) CONDITIONS

Consider examples of **necessary** (but **not sufficient**) conditions:

    (4) *Your buying a ticket* is a necessary condition for your winning a lottery.

    (5) *Gabby's being a woman* is a necessary condition for her being a mother.

    (6) *Being cloudy* is a necessary condition of raining.

Necessary conditions are best captured by "only if" conditionals, which can be paraphrased in terms of standard if-then conditionals.

    You must buy the ticket to win a lottery but buying the ticket does not guarantee that you will win. Buying the ticket is not a sufficient condition for winning the lottery.

(4′) Only if *you buy a lottery ticket* will you win a lottery.

(4″) You will win a lottery only if *you buy a lottery ticket.*

(4‴) If you have won a lottery then *you have bought a lottery ticket.*

(4⁗) If *you* do not *buy a lottery ticket* then you will not win a lottery.

Being a woman is a necessary (not a sufficient) condition for being a mother. Being a woman is not a sufficient condition for being a mother since there are women who are not mothers.

(5′) Only if *Gabby is a woman* is she a mother.

(5″) Gabby is a mother only if *Gabby is a woman.*

(5‴) If Gabby is a mother then *Gabby is a woman.*

(5⁗) If *Gabby is* not *a woman* then Gabby is not a mother.

Being cloudy is a necessary (but not sufficient) condition for rain. Being cloudy is not a sufficient condition for rain because it does not always rain if it is cloudy (sometimes there are clouds without precipitation, sometimes it snows when it is cloudy, etc.).

(6′) Only if *it is cloudy* does it rain.

(6″) It rains only if *it is cloudy.*

(6‴) If it rains then *it is cloudy.*

(6⁗) If *it is* not *cloudy* then it does not rain.

SUMMARY

We can express conditions (1)-(6) in the following way:

(1″) Logi is a mammal if *Logi is a hamster.*

(2″) Ann will be angry if *Stan forgets about their anniversary.*

(3″) John is an adult if *he is 28 years old.*

(4″) You will win the lottery only if *you buy the ticket.*

(5″) Gabby is a mother only if *Gabby is a woman.*

(6″) It rains only if *it is cloudy.*

Note that the italicized phrases constitute the **sufficient** conditions (in (1″)-(3″)) and **necessary** conditions (in (4″)-(6″)) for what is not italicized.

p if *r*	*r* is a sufficient condition of *p*	*r* ⊃ *p*
p only if *r*	*r* is a necessary condition of *p*	~*r* ⊃ ~*p* *p* ⊃ *r*
p if and only if *r*	*r* is a necessary and sufficient condition of *p*	*r* ≡ *p*

Exercise C.1 Necessary and Sufficient Conditions

> In Ex. C.1-C.3, determine whether the proposition indicates a necessary or a sufficient condition.

(a)   It hails only if it is cloudy.

Being cloudy is   ○ necessary   for hail.
                       ○ sufficient

(b)   It rains if it drizzles.

Drizzle is   ○ necessary   for rain.
                       ○ sufficient

(c)   Pully is a hamster only if Pully has cheek pouches.

Having cheek pouches is   ○ necessary   for Pully's being a hamster.
                           ○ sufficient

(d)   Pully is a hamster if Pully has cheek pouches.

Having cheek pouches is   ○ necessary   for Pully's being a hamster.
                           ○ sufficient

Exercise C.2 Necessary and Sufficient Conditions

(a)   Pully is a hamster if and only if Pully has cheek pouches.

Having cheek pouches is   ○ necessary   for Pully's being a hamster.
                           ○ sufficient

(b)   Susan will pass logic if she makes 55% on the test.

Making 55% on the test is   ○ necessary   for Susan's passing logic.
                             ○ sufficient

(c)   Susan will not get an A if she makes 85% on the test.

Making 85% on the test is   ○ necessary   for Susan's not getting A.
                             ○ sufficient

(d)   Susan will get an A+ if but only if she makes 100% on the test.

Making 100% on the test is   ○ necessary   for Susan's getting A+.
                              ○ sufficient

Exercise C.3 Necessary and Sufficient Conditions

(a)   Jack will get a B only if he gets 100% on the project.

Getting 100% on the project is   ○ necessary   for Jack's getting B.
                                  ○ sufficient

(b)   Jack will get a B if he gets 100% on the project.

Getting 100% on the test is   ○ necessary   for Jack's getting B.
                               ○ sufficient

(c)   Tim will lose weight only if he goes on a diet.

Tim's going on a diet is   ○ necessary   for his losing weight.
                            ○ sufficient

(d)   Jane will go on a diet if she loses weight.

Jane's losing weight is   ○ necessary   for her going on a diet.
                           ○ sufficient

In Ex. C.4-C.5, first determine which conditionals are true.

Then, determine whether the indicated condition is necessary, sufficient, or both.

Exercise C.4 Necessary and Sufficient Conditions

(a) Logi is a mammal **if** *Logi is a hamster*.   ○ true ○ false

Logi is a mammal **only if** *Logi is a hamster*.   ○ true ○ false

Logi's being a hamster is   ○ sufficient   ○ necessary   for Logi's being a mammal.

(b) Ann will be angry **if** *Stan forgets about the anniversary*.   ○ true ○ false

Ann will be angry **only if** *Stan forgets about the anniversary*.   ○ true ○ false

Stan's forgetting about the anniversary is   ○ sufficient   ○ necessary   for Ann's anger

(c) John is an adult **only if** *he is 28 years old*   ○ true ○ false

John is an adult **if** *he is 28 years old*   ○ true ○ false

John's being 28 years old is   ○ sufficient   ○ necessary   for his being an adult.

Exercise C.5 Necessary and Sufficient Conditions

(a) You will win the lottery **if** *you buy the ticket*.   ○ true ○ false

You will win the lottery **only if** *you buy the ticket*.   ○ true ○ false

Your buying the ticket is   ○ sufficient   ○ necessary   for your winning the lottery.

(b) Ben is a father **only if** *Ben is a man*.   ○ true ○ false

Ben is a father **if** *Ben is a man*.   ○ true ○ false

Ben being a man is   ○ sufficient   ○ necessary   for Ben's being a father.

(c) It hails **if** *it is cloudy*.   ○ true ○ false

It hails **only if** *it is cloudy*.   ○ true ○ false

Being cloudy is   ○ sufficient   ○ necessary   for hail.

In Ex. C.6-C.8, fill the missing information (see Example)

HINT: The implication $s \supset r$ can be read in two ways:
r if s s is a sufficient condition for r
s only if r r is a necessary condition for s

Example

If   Zorro is a poodle   then   Zorro is a dog

Zorro is a dog	if	Zorro is a poodle
Zorro is a poodle	only if	Zorro is a dog
Zorro's being a poodle	is a sufficient condition of	Zorro's being a dog
Zorro's being a dog	is a necessary condition of	Zorro's being a poodle

Exercise C.6 Necessary and Sufficient Conditions

(a)   If Aristo is a Maine Coon then Aristo is a cat.

	if	
	only if	
	is a sufficient condition of	
	is a necessary condition of	

(b)   If it rains then it is cloudy.

	if	
	only if	
	is a sufficient condition of	
	is a necessary condition of	

Exercise C.7 Necessary and Sufficient Conditions

(a)   If Burr barks then Burr is a dog.

	if	
	only if	
	is a sufficient condition of	
	is a necessary condition of	

(b)   If Pum is a hamster then Pum has cheek pouches

	if	
	only if	
	is a sufficient condition of	
	is a necessary condition of	

Exercise C.8 Necessary and Sufficient Conditions

(a)   If ABCD is a square then ABCD is a rectangle

	if	
	only if	
	is a sufficient condition of	
	is a necessary condition of	

(b)   If ABC is a triangle then ABC is a polygon.

	if	
	only if	
	is a sufficient condition of	
	is a necessary condition of	

In Ex. C.9-C.10, determine whether the mentioned condition is necessary or sufficient.

HINT: Be careful about what is supposed to be a condition of what. In some cases, you should reformulate the original proposition so that the mentioned condition follows "if" or "only if." See Examples.

HINT: s ⊃ r can be read in two ways:
r if s
s only if r

Example 1

Arrow is a terrier only if Arrow is a dog.

Arrow is a dog **if Arrow is a terrier**.

Arrow's being a terrier is   ○ necessary   ● sufficient   for Arrow's being a dog.

Example 2

Keb is a Russian blue **only if Keb is a cat.**

Keb's being a cat is   ● necessary   ○ sufficient   for Keb's being a Russian Blue.

Exercise C.9 Necessary and Sufficient Conditions

(a)   It rains only if it's cloudy

Being cloudy is   ○ necessary   ○ sufficient   for rain.

(b)   It rains if it drizzles.

Rain is   ○ necessary   ○ sufficient   for drizzle.

(c)   Daphie is a sheltie only if Daphie is a dog.

Daphie's being a sheltie is   ○ necessary   ○ sufficient   for Daphie's being a dog.

(d)   Mela is a cat if Mela is a Russian blue.

Mela's being a cat is   ○ necessary   ○ sufficient   for Mela's being a Russian Blue.

Exercise C.10 Necessary and Sufficient Conditions

(a)   ABCD is a polygon if it is a rhombus.

ABCD's being a rhombus is   ○ necessary   for its being a polygon.
                             ○ sufficient

(b)   ABCD is a polygon if it is a parallelogram.

ABCD's being a polygon is   ○ necessary   for its being a parallelogram.
                             ○ sufficient

(c)   ABCD is a rectangle only if it is a polygon.

ABCD's being a rectangle is   ○ necessary   for its being a polygon.
                               ○ sufficient

(d)   ABCD is a square only if it is a polygon.

ABCD's being a polygon is   ○ necessary   for its being a square.
                             ○ sufficient

Summary

You have learned to symbolize the "only if" phrase. You have also learned that "if" often expresses a sufficient condition while "only if" expresses a necessary condition. You have further enhanced your symbolization skills.

.

p if *r*	*r* ⊃ *p*	if *r* then *p*
p only if *r*	~*r* ⊃ ~*p*	if not *r* then not *p*
	p ⊃ *r*	if *p* then [this must mean that] *r*

For complex symbolizations, it is helpful to use the "only if" template.

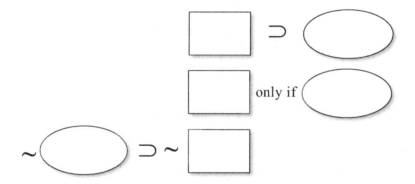

Unit 1.6

"... Unless ..." in Symbolizations

Overview

In this unit, you will learn about the connective phrase "unless."

In this unit, you will learn how to:
- symbolize "unless,"
- symbolize more complicated English sentences.

Time:	2-3 hours
Difficulty:	●●●●○○○
Status:	Essential/**Recommended**/Optional
Number of exercises:	8
Prerequisites:	Introduction, Unit 1.2, Unit 1.3

You won't learn to symbolize "unless" unless you do the exercises!

A. "Unless"

Example 1

Suppose Ann says to Ken:

    (1) I will divorce you unless *you change.*

What, aside from family trouble, does (1) mean? (1) can be expressed in two different but, as it turns out, logically equivalent ways:

    (1a) If *Ken* does not *change* then Ann will divorce him

    (1b) Either *Ken changes* or Ann will divorce him.

We can symbolize the propositions, respectively, as:

        D unless C

  [1a] ~C ⊃ D

  [1b] C ∨ D

> **C**: Ken **c**hanges
> **D**: Ann **d**ivorces Ken

Two points are worth noting.

    First, if we render proposition (1) as the implication [1a], then the proposition following the "unless" clause (italicized above) becomes negated. However, if we render (1) as the disjunction [1b], that proposition is not negated.

    Second, in both cases [1a] and [1b], the italicized proposition "travels" from being the second term to being the first term. In the case of conditional [1a], the italicized proposition becomes the antecedent of the conditional. In the case of disjunction [1b], the italicized proposition becomes the first disjunct.

    As you will learn later, disjunction is commutative, i.e., the order of the disjuncts does not affect the truth value of the disjunction. This means that the disjunctive symbolization of "*r* unless *p*" can be either "*p* ∨ *r*" or "*r* ∨ *p*." The latter is particularly useful because it is so simple. You just replace "unless" with "∨." You don't need to worry about adding negations or changing the order of the terms. This is a lifesaver in complex symbolizations. The only problem is that the symbolization loses some of its intuitive appeal. Consider:

  [1c] D ∨ C   Either Ann divorces Ken or *Ken will change.*

There is some question whether [1c] is as intuitive as [1b] when it comes to the symbolization of (1). Bear in mind, however, that propositional logic provides very simplified tools for representing what we mean and say. Recall our discussion of the material conditional, for example.

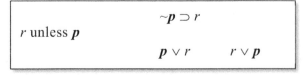

    In general:

r unless *p*	$\sim\!p \supset r$	
	$p \vee r$	$r \vee p$

Exercise A.1 "Unless"

A: **A**nn will go on a diet
B: **B**etty will go on a diet
C: **C**harlie will go on a diet
D: Ann's **d**octor objects to Ann going on a diet
E: **E**velyn forbids Betty to go on a diet
G: **G**arry will go on a diet

In Ex. A.1-A.2, provide two paraphrases of each proposition in English, then symbolize them.

(a)   Ann will go on a diet unless her doctor objects to her going on a diet.

If Ann's doctor does not object to her going on a diet then she will go on a diet.	
Either Ann's doctor objects to her going on a diet or she will go on a diet.	

(b)   Betty will go on a diet unless Evelyn forbids her to do so.

(c)   Charlie will go on a diet unless Garry goes on a diet.

(d)   Garry will go on a diet unless Charlie goes on a diet.

Exercise A.2 "Unless"

> A: **A**nn will go on a diet   D: Ann's **d**octor objects to Ann going on a diet
> B: **B**etty will go on a diet   E: **E**velyn forbids Betty to go on a diet
> C: **C**harlie will go on a diet   G: **G**arry will go on a diet

(a)   Betty will go on a diet unless Ann's doctor objects to Ann's going on a diet.

(b)   Betty will not go on a diet unless Ann goes on a diet.

(c)   Betty and Ann will both go on a diet unless Ann's doctor objects to Ann's going on a diet.

(d)   Ann will go on a diet unless Charlie or Garry goes on a diet.

Example 2

Consider a slightly more complex example. Ken says to Ann: "I will not tell you what happened unless *you shut up*." Let's transform what Ken says into a proposition and mark all the connectives:

(2)   Ken will not tell Ann what happened unless *Ann shuts up.*

"Unless" is the main connective (it is a proposition of the form "something unless something else" rather than a proposition of the form "it is not the case that something").

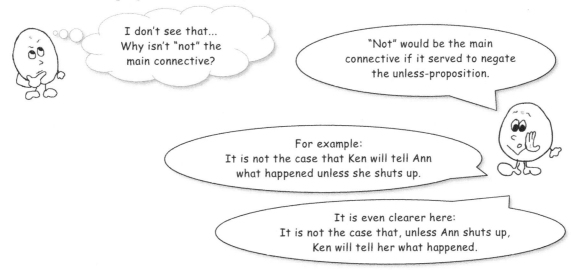

It is useful to do a partial symbolization:

~K unless A

A: **A**nn shuts up
K: **K**en tells Ann what happened

For complex propositions, it is useful to use the symbolization templates.

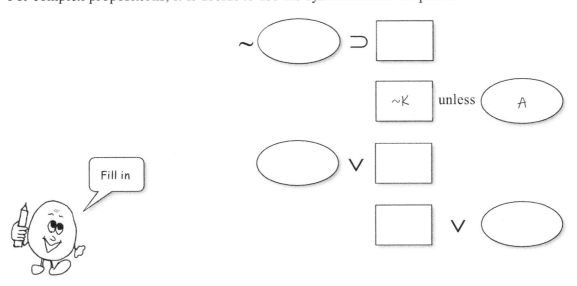

We thus obtain the following symbolizations:

  [2a] ~A ⊃ ~K

  [2b] A ∨ ~K

  [2c] ~K ∨ A

These symbolizations correspond to two equivalent ways of understanding our original proposition (2):

  (2a) $\boxed{\text{If}}$ *you do* $\boxed{\text{not}}$ *shut up* $\boxed{\text{then}}$ I will not tell you what happened

  (2b) $\boxed{\text{Either}}$ *you shut up* $\boxed{\text{or}}$ I will not tell you what happened

Is the third symbolization as intuitive as the first two? I leave it to you to ponder.

  (2c) $\boxed{\text{Either}}$ I will not tell you what happened $\boxed{\text{or}}$ *you will shut up*.

When the terms of the *unless* proposition are simple, you can rely on your intuitions in doing the symbolizations. However, when they are complex, it is safer to check your symbolizations against the template.

Example 3

Ann says to Ken "I will do the assignment unless *you interrupt me or play loud music.*" Ann expresses the following proposition:

  (3) Ann will do the assignment $\boxed{\text{unless}}$ *Ken interrupts her* $\boxed{\text{or}}$ *plays loud music.*

Let's do a partial symbolization:

    A unless (K ∨ M)

A: **A**nn does the assignment
K: **K**en interrupts Ann
M: Ken plays loud **m**usic

Again, it's useful to use the template:

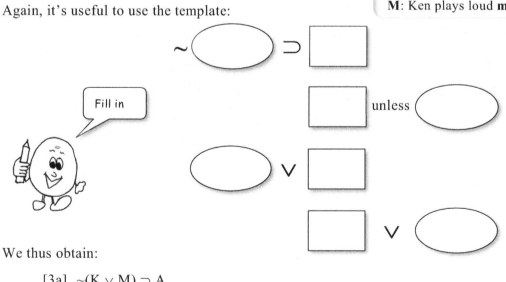

We thus obtain:

  [3a] ~(K ∨ M) ⊃ A

  [3b] (K ∨ M) ∨ A

  [3c] A ∨ (K ∨ M)

Example 4

(4) Adler's theory is true unless *Jung's theory is false.*

When we make the negations explicit, we obtain:

Adler's theory is true unless *Jung's theory is* not *true.*

After partial symbolization:

A unless ~J

After plugging into the symbolization template

A: **Adler's theory is true**
J: **Jung's theory is true**

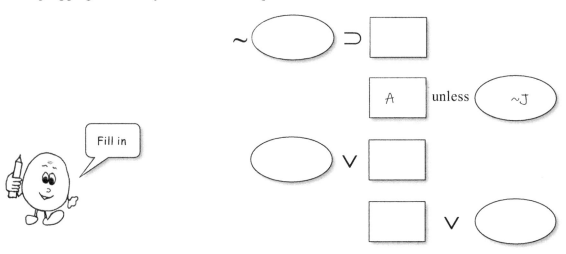

[4a] ~~J ⊃ A

[4b] ~J ∨ A

[4c] A ∨ ~J

Could we not drop the double negations in [4a]?

Don't be tempted to transform propositions before you learn proofs!

A: **A**nn is happy   **C**: **C**harlie is sad
B: **B**etty is happy   **D**: **D**irk is sad

In Ex. A.3-A.4, formulate the "unless" proposition in English and provide two symbolizations (see Example).

Example
C unless B

Charlie is sad unless Betty is happy	$B \lor C$ $\sim B \supset C$

Exercise A.3 "Unless" – Complex Terms

(a)   ~A unless C

(b)   A unless ~C

(c)   ~B unless ~D

(d)   (C ∨ D) unless (A • B)

Exercise A.4 "Unless" – Complex Terms

(a)   (C • D) unless (A ∨ B)

(b)   (A ⊃ B) unless (B unless A)

(c)   (A ≡ B) unless (A ≡ ~B)

In Ex. A.5-A.6, symbolize each proposition in two equivalent ways (one of which uses the conditional paraphrase).

Use the symbolization template for complex propositions.

A: **A**nn will go on a diet
B: **B**etty will go on a diet
C: **C**harlie will go on a diet
D: Ann's **d**octor objects to Ann going on a diet
G: **G**arry will go on a diet

Exercise A.5 Symbolizations

(a)   Ann will not go on a diet unless Betty goes on a diet.

(b)   Unless Ann goes on a diet, Betty will not go on a diet.

(c)   Betty will not go on a diet unless Charlie and Garry both go on a diet.

(d)   Ann will not go on a diet unless either Charlie or Garry goes on a diet.

Exercise A.6 Symbolizations

(a)   Ann will go on a diet just in case Betty goes on a diet, unless Ann's doctor objects to Ann's going on a diet.

(b)   Ann will go on a diet, unless Garry does not go on a diet but Betty does go on a diet.

(c)   Neither Charlie nor Garry will go on a diet unless Betty and Ann both go on a diet.

(d)   Either Ann or Betty will not go on a diet unless either Charlie or Garry goes on a diet.

B. Complicated Symbolizations

Let's do some more complex examples together.

Example 1

(1) Ben won't get an A in logic or math unless Jim gets an A in logic or math.

Let's mark the connectives:

Ben won't get an A in logic or math unless Jim gets an A in logic or math.

The structure of the sentence indicates that "unless" is the main connective:

Not (B or M) unless (J or H)

> **B**: **B**en gets an A in logic
> **M**: Ben gets an A in **m**ath
> **J**: **J**im gets an A in logic
> **H**: Jim gets an A in ma**t**h

We can replace the obvious connectives and obtain:

~(B ∨ M) unless (J ∨ H)

Once again we need to recall the ways of symbolizing "unless." Given that its terms are complex, it's useful to use the template:

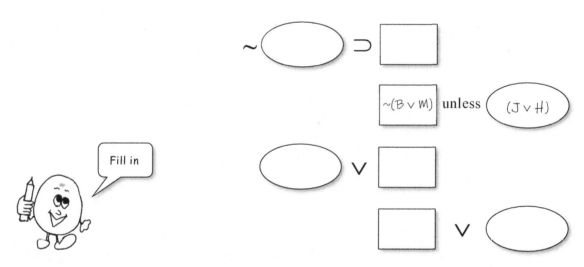

We thus obtain:

[1a] ~(J ∨ H) ⊃ ~(B ∨ M)

[1b] (J ∨ H) ∨ ~(B ∨ M)

[1c] ~(B ∨ M) ∨ (J ∨ H)

Note: [1b] is more intuitive but [1c] is simpler and structurally closer to (1).

Example 2

    (2) If Brad will get an A in logic provided that he works hard then, unless a pandemic breaks out, Jane will get an A in logic provided that she works hard and completes all the exercises.

Let's mark the connectives:

    If Brad will get an A in logic provided that he works hard then, unless a pandemic breaks out, Jane will get an A in logic provided that she works hard and completes all the exercises.

This is a very complex proposition. The main connective here is "if-then," which is partly determined by the sentence structure and partly by the meaning of what is said. Let's put parentheses around its antecedent and consequent, so that we can think about their complexity more clearly:

    If (Brad will get an A in logic provided that he works hard) then (unless a pandemic breaks out, Jane will get an A in logic provided that she works hard and completes all the exercises)

What is the main connective in the consequent:

    unless a pandemic breaks out, Jane will get an A in logic provided that she works hard and completes all the exercises

There are three connective phrases here: "unless," "provided that," and "and." The position of "unless," underscored by the comma, shows that "unless" is the main connective. We can paraphrase the consequent and insert the remaining parentheses:

If (Brad will get an A in logic provided that he works hard) then [(Jane will get an A in logic provided that (she works hard and completes all the exercises)) unless a pandemic breaks oud	**B**: **B**rad gets an A in logic **H**: **B**rad works **h**ard **J**: **J**ane gets an A in logic **W**: Jane **w**orks hard **X**: Jane completes all e**x**ercises **P**: **P**andemic breaks out

After a partial symbolization:

    (B provided that H) ⊃ [(J provided that (W • X)) unless P]

Now we need to recall the ways to symbolize the connective phrases. Recall that "*p* provided that *q*" is to be paraphrased as "if *q* then *p*." We thus obtain:

    (H ⊃ B) ⊃ [((W • X) ⊃ J) unless P]

We could symbolize "unless" in three ways, as we used to do. However, given the complexity of the sentence, let's stick to the simplest symbolization:

    [3c] (H ⊃ B) ⊃ [((W • X) ⊃ J) ∨ P]

Of course, there are other possible symbolizations:

    [3a] (H ⊃ B) ⊃ [P ∨ ((W • X) ⊃ J)]

    [3b] (H ⊃ B) ⊃ [~P ⊃ ((W • X) ⊃ J)]

A: Amy is nice	**E**: Betty will go out with Chris
B: Betty is nice	**K**: Betty will go out with Dirk
C: Chris is nice	**M**: Amy will go out with Chris
D: Dirk is nice	**Y**: Amy will go out with Dirk

Exercise B.1. Symbolization

(a)   Amy will go out with Dirk unless Betty goes out with him, provided, however, that Dirk is nice.

(b)   Chris will not be nice unless either Amy or Betty goes out with him.

(c)   Amy will go out with Dirk if and only if he is nice, unless Dirk goes out with Betty.

(d)   Amy or Betty will go out with Dirk, unless he is not nice or one of the girls goes out with Chris.

Exercise B.2 Symbolizations

(a)   Either Amy or Betty will go out with Chris; however, Amy will go out with Chris unless she goes out with Dirk, and Betty will go out with Chris if she does not go out with Dirk.

(b)   Either if Chris is nice then Amy will go out with him unless Betty does or if Dirk is nice then Betty will go out with him unless Amy does.

(c)   Dirk will not be nice unless, first, Amy is nice and goes out with him and, second, Betty is nice and Betty goes out with Chris.

(d)   Neither Amy nor Betty will go out with Dirk unless he is nice, but if Dirk is nice then Amy or Betty will go out with Dirk unless Chris is nice.

Summary

You have learned to symbolize "unless" phrases.

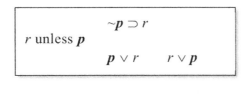

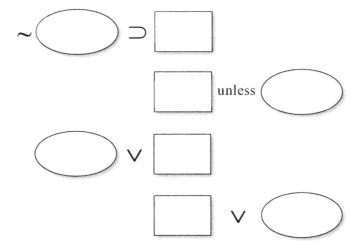

You have further enhanced your symbolization skills.

Concluding Remarks: Tricky Symbolizations

You have learned quite a lot. The more exercises you do, the more confident you should be. However, the difficulty in symbolization goes beyond complexity. Some symbolizations are just tricky. Here are some examples.

NOT ALL THAT LOOKS LIKE A CONJUNCTION IS A CONJUNCTION

You already know that symbolization need not be so straightforward. Consider a straightforward case first:

(1) Susan and Mary wear glasses.

This is a straightforward conjunction. It can be rendered as a conjunction of two simple propositions:

(1′) Susan wears glasses and Mary wears glasses.

The logical structure of this proposition is thus:

[1] S • M

S: Susan wears glasses
M: Mary wears glasses

The same is true for many of the occurrences of "and."

However, there are some uses of "and" where a conjunction is more difficult to find. Consider:

(2) Susan and Will are related.

Surely, we cannot interpret this proposition as the following conjunction:

Susan is related *and* Will is related.

S • W

We do not even understand what such a proposition means. What does it mean to say that Susan is related? What does it mean to say that Will is related? And to whom? Furthermore, suppose that we had a more complex conjunction: Susan and Will are related, and Ann and Tim are related as well. Should we represent it as: (S • W) • (A • T)? As we said, conjunctions are associative; the placement of parentheses does not affect the truth value of the conjunction. Conjunctions are also commutative; the truth value of the conjunction is not affected by the order in which the conjuncts occur. Given these two properties of conjunction, (S • W) • (A • T) is equivalent to (A • W) • (S • T). However, from the fact that Susan and Will are related and that Ann and Tim are related as well, it certainly does not follow that Ann and Will are related or that Susan and Tim are related.

Contrary to appearances, (2) is not a conjunction, at least not of the kind suggested above. In fact, (2) can be paraphrased as:

(2′) Susan and Will are related to each other.

The proposition represents a relation between two people. Propositional logic is ill-equipped to handle relations (quantifier logic allows one to do that much better). In propositional logic, such propositions are best treated either as simple propositions or as conjunctions whose conjuncts mention the relation more explicitly:

(2″) Susan is related to Will and Will is related to Susan.

There are other examples where one has to be careful with "and." Consider:

(3) Jack and Jill are married;

(4) Fichte and Hegel were contemporaries;

and so on.

"NOT ONLY ... BUT..."

Consider the proposition:

(1) Ann is not only a loving mother but also a dedicated scientist.

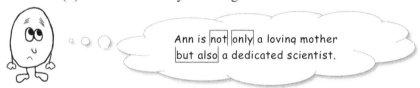

The presence of "not" might suggest that some negation is in sight. The presence of "only" might wake you up. The presence of "but also" suggests a conjunction. Two or three connectives?

However, when you reflect on what is being said, you will see that what the person means to say (from the point of view of propositional logic) is just:

(1′) Ann is both a loving mother and a dedicated scientist.

(1) is simply a conjunction:

[1] L • D

L: Ann is a loving mother
D: Ann is a dedicated scientist

NON-TRUTH-FUNCTIONAL OPERATORS

So far, we have only considered truth-functional operators. All connectives are truth-functional operators, as are phrases such as "it is the case that."

There are other non-truth-functional (opaque, intensional) operators for which propositional logic is insufficient. They include such operators as:

x believes that *p*	it is possible that *p*
x thinks that *p*	it is necessary that *p*
x doubts whether *p*	it is permissible that *p*
x wants it to be the case that *p*	it is obligatory that *p*

Sometimes what follows such operators can include propositional connectives. However, stronger logical theories are needed to handle such contexts properly (e.g., modal logic, deontic logic, intensional logic). Whatever falls within the scope of such operators cannot be treated as a complex proposition in propositional logic. Consider, for example, the following propositions:

(1) John believes that there are seven days in a week.

(2) John believes that whales and sharks are fish.

(3) John believes that whales are not mammals but fish.

All of these propositions can be captured in propositional logic only as simple propositions:

[1] S

[2] W

[3] M

S: John believes that there are seven days in a week
W: John believes that whales and sharks are fish
M: John believes that whales are not mammals but fish

Propositional logic does not "see" their complexity or even the propositional connectives that are embedded in the scope of the "…believes that" operator.

* * *

You have learned a lot but there is a lot more to learn.

Solutions to Unit 1.1 Exercises

Exercise A.1 Propositions

Sentences marked by '●' express a proposition.

●   (a) Dick Cheney overcooked the cauliflower.

⊗   (b) No force could stop <u>you</u>. ['you' is an indexical]

⊗   (c) It was very dark <u>there</u>. ['there' is an indexical]

⊗   (d) <u>My</u> friends went to the forest to pick mushrooms. ['My' is an indexical]

●   (e) Henry Fonda sneaked into the kitchen.

●   (f) Hillary Clinton attached herself to the painted wall.

●   (g) If Fred Astaire were not a dancer, Greta Garbo would not be an actress.

⊗   (h) If only children knew more than their parents<u>!</u> [Exclamations are not propositions]

⊗   (i) Will Henry ever come to like girls<u>?</u> [Questions are not propositions]

●   (j) Bill Clinton is a woman.

Exercise A.2 Propositions

(a) An unambiguous declarative sentence expresses a proposition.	● true	○ false
(b) An ambiguous declarative sentence expresses a proposition.	○ true	● false
(c) A non-declarative sentence expresses a proposition.	○ true	● false
(d) All propositions are either true or false.	● true	○ false
(e) All sentences are either true or false. (E.g., questions are sentences but are neither true nor false.)	○ true	● false
(f) One proposition can be expressed by means of more than one sentence.	● true	○ false
(g) One unambiguous declarative sentence expresses only one proposition.	● true	○ false

Exercise B.1 Arguments

(a) All arguments have exactly one premise.   ○ true   ● false

(b) All arguments have at least one premise.   ● true   ○ false

(c) All arguments have at least two premises.   ○ true   ● false

(d) An argument can have no premises.   ○ true   ● false

(e) An argument can have only one premise.   ● true   ○ false

(f) An argument can have only two premises.   ● true   ○ false

(g) An argument can have one hundred premises.   ● true   ○ false

(h) It is impossible for an argument to have exactly seven premises.   ○ true   ● false

(i) All arguments have exactly one conclusion.   ● true   ○ false

(j) All arguments have at least two conclusions.   ○ true   ● false

(k) Some arguments can have no conclusions.   ○ true   ● false

(l) Some arguments can have two conclusions.   ○ true   ● false

(m) In an argument, one proposition is accepted on the basis of others.   ● true   ○ false

(n) In an argument, one sentence is accepted on the basis of others.   ○ true   ● false

Exercise B.2 Argument Recognition

(a)

All killing of innocent human beings is wrong.

Abortion is the killing of an innocent human being.

So, abortion is wrong.

(b)

People have the right to decide what to do with their bodies.

Nobody can be forced to save the life of a human being by giving them a kidney or even bone marrow or blood.

So, women have the right to terminate an unwanted pregnancy.

(c)

Human actions are either causally determined or mere random occurrences.
If human actions are causally determined, there is no free will; if they are merely random events, there is no free will.

So, there is no free will.

(d)

Nothing can be prior to itself.
So, nothing can cause itself.

(e)

We want our children to grow up strong and independent.
If we bought a car for each of our children, they would get spoiled and they would fail to become strong and independent.
So, We cannot buy a car for each of our children.

(f)

It is impossible to think of anything greater than God.
Something that exists in reality is greater than something that exists only in the mind.
If God did not exist in reality, it would be possible to think of something greater than God, i.e. a being just like God that in addition existed in reality.
So, God exists in reality.

(g)

If an all-good, all-powerful, and all-knowing God existed, God would eliminate all evil.
Evil exists.
So, God does not exist.

Exercise B.3 Deduction in Practice

(a) If the Philadelphia Eagles win the game against the Dallas Cowboys, they will enter the playoffs.
      The Eagles did not enter the playoffs.

So, Philadelphia Eagles did not win the game with Dallas Cowboys.

(b) You can't go wrong with this salad: if you follow the recipe, it will be perfect.
      The salad was not perfect.

So, you did not follow the recipe.

(c) If it rains, Abe always takes an umbrella.
      If Abe takes an umbrella, he's uncomfortable.
      Yesterday, Abe was not uncomfortable.

So, it did not rain.

(d) If you get either 85 or 86 points on a quiz, you get a B.
      Al got 85 points on a quiz.

So, Al got a B.

(e)   If it either rains or snows, Joe never goes out.
      Joe did go out yesterday.
      _____
      | So, it neither rained nor snowed. |

(f)   All metals conduct electricity.
      But no sotones conduct electricity.
      _____
      | So, no sotones are metals. |

Exercise B.4 Logical Form – Disjunctive Syllogism

(i)

| John will turn right | or | John will turn left |

It is not the case that | John turned left |

So, | John turned right |

(ii)

| Kay will have fruit. | or | Kay will have ice-cream. |

It is not the case that | Kay had ice-cream. |

So, | Kay had fruit. |

(iii)

| Tim will get a rabbit | or | Tim will get a hamster. |

It is not the case that | Tim got a hamster. |

So, | Tim got a rabbit |

(iv)

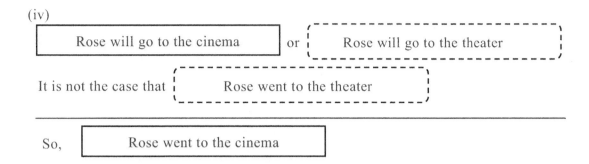

So, | Rose went to the cinema |

Exercise E Soundness

A sound argument is an argument that is valid and whose premises are true. To say that an argument is valid is to say that it is impossible for its conclusion to be true given that its premises are false.

Take an arbitrary sound argument. Let us call it α. To say that α is sound is to say that α is valid and α's premises are true (from the Definition of Soundness). To say that α is valid is to say that it is impossible for α's conclusion to be false if α's premises are true (from the Definition of Validity). But we know that α's premises are true (because the argument is sound). So, it is impossible for α's conclusion to be false. So, α's conclusion must be true. This reasoning establishes that the conclusion of any sound argument must be true.

Exercise F Hidden Premises

(a)
Capital punishment is killing.
All killing is wrong.
So, capital punishment is wrong.

(b)
Abortion is the killing of an innocent child.
All killing of innocent children is wrong.
So, abortion is wrong.

(c)
Alcohol or drugs taken by pregnant women may have a detrimental impact on the development of the fetus.
Pregnant women should never do anything that has a detrimental impact on the development of the fetus.
So, pregnant women should never drink alcohol or take drugs.

(d)
Sally has never received a violation from the Federal Aviation Administration during her 16-year flying career.
Anybody who has never in their career received a violation from the FAA is a great pilot.
So, Sally is a great pilot.

(e)
The government of Zunimagua has refused to schedule free elections, release political prisoners, or restore freedom of speech.
The United States should only provide financial aid to governments abiding by democratic principles: allowing free elections and free speech.
So, no more financial aid from the United States should be provided to Zunimagua.

Solutions to Unit 1.2 Exercises

Exercise B. Simple vs. Complex Propositions

Simple propositions are marked by ✓

(a) ✓   John is one of those extraordinarily nice men who hate all women that wear big hats.

(b)   John invited Susan out ⟦and⟧ she agreed.

(c)   ⟦If⟧ Susan does ⟦not⟧ come on time ⟦then⟧ John will be distraught.

(d) ✓   Susan was quite punctual.

(e)   John did ⟦not⟧ believe his eyes.

(f) ✓   Susan was wearing the biggest hat John has ever seen in his entire life.

(g) ✓   John started pleading for Susan to take off what seemed to him to be one of the ugliest things ever produced by a human hand.

(h)   Susan agreed to take off the hat ⟦if and only if⟧ John takes off the bow tie ⟦and⟧ the cowboy boots.

(i)   Susan's ex-husband wore bow ties ⟦and⟧ her ex-father-in-law wore cowboy boots.

Exercise C.1. Symbolization Key Errors

(a)   John invited Susan out and she agreed.

J: John invites Susan out.
S: She agrees.

An indexical is used. "She agreed" is not a proposition.

(b)   John did not believe his eyes.

J: John did not believe his eyes.

The "No Complexity" Rule is violated: negations are complex propositions.

(c)   Susan's ex-husband wore bow ties and her ex-father-in-law wore cowboy boots.

      B: bow ties
      C: cowboy boots

The symbolization key must list complete propositions. No shortcuts are allowed.

(d)   Susan agreed to take off the hat if and only if John takes off the bow tie and the cowboy boots.

      S: Susan agrees to take off the hat.
      J: John takes off the bow tie.
      J: John takes off the cowboy boots.

The "1-1" Rule is violated: the same letter is assigned to two different propositions.

Exercise C.2. Symbolization Key Errors

(a)   John will be distraught if and only if Susan does not come on time.
Susan was quite punctual.
So, John was not distraught.

      J: John is distraught.
      S: Susan comes on time.
      P: Susan is quite punctual.

The "1-1" Rule is violated: the same proposition is assigned two different letters (S and P). Note that "Susan came on time" and "Susan was punctual" convey the same meaning (proposition) in the context of this argument.

(b)   John will be distraught if and only if Susan does not come on time.
Susan was punctual.
So, John was not distraught.

      S: Susan comes on time.
      J: John will be distraught.
      W: John was distraught.

The "1-1" Rule is violated: the same proposition is assigned two different letters (J and W). This is because of the rule to disregard tense.

(c)   John will be distraught if and only if Susan does not come on time.
Susan was punctual.
So, John was not distraught.

      John: John will be distraught.
      Susan: Susan comes on time.

Only single capital letters are assigned to propositions in a symbolization key.

Exercise C.3. Symbolization Key Errors

(a)   John invited Susan out and she didn't agree to go out with him.
      If Susan agrees to go out with John then she will wear a big hat.
      Susan will wear a big hat if and only if she will want to teach John a lesson.
      If Susan wants to teach John a lesson, then he will not invite her out.

   J: John invited Susan out.
   S: **She** did**n't** agree to go out with **him**.
   A: Susan agrees to go out with John.
   S: Susan will wear a big hat.
   J: **She** will want to teach John a lesson.
   W: Susan wants to teach John a lesson.
   H: **He** will **not** invite her out.

   Error 1. 2nd (S), 5th (J), and 7th (H) entries include indexical terms.

   Error 2. "1-1" Rule violation: letters 'J' and 'S' have dual assignments.

   Error 3. "No Complexity" Rule violation: 2nd entry (S) and 7th entry (H) include a negation.

(b)   If Ben swims, then he will jog or he will diet.
      If Ben diets then she will not jog.
      If Ben does not jog, then he will not swim.
      If Ben is on a diet, then he will not swim and he will not jog.

   S: Ben swims.
   J: Ben will jog.
   D: Ben will diet
   B: Ben diets.
   N: Ben does **not** jog.
   A: Ben is on a diet.
   H: **He** swims.
   E: **He** jogs.

   Error 1: H and E are assigned to sentences with indexical terms.

   Error 2: "No Complexity" Rule violation: N is assigned to a complex proposition, a negation.

   Error 3: "1-1" Rule violation: D, B, and A are assigned to the same proposition (tense ought to be disregarded).

Exercise C.4. Symbolization Key

[Bear in mind that you may have used different letters.]

(a)   John invited Susan out and she agreed.

> **J**: John invited Susan out.
> **S**: Susan agreed to go out with John.

(b)   John did not believe his eyes.

> **J**: John believed his eyes.

Note that we can choose 'J' because we are not treating (a) and (b) as a group of propositions. If you were asked to construct a symbolization key for the group of propositions that included the sentences from (a) and (b), then if you made the above assignments for (a), you would have to choose a different letter for "John believed his eyes".

(c)   Susan's ex-husband wore bow ties and her ex-father-in-law wore cowboy boots.

> **B**: Susan's ex-husband wore **bow tie**s.
> **C**: Susan's ex-father-in-law wore **c**owboy boots.

(d)   Susan agreed to take off the hat if and only if John takes off the bow tie and the cowboy boots.

> **S**: Susan agrees to take off the hat.
> **B**: John takes off the **bow tie**.
> **C**: John takes off the **c**owboy boots.

Exercise C.5. Symbolization Key

(a)   John will be distraught if and only if Susan does not come on time.
       Susan was punctual.
       So, John was not distraught.

> **J**: John is distraught.
> **S**: Susan comes on time.

or

> **J**: John is distraught.
> **S**: Susan is punctual.

(b)   John invited Susan out and she didn't agree to go out with him.
       If Susan agrees to go out with John then she will wear a big hat.
       Susan will wear a big hat if and only if she will want to teach John a lesson.
       If Susan wants to teach John a lesson, then he will not invite her out.

> J: John invites Susan out
> S: Susan agrees to go out with John
> H: Susan wears a big **h**at
> L: Susan wants to teach John a **l**esson.

Exercise D.1. Match Negations

A: **A**nn makes dinner   B: **B**en makes lunch

~A [4]   1. It's not the case that Ben didn't make lunch.

~~A [2]   2. Ann didn't fail to make dinner.

~B [3]   3. Ben didn't make lunch.

~~B [1]   4. Ann failed to make dinner.

Exercise D.2. Match Negations

A: **A**nn makes dinner

~~A [1 / 2]

~~~A [3 / 5]

~~~~A [4]

1. Ann didn't fail to make dinner.

2. It's false that Ann didn't make dinner.

3. It's a falsehood that Ann didn't fail to make dinner.

4. It's not false that Ann didn't fail to make dinner.

5. It's not true that Ann didn't fail to make dinner.

Exercise D.3. Match Negations

B: **B**en makes lunch

~~B [1 / 3]

~~~B [2 / 5]

~~~~B [4]

1. Ben didn't fail to make lunch.

2. It is false that Ben didn't fail to make lunch.

3. It is false that Ben didn't make lunch.

4. It isn't false that Ben didn't fail to make lunch.

5. It isn't false that Ben didn't make lunch.

Exercise D.4. Match Negations

J: **J**ung's theory is true

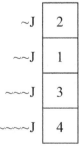

~J [2]   1. Jung's theory isn't false.

~~J [1]   2. Jung's theory is false.

~~~J [3]   3. It is not the case that Jung's theory isn't false.

~~~~J [4]   4. It is not the case that it is false that Jung's theory isn't false.

Exercise D.5. Match Negations

A: Adler's theory is true

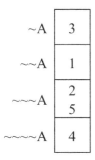

1. It's not the case that Adler's theory isn't true.

2. It is false that it's not the case that Adler's theory isn't true.

3. Adler's theory isn't true.

4. It's wrong to think that it is false that it's not the case that Adler's theory isn't true.

5. It's not the case that Adler's theory isn't false.

Exercise D.6 Negations

A: Abe will make dinner   **B**: Betty will make dinner

(a)   Abe will not make dinner

(b)   It would be false to say that Betty will make dinner.

(c)   It would be false to say that Betty will not make dinner.

(d)   It would be preposterous to think that Abe will make dinner.

(e)   It would be preposterous to think that it would not be the case that Betty will not make dinner.

(f)   Abe failed to make dinner

~A
~B
~~B
~A
~~B
~A

Exercise E.1. Match Conjunctions

A: Ann has a dog   **B**: Ben has a dog   **C**: Ann has a cat   **D**: Dan has a cat

A • B	1, 4
A • C	5
B • D	6
C • D	2
D • C	7, 8
C • A	3

1. Ann and Ben both have a dog.

2. Ann and Dan have a cat.

3. Ann has a cat and, moreover, she has a dog.

4. Ann has a dog, however, Ben also has a dog.

5. Ann has both a dog and a cat.

6. Ben has a dog but Dan has a cat.

7. Dan has a cat even though Ann has a cat as well.

8. Dan and Ann have a cat.

Exercise E.2. Match Conjunctions

A: Ann has a dog   **B**: Ben has a dog   **C**: Ann has a cat   **D**: Dan has a cat

A • ~B	5
~B • A	4
~D • C	1 / 7
B • (A • C)	2
~B • (A • C)	3
(C • D) • (A • B)	6

1. Dan doesn't have a cat despite the fact that Ann has a cat.

2. Ben has a dog but Ann has a dog and a cat.

3. Ben does not have a dog while Ann has both a dog and a cat.

4. Ben does not have a dog but Ann does.

5. Ann has a dog although Ben doesn't.

6. Ann and Dan both have a cat while Ann and Ben both have a dog.

7. Although Dan does not have a cat, Ann does.

Exercise E.3. Match Conjunctions

A: Adler's theory is true.   **J**: Jung's theory is true.   **R**: Freud's theory is true

A • ~J	5
A • ~R	1 / 6
~J • ~R	2 / 3
A • (J • R)	4
(A • J) • R	4

1. While Adler's theory is true Freud's theory is false.

2. Jung's theory is false and so is Freud's.

3. Jung's theory and Freud's theory are both false.

4. Adler's theory, Jung's theory, and Freud's theory are true.

5. Adler's theory is true but Jung's theory is false.

6. Adler's theory is true but Freud's theory is not true.

Exercise E.4. Conjunctions

A: Abe will make dinner   **B**: Betty will make dinner   **C**: Chris will make lunch

(a)	Abe and Betty will both make dinner.	A • B
(b)	Abe will make dinner but Betty will also make dinner.	A • B
(c)	Abe will make dinner but Betty will not.	A • ~B
(d)	Abe will not make dinner but Betty will.	~A • B
(e)	Abe will make dinner while Chris will make lunch.	A • C
(f)	Chris will not make lunch even though Abe will make dinner.	~C • A
(g)	Despite the fact that Abe will not make dinner, Betty will make it.	~A • B
(h)	Abe will not make dinner despite the fact that Chris will make lunch.	~A • C

Exercise F.1. Match Disjunctions

A: Ann diets   **B**: Ben diets   **E**: Ann exercises   **J**: Ann jogs   **S**: Ben swims

A ∨ B	3	1. Ann either exercises or jogs
	6	2. Ann exercises or jogs.
E ∨ J	1	
	2	3. Ann or Ben is on a diet.
~A ∨ ~B	5	4. Ben does not swim or does not diet.
		5. Either Ann does not diet or Ben does not diet.
~S ∨ ~B	4	6. Either Ann or Ben diets.

Exercise F.2. Match Disjunctions

A: Ann diets   **B**: Ben diets   **E**: Ann exercises   **J**: Ann jogs   **S**: Ben swims

J ∨ (A • E)	1	1. Ann either jogs or both diets and exercises.
(A • E) ∨ (A • J)	2	2. Either Ann diets and exercises or she diets and jogs.
(J • S) ∨ (A • B)	4	3. Either Ann diets or jogs or Ben diets or swims.
(A ∨ J) ∨ (B ∨ S)	3	4. Either Ann jogs and Ben swims or they both diet.

Exercise F.3. Disjunctions

A: Abe will make dinner   **C**: Chris will make lunch
B: Betty will make dinner   **D**: Dan will make lunch

(a) Abe or Betty will make dinner.	A ∨ B
(b) Either Betty or Abe will make dinner.	B ∨ A
(c) Either Chris will not make lunch or Abe will make dinner.	~C ∨ A
(d) Either Chris will make lunch or Betty will not make dinner.	C ∨ ~B
(e) Either Chris will not make lunch or Dan will not make lunch.	~C ∨ ~D
(f) Abe will make dinner or either Chris or Dan will make lunch.	A ∨ (C ∨ D)
(g) Either Abe and Betty will make dinner or Chris and Dan will make lunch.	(A • B) ∨ (C • D)

Exercise G.1. Match Biconditionals

A: Ann diets   **B**: Ben diets   **E**: Ann exercises   **J**: Ann jogs   **S**: Ben swims

$A \equiv B$ | 1 |
| | 3 |

$E \equiv J$ | 2 |

$\sim E \equiv \sim J$ | 5 |

$\sim B \equiv S$ | 4 |

1. Ann diets if and only if Ben diets.

2. Ann exercises if and only if she jogs.

3. Ann diets exactly if Ben diets.

4. Ben does not diet when and only when he swims.

5. Ann does not exercise if and only if she does not jog.

Exercise G.2. Match Biconditionals

A: Ann diets   **B**: Ben diets   **E**: Ann exercises   **J**: Ann jogs   **S**: Ben swims

$B \equiv (A \vee E)$ | 2 |

$\sim S \equiv (\sim E \bullet \sim J)$ | 3 |

$J \equiv (A \bullet \sim E)$ | 1 |

1. Ann jogs if and only if she diets but does not exercise.

2. Ben diets just in case Ann either diets or exercises.

3. Ben does not swim just in case Ann does not exercise and does not jog.

Exercise G.3. Match Biconditionals

A: Ann diets   **B**: Ben diets   **E**: Ann exercises   **J**: Ann jogs   **S**: Ben swims

$(J \bullet E) \equiv A$ | 1 |

$(A \bullet B) \equiv (J \bullet S)$ | 3 |

$(A \vee J) \equiv (B \vee S)$ | 2 |

1. Ann both jogs and exercises just in case she diets.

2. Ann diets or jogs if but only if Ben diets or swims.

3. Ann and Ben both diet just in case Ann jogs and Ben swims.

Exercise G.4. Biconditionals

A: Abe will make dinner   **B**: Betty will make dinner   **C**: Chris will make lunch

(a)   Abe will make dinner if and only if Betty will.

(b)   Chris will make lunch just in case Betty makes dinner.

(c)   Abe makes dinner when and only when Betty does not.

(d)   Abe will not make dinner just in case Chris will not make lunch.

(e)   Chris will make lunch just in case Abe or Betty makes dinner.

(f)   Chris will not make lunch just in case Abe and Betty both make dinner.

$A \equiv B$
$C \equiv B$
$A \equiv \sim B$
$\sim A \equiv \sim C$
$C \equiv (A \vee B)$
$\sim C \equiv (A \bullet B)$

Exercise H.1. Match Conditionals

B: Ann goes out with **Ben**   **H**: Ben invites Ann to the theater   **M**: Ben invites Ann to the movies

M ⊃ B	1
	4
H ⊃ ~B	2
	3

1. If Ben invites Ann to the movies, she will go out with him.

2. If Ben invites Ann to the theater then she will not go out with him.

3. Ann will not go out with Ben if he invites her to the theater.

4. Ann will go out with Ben if he invites her to the movies.

Exercise H.2. Match Conditionals

B: Ann goes out with **Ben**   **C:** Ann goes out with **Chris**   **H**: Ben invites Ann to the theater

H ⊃ C	1
	6
C ⊃ ~B	2
	5
B ⊃ ~C	3
	4

1. If Ben invites Ann to the theater, she will go out with Chris.

2. If Ann goes out with Chris, she will not go out with Ben.

3. If Ann goes out with Ben then she will not go out with Chris.

4. Ann will not go out with Chris if she goes out with Ben.

5. Ann will not go out with Ben if she goes out with Chris.

6. Ann will go out with Chris if Ben invites her to the theater.

Exercise H.3. Match Conditionals

A: Ann walks her dog   **B:** Ben walks his dog   **C:** Chris walks his dog   **D:** Deb walks her dog

A ⊃ B	1
D ⊃ C	2
B ⊃ D	3

1. Assuming that Ann walks her dog, Ben will walk his dog.

2. Chris will walk his dog provided that Deb walks her dog.

3. Deb will walk her dog in case Ben walks his.

Exercise H.4. Match Conditionals

A: Ann walks her dog   **B:** Ben walks his dog   **C:** Chris walks his dog   **D:** Deb walks her dog

C ⊃ A	2
A ⊃ ~C	1
~A ⊃ C	3

1. If Ann walks her dog, then Chris will not walk his dog.

2. Ann will walk her dog given that Chris walks his dog.

3. Chris will walk his dog as long as Ann does not walk her dog.

Exercise H.5. Match Conditionals

A: Ann walks her dog   **B:** Ben walks his dog   **C:** Chris walks his dog   **D:** Deb walks her dog

$(A \vee D) \supset B$ | 2 |

$A \supset (B \vee C)$ | 1 |

1. If Ann walks her dog, Ben or Chris will walk their dogs.

2. Ben will walk his dog when either Ann or Deb walks their dogs.

Exercise H.6. Match Conditionals

A: Ann walks her dog   **B:** Ben walks his dog   **C:** Chris walks his dog   **D:** Deb walks her dog

$(B \bullet C) \supset {\sim}A$ | 2 |

$D \supset (A \bullet B)$ | 1 |

1. Ann and Ben will walk their dogs on the condition that Deb walks her dog.

2. Supposing that both Ben and Chris walk their dogs, Ann will not walk her dog.

Exercise H.7. Conditionals

A: Abe will make dinner   **C: C**hris will make lunch
B: Betty will make dinner   **D: D**an will make lunch

(a)   Betty will make dinner if Dan makes lunch.

$D \supset B$

If | Dan makes lunch | then | Betty will make dinner |

(b)   Chris will make lunch given that Abe makes dinner.

$A \supset C$

If | Abe makes dinner | then | Chris will make lunch |

(c)   Assuming that Chris makes lunch, Abe will make dinner.

$C \supset A$

If | Chris makes lunch | then | Abe will make dinner |

(d)   Given that Betty makes dinner, Chris makes lunch.

$B \supset C$

If | Betty makes dinner | then | Chris makes lunch |

(e)   On the supposition that Chris makes lunch, Abe makes dinner.

$C \supset A$

If | Chris makes lunch | then | Abe makes dinner

(f)   Chris will make lunch provided that Betty will not make dinner.

$\sim B \supset C$

If | Betty will not make dinner | then | Chris will make lunch

(g)   Provided that Dan makes lunch, Abe will not make dinner.

$D \supset \sim A$

If | Dan makes lunch | then | Abe will not make dinner

Exercise H.8. Conditionals

A: **A**be will make dinner   **C**: **C**hris will make lunch
B: **B**etty will make dinner   **D**: **D**an will make lunch

(a)   On the condition that Betty makes dinner, Chris will make lunch.

$B \supset C$

If | Betty makes dinner | then | Chris will make lunch

(b)   Dan will not make lunch if Abe does not make dinner.

$\sim A \supset \sim D$

If | Abe does not make dinner | then | Dan will not make lunch

(c)   Dan will make lunch if either Abe or Betty make dinner.

$(A \vee B) \supset D$

If | either Abe or Betty make dinner | then | Dan will make lunch

(d)   Abe will make dinner on the assumption that Betty does not.

$\sim B \supset A$

If | Betty does not make dinner | then | Abe will make dinner

(e)   Abe will make dinner provided that either Chris or Dan make lunch. $(C \lor D) \supset A$

If | either Chris or Dan make lunch | then | Abe will make dinner |

(f)   Given that either Chris or Dan make lunch, Abe or Betty will make dinner. $(C \lor D) \supset (A \lor B)$

If | either Chris or Dan make lunch | then | Abe or Betty will make dinner |

(g)   Chris and Dan will both make lunch given that Abe and Betty both make dinner. $(A \bullet B) \supset (C \bullet D)$

If | Abe and Betty both make dinner | then | Chris and Dan will both make lunch |

Exercise H.9. Conditionals

D: Ann is on a **d**iet   **H**: Ann gets **h**ealthier   **I**: Bill is on a diet   **W**: Bill gains **w**eight
E: Ann **e**xercises regularly   **G**: Ann **g**ains weight   **J**: Bill **j**ogs regularly

(a)   Ann will get healthier if she goes on a diet and does not gain weight. $(D \bullet \sim G) \supset H$

If | Ann goes on a diet and does not gain weight | then | Ann will get healthier |

(b)   Ann will go on a diet and will exercise regularly on the condition that Billy goes on a diet. $I \supset (D \bullet E)$

If | Billy goes on a diet | then | Ann will go on a diet and will exercise regularly |

(c)   Billy will go on a diet provided that Ann goes on a diet and does not gain weight. $(D \bullet \sim G) \supset I$

If | Ann goes on a diet and does not gain weight | then | Billy will go on a diet |

(d)   Given that Billy jogs regularly or is on a diet, he does not gain weight. $(J \lor I) \supset \sim W$

If | Billy jogs regularly or is on a diet | then | Billy does not gain weight |

(e)   Ann will exercise regularly provided that Billy jogs regularly and does not gain weight.

$(J \cdot \sim W) \supset E$

| If | Billy jogs regularly and does not gain weight | then | Ann will exercise regularly |

(f)   Ann will exercise regularly given that she gets healthier or doesn't gain weight.

$(H \vee \sim G) \supset E$

| If | Ann gets healthier or doesn't gain weight | then | Ann will exercise regularly |

(g)   Provided that Ann goes on a diet and exercises regularly, she will be healthy and will not gain weight.

$(D \cdot E) \supset (H \cdot \sim G)$

| If | Ann goes on a diet and exercises regularly | then | Ann will be healthy and will not gain weight |

Solutions to Unit 1.3 Exercises

D: Ann diet   **E**: Ann exercises   **J**: Ann jogs

Exercise A.1 Match Propositions

Proposition	Match
E ∨ (D • J)	2
(E ∨ D) • J	1

1   Ann will exercise or diet but, in either case, she will jog.

2   Either Ann will exercise or she will both diet and jog.

Exercise A.2 Match Propositions

Proposition	Match
(D ∨ E) • J	3
(D ∨ E) ∨ J	2
D ∨ (E • J)	1
D ∨ (E ∨ J)	2

1   Either Ann will diet or she will both exercise and jog.

2   Ann will diet, exercise, or jog.

3   Ann will diet or exercise but, in any event, she will jog.

Exercise A.3 Match Propositions

Proposition	Match
(D • E) • J	3
(D • E) ∨ J	4 / 5
D • (E • J)	3
D • (E ∨ J)	1 / 2

1   Ann will diet and she will exercise or jog.

2   Ann will diet but she will either exercise or jog.

3   Ann will diet, exercise, and jog.

4   Ann will either diet and exercise or jog.

5   Either Ann will both diet and exercise or she will jog.

D: Ann diet   **E**: Ann exercises   **H**: Ann is healthy

Exercise A.4 Match Propositions

Proposition	Match
D ⊃ H	1 / 3
~D ⊃ H	2 / 4

1   If Ann diets then she will be healthy.

2   Ann will be healthy if she does not diet.

3   Ann will be healthy if she diets.

4   If Ann does not diet then she will be healthy.

Exercise A.5 Match Propositions

D ⊃ ~H	4		

D ⊃ ~H | 4 | 1 | If Ann is healthy then she will not diet.

~D ⊃ ~H | 3 | 2 | If Ann is healthy then she will diet.

H ⊃ D | 2 | 3 | If Ann does not diet then she will not be healthy.

H ⊃ ~D | 1 | 4 | If Ann diets then she will not be healthy.

Exercise A.6 Match Propositions

(D • E) ⊃ H | 2 | 1 | Ann diets and if she exercises then she will be healthy.

2 | If Ann diets and exercises then she will be healthy.

D • (E ⊃ H) | 1 | 3 | If Ann diets then she will both exercise and be healthy.

D ⊃ (E • H) | 3 | 4 | If Ann diets then she will exercise but, in any event, she will be healthy.

(D ⊃ E) • H | 4 |

Exercise A.7 Match Propositions

(D ∨ E) ⊃ H | 4 | 1 | Ann will be healthy on the condition that if she diets then she will exercise.

D ∨ (E ⊃ H) | 2 | 2 | Either Ann will diet or if she exercises then she will be healthy.

D ⊃ (E ⊃ H) | 3 | 3 | If Ann diets then if she exercises then she will be healthy.

(D ⊃ E) ⊃ H | 1 | 4 | If Ann either diets or exercises then she will be healthy.

Example

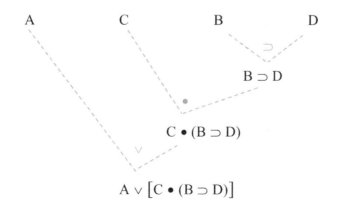

Exercise B.1 Main Connective

1. (A • B) ∨ (C ⊃ D)

2. A • (B ∨ (C ⊃ D))

3. ((A • B) ∨ C) ⊃ D

4. A • ((B ∨ C) ⊃ D)

5. (A • (B ∨ C)) ⊃ D

6. (A ⊃ A) ⊃ (A ⊃ B)

7. A ⊃ (A ⊃ (A ⊃ B))

8. ((A ⊃ A) ⊃ A) ⊃ B

Exercise B.2 Main Connective

1. (((A • B) • C) ≡ (A ∨ C)) ⊃ (A • (B ∨ C))

2. (((A ≡ B) ⊃ (B ≡ C)) • (C ⊃ D)) ∨ (B ⊃ ((A • B) ≡ C))

3. (((A ∨ B) • (C ∨ D)) ⊃ C) ≡ ((A ⊃ ((C ⊃ D) ⊃ B)) ⊃ D)

Example

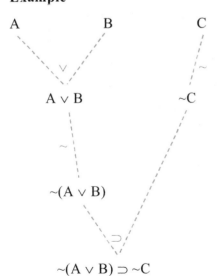

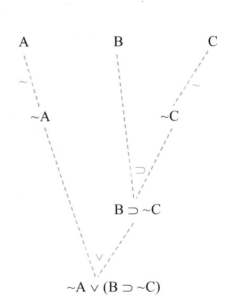

Exercise C.1 Main Connective

1. $\sim A \supset (B \vee A)$

2. $\sim(A \supset B) \vee A$

3. $\sim((A \supset B) \vee A)$

4. $\sim\sim A \vee (B \supset C)$

5. $\sim(\sim A \vee B) \supset C$

6. $\sim(\sim A \vee (B \supset C))$

7. $\sim\sim(A \vee (B \supset C))$

8. $\sim\sim(A \vee B) \supset C$

Exercise C.2 Main Connective

1. $\sim(\sim(\sim A \vee \sim B) \supset \sim(A \cdot B)) \supset \sim(\sim A \vee \sim A)$

2. $\sim(\sim(A \supset (B \cdot A)) \equiv \sim\sim\sim(\sim B \supset \sim A))$

3. $\sim\sim(\sim A \vee \sim(B \cdot \sim C)) \supset \sim((\sim C \vee B) \equiv A)$

D: Ann **d**iets	**G**: Ann **g**ains weight	**I**: Billy d**i**ets
E: Ann **e**xercises	**H**: Ann is **h**ealthy	**O**: Billy j**o**gs
J: Ann **j**ogs		**W**: Billy gains **w**eight
S: Ann **s**wims		

Exercise D.1 Symbolization

(a)	If Ann exercises then she will not gain weight.	$E \supset \sim G$
(b)	If Ann does not exercise then she will gain weight.	$\sim E \supset G$
(c)	If Ann either diets or exercises then she will be healthy.	$(D \vee E) \supset H$
(d)	If Ann diets and swims then she will be healthy.	$(D \cdot S) \supset H$
(e)	If Ann diets and jogs then she will not gain weight.	$(D \cdot J) \supset \sim G$

Exercise D.2 Symbolization

(a)	If Ann swims then she will not jog.	S ⊃ ~J
(b)	If Billy diets then he will not jog	I ⊃ ~O
(c)	If Billy diets or jogs then he will not gain weight.	(I ∨ O) ⊃ ~W
(d)	If Billy and Ann are on a diet, they will both jog.	(I • D) ⊃ (O • J)
(e)	If Billy either jogs or is on a diet then Ann will either swim or jog.	(O ∨ I) ⊃ (S ∨ J)

Exercise D.3 Symbolization

(a)	If either Ann or Billy gains weight then if Ann does not diet then Billy will not diet.	(G ∨ W) ⊃ (~D ⊃ ~I)
(b)	If Ann and Billy are both on a diet then Ann will jog if and only if Billy jogs.	(D • I) ⊃ (J ≡ O)
(c)	Either Ann and Billy will diet or they will both jog.	(D • I) ∨ (J • O)
(d)	Either Ann will diet or she will both swim and jog.	D ∨ (S • J)

Exercise D.4 Disambiguation

(a)   Abe will read a couple of textbooks or listen to some lectures and solve some problems.

1:	Either Abe will read a couple of textbooks or both listen to some lectures and solve some problems.
2:	Abe will both either read a couple of textbooks or listen to some lectures and solve some problems.
or:	Abe will read a couple of textbooks or listen to some lectures, but, in any event, he will solve some problems.

L: Abe will listen to some lectures **R**: Abe will read some textbooks **S**: Abe will solve some problems	[1] R ∨ (L • S)
	[2] (R ∨ L) • S

(b)   If Ann finishes her graduate studies then she will work as a scientist or she will become a teacher.

1:	If Ann finishes her graduate studies then she will either work as a scientist or become a teacher.
2:	Either Ann will work as a scientist if she finishes her graduate studies or Ann will become a teacher.
or:	Either if Ann finishes her graduate studies then she will work as a scientist or Ann will become a teacher.

G: Ann finishes her graduate studies **S**: Ann will work as a scientist **R**: Ann will become a teacher	[1] G ⊃ (S ∨ R)
	[2] (G ⊃ S) ∨ R

(c)   Claire will go to Hawaii and Ben will go to Florida if Ann will go to the Bahamas.

1:	Claire will go to Hawaii and if Ann will go to the Bahamas then Ben will go to Florida.
2:	If Ann will go to the Bahamas then both Claire will go to Hawaii and Ben will go to Florida.

A: Ann will go to the Bahamas **B**: Ben will go to Florida **C**: Claire will go to Hawaii	[1] C • (A ⊃ B)
	[2] A ⊃ (C • B)

(d)   Ann will finish her graduate studies and she will work as a scientist or she will become a teacher if she can live with little pay.

1:	Either Ann will both finish her graduate studies and work as a scientist or she will become a teacher if she can live with little pay.
2:	Ann will finish her graduate studies and if she can live with little pay then she will either work as a scientist or become a teacher.
3:	Ann will finish her graduate studies and either she will work as a scientist or if she can live with little pay then she will become a teacher.
4:	If Ann can live with little pay then she will both finish her graduate studies and either work as a scientist or become a teacher.
5:	If Ann can live with little pay then either she will both finish her graduate studies and work as a scientist or she will become a teacher.

	[1]	(G • S) ∨ (L ⊃ R)
	[2]	G • (L ⊃ (S ∨ R))
G: Ann finishes her graduate studies **L**: Ann can live with little pay **S**: Ann will work as a scientist **R**: Ann will become a teacher	[3]	G • (S ∨ (L ⊃ R))
	[4]	L ⊃ (G • (S ∨ R))
	[5]	L ⊃ ((G • S) ∨ R)

Exercise D.5 Symbolization (Main Connective Determined by Meaning)

> **D**: Ann **d**iets   **G**: Ann **g**ains weight   **I**: Billy d**i**ets
> **E**: Ann **e**xercises   **H**: Ann is **h**ealthy   **O**: Billy j**o**gs
> **J**: Ann **j**ogs   **W**: Billy gains **w**eight
> **S**: Ann **s**wims

(a)	If Ann swims then she will not jog and if she jogs then she will not swim.	$(S \supset {\sim}J) \bullet (J \supset {\sim}S)$
(b)	If Ann jogs then Billy jogs and if she swims then Billy diets.	$(J \supset O) \bullet (S \supset I)$
(c)	If Ann jogs then Billy jogs and if, in addition, she swims then Billy diets.	$J \supset (O \bullet (S \supset I))$
(d)	Ann will jog just in case Billy jogs and Billy will go on a diet just in case Ann goes on a diet.	$(J \equiv O) \bullet (I \equiv D)$
(e)	Billy does not gain weight just in case he diets and he also jogs.	${\sim}W \equiv (I \bullet O)$
(f)	Billy does not gain weight just in case he diets and, incidentally, it so happens that he also jogs.	$({\sim}W \equiv I) \bullet O$

Exercise D.6 Symbolization (Main Connective Determined by Meaning)

> **D**: Ann **d**iets   **G**: Ann **g**ains weight   **I**: Billy d**i**ets
> **E**: Ann **e**xercises   **H**: Ann is **h**ealthy   **O**: Billy j**o**gs
> **J**: Ann **j**ogs   **W**: Billy gains **w**eight
> **S**: Ann **s**wims

(a)	If Ann diets then so does Billy but if she does not diet then Billy gains weight.	$(D \supset I) \bullet ({\sim}D \supset W)$
(b)	Billy will gain weight just in case Ann gains weight and Billy will jog just in case Ann swims, jogs, or exercises.	$(W \equiv G) \bullet (O \equiv ((S \vee J) \vee E))$
(c)	If Billy diets then Ann also diets and if he jogs then she also jogs.	$(I \supset D) \bullet (O \supset J)$
(d)	If Billy diets then Ann also diets and if, in addition, he jogs then she also jogs.	$I \supset (D \bullet (O \supset J))$
(e)	Ann will be healthy just in case she diets and either jogs, swims, or exercises.	$H \equiv (D \bullet ((J \vee S) \vee E))$
(f)	Ann will be healthy just in case she diets and, incidentally, it so happens that she either jogs, swims, or exercises.	$(H \equiv D) \bullet ((J \vee S) \vee E)$

Exercise D.7 Symbolization (Comma Placement)

D: Ann **d**iets	**G**: Ann **g**ains weight
E: Ann **e**xercises	**H**: Ann is **h**ealthy
J: Ann **j**ogs	
S: Ann **s**wims	

I: Billy diets		
O: Billy j**o**gs		
W: Billy gains **w**eight		

(a) If Ann swims, then she will not jog though she will diet.

$$S \supset (\sim J \bullet D)$$

(b) If Ann swims then she will not jog, but she will diet.

$$(S \supset \sim J) \bullet D$$

(c) If Ann is on a diet then Billy will be on a diet, but he will not jog.

$$(D \supset I) \bullet \sim O$$

(d) If Ann is on a diet, then Billy will be on a diet but he will not jog.

$$D \supset (I \bullet \sim O)$$

(e) If Ann jogs, then she will not gain weight provided that she goes on a diet.

$$J \supset (D \supset \sim G)$$

(f) If Ann jogs then she will not gain weight, provided that she goes on a diet.

$$D \supset (J \supset \sim G)$$

Exercise D.8 Symbolization (Comma Placement)

D: Ann **d**iets	**G**: Ann **g**ains weight
E: Ann **e**xercises	**H**: Ann is **h**ealthy
J: Ann **j**ogs	
S: Ann **s**wims	

I: Billy diets		
O: Billy j**o**gs		
W: Billy gains **w**eight		

(a) If Ann diets then she will not gain weight, assuming that she is healthy.

$$H \supset (D \supset \sim G)$$

(b) If Ann diets, then she will not gain weight assuming that she is healthy.

$$D \supset (H \supset \sim G)$$

(c) If Billy and Ann diet, then they will jog provided that Ann is healthy.

$$(I \bullet D) \supset (H \supset (O \bullet J))$$

(d) If Billy and Ann diet then they will jog, provided that Ann is healthy.

$$H \supset ((I \bullet D) \supset (O \bullet J))$$

(e) Ann and Bill will jog or they will diet, provided that Ann is healthy.

$$H \supset ((J \bullet O) \vee (D \bullet I))$$

(f) Ann and Bill will jog, or they will diet provided that Ann is healthy.

$$(J \bullet O) \vee (H \supset (D \bullet I))$$

Exercise D.9 Symbolization

> **A**: Ann is on a diet   **L**: Larry is getting fat
> **B**: Betty is on a diet.   **M**: Martin is getting fat
> **C**: Charlie is on a diet   **N**: Newt is getting fat

(a)	Either Ann is on a diet or Betty and Charlie are both on a diet.	$A \vee (B \bullet C)$
(b)	It is both the case that either Ann or Betty is on a diet and that Charlie is on a diet.	$(A \vee B) \bullet C$
(c)	Either Ann or Betty is on a diet and, in any event, Charlie is on a diet.	$(A \vee B) \bullet C$
(d)	Either Larry and Martin are getting fat or Martin and Newt are getting fat	$(L \bullet M) \vee (M \bullet N)$
(e)	Either Ann or Betty is on a diet; however, it is also the case that either Betty or Charlie is on a diet.	$(A \vee B) \bullet (B \vee C)$
(f)	Either both Larry and Martin are getting fat or Newt is not getting fat.	$(L \bullet M) \vee {\sim}N$

> **D**: Ann diets   **G**: Ann gains weight   **I**: Billy diets
> **E**: Ann exercises   **H**: Ann is healthy   **O**: Billy jogs
> **J**: Ann jogs   **W**: Billy gains weight
> **S**: Ann swims

Exercise D.10 Symbolization

(a)	If Ann does not exercise then she will both gain weight and lose health.	${\sim}E \supset (G \bullet {\sim}H)$
(b)	If Ann swims or jogs then Billy diets or jogs.	$(S \vee J) \supset (I \vee O)$
(c)	Either Ann will diet and swim or Billy will diet and jog.	$(D \bullet S) \vee (I \bullet O)$
(d)	Ann will either diet and swim or she will diet and jog.	$(D \bullet S) \vee (D \bullet J)$
(e)	If Ann swims or Billy jogs then both Ann and Billy will be on a diet.	$(S \vee O) \supset (D \bullet I)$

D: Ann **d**iets   **G**: Ann **g**ains weight   **I**: Billy d**i**ets
E: Ann **e**xercises   **H**: Ann is **h**ealthy   **O**: Billy j**o**gs
J: Ann **j**ogs   **W**: Billy gains **w**eight
S: Ann **s**wims

Exercise D.11 Symbolization

(a)	Ann will be healthy just in case both she and Billy will jog.	$H \equiv (J \bullet O)$
(b)	Billy will jog if but only if either Ann jogs or exercises.	$O \equiv (J \vee E)$
(c)	If Ann is on a diet but Billy is not, they will both be jogging.	$(D \bullet \sim I) \supset (J \bullet O)$
(d)	Ann will either swim or jog if Billy either jogs or is on a diet.	$(O \vee I) \supset (S \vee J)$
(e)	If either Ann or Billy gains weight then if Ann does not diet then Billy will not diet.	$(G \vee W) \supset (\sim D \supset \sim I)$

Exercise D.12 Symbolization

(a)	If Ann and Billy are both on a diet then Ann will jog if and only if Billy jogs.	$(D \bullet I) \supset (J \equiv O)$
(b)	Either Ann and Billy will diet or they will both jog.	$(D \bullet I) \vee (J \bullet O)$
(c)	If Ann both diets and either swims or jogs then she will be healthy.	$(D \bullet (S \vee J)) \supset H$
(d)	If either Ann and Billy both diet or they both jog then if Ann does not gain weight then Billy will not gain weight.	$((D \bullet I) \vee (J \bullet O)) \supset (\sim G \supset \sim W)$

Solutions to Unit 1.4 Exercises

Exercise B.1 Neither nor, Not both

(a)	Ann and Betty are not both on a diet.	~(A • B)
(b)	Neither Ann nor Betty is on a diet.	~A • ~B
(c)	Betty and Dirk are not both on a diet.	~(B • D)
(d)	Neither Evelyn nor Betty is on a diet.	~E • ~B
(e)	Ann and Dirk are not both on a diet.	~(A • D)

Exercise B.1+ Neither nor, Not both

(a)	Neither Evelyn nor Garry is on a diet.	~E • ~G
(b)	Dirk and Evelyn are not both on a diet.	~(D • E)
(c)	Neither Garry nor Charlie is on a diet.	~G • ~C
(d)	Neither Dirk nor Garry is on a diet.	~D • ~G
(e)	Dirk and Garry are not both on a diet.	~(D • G)

Exercise B.2 Neither nor, Not both

(a)	Neither Dirk nor Charlie is on a diet.	~D • ~C
(b)	Betty and Dirk are not both on a diet.	~(B • D)
(c)	Neither Garry nor Evelyn is on a diet.	~G • ~E
(d)	Ann is on a diet but neither Betty nor Charlie is on a diet.	A • (~B • ~C)
(e)	If Ann is on a diet then Betty and Garry are not both on a diet.	A ⊃ ~(B • G)

Exercise B.3 Both-Not, Not both

(a)	Ann and Betty are both not on a diet.	~A • ~B
(b)	Charlie and Ann are not both on a diet.	~(C • A)
(c)	Evelyn and Ann are both not on a diet.	~E • ~A
(d)	Charlie and Betty are both not on a diet.	~C • ~B
(e)	Charlie and Dirk aren't both on a diet.	~(C • D)

Exercise B.4 Neither nor-Nor

(a)	Neither Ann nor Betty nor Evelyn is on a diet.	~A • (~B • ~E) (~A • ~B) • ~E
(b)	Neither Charlie, Dirk, nor Garry is on a diet.	~C • (~D • ~G) (~C • ~D) • ~G
(c)	Neither Garry nor Betty nor Evelyn is on a diet.	(~G • ~B) • ~E ~G • (~B • ~E)
(d)	Charlie, Dirk, and Garry are all not on a diet.	~C • (~D • ~G) (~C • ~D) • ~G
(e)	Charlie, Dirk, and Garry are not all on a diet.	~(C • (D • G)) ~((C • D) • G)

Exercise B.5 Neither nor – Complex Terms

(a) Neither A nor B

Neither Ann nor Betty is sick.	~A • ~B

(b) Neither ~A nor ~B

Neither Ann is not sick nor Betty is not sick.	~~A • ~~B

(c) Neither (A • B) nor (C • D)

Neither both Ann and Betty are sick nor both Charlie and Dirk are sick.	~(A • B) • ~(C • D)

(d) Neither (A ∨ B) nor (A • B)

Neither is it the case that Ann or Betty is sick nor is it the case that both Ann and Betty are sick.	~(A ∨ B) • ~(A • B)

(e) Neither (A ⊃ B) nor (B ⊃ A)

Neither is it the case that if Ann is sick then so is Betty nor is it the case that if Betty is sick then so is Ann.	~(A ⊃ B) • ~(B ⊃ A)

(f) Neither (A ≡ B) nor (B ≡ A)

Neither is it the case that Ann is sick if and only if Betty is nor is it the case that Betty is sick just in case Ann is.	~(A ≡ B) • ~(B ≡ A)

Exercise B.6 Neither nor – Complex Terms

(a)	Neither is it the case that both Ann and Betty are sick nor is it the case that Dirk is while Chris is not sick.	$\sim(A \bullet B) \bullet \sim(D \bullet \sim C)$
(b)	Neither is it so that either Dirk or Charlie are sick nor is it so that Charlie is not sick if and only if Dirk is not sick.	$\sim(D \vee C) \bullet \sim(\sim C \equiv \sim D)$
(c)	Neither Charlie is not sick nor Betty and Ann are both sick.	$\sim C \bullet \sim(B \bullet A)$
(d)	Neither is it true that if Charlie is sick then Betty or Dirk is sick nor is it true that if Betty or Dirk is sick then so is Charlie.	$\sim(C \supset (B \vee D)) \bullet \sim((B \vee D) \supset C)$
(e)	Either neither Ann nor Betty is not sick or neither Betty nor Charlie is not sick.	$\sim(\sim A \bullet \sim B) \vee \sim(\sim B \bullet \sim C)$

Exercise B.7 Not both – Complex Terms

(a) Not both A and B

Not both Ann and Betty are rich.	$\sim(A \bullet B)$

(b) Not both ~A and ~B

It's not both the case that Ann isn't rich and Betty isn't rich.	$\sim(\sim A \bullet \sim B)$

(c) Not both (A • B) and (C • D)

It's not both the case that Ann and Betty are both rich and Charlie and Dirk are both rich.	$\sim((A \bullet B) \bullet (C \bullet D))$

(d) Not both (A ∨ B) and (A • B)

It's not both the case that either Ann or Betty is rich and that Ann and Betty are both rich.	$\sim((A \vee B) \bullet (A \bullet B))$

(e) Not both (A ⊃ B) and (B ⊃ A)

It's not both the case that if Ann is rich then so is Betty and that if Betty is rich then so is Ann.	$\sim((A \supset B) \bullet (B \supset A))$

(f) Not both (A ≡ B) and (B ≡ A)

It's not both the case that Ann is rich if and only if Betty is and that Betty is rich just in case Ann is.	$\sim((A \equiv B) \bullet (B \equiv A))$

Exercise B.8 Not both – Complex Terms

(a)	It is not both the case that Ann and Betty are both rich and that Dirk and Chris are not rich.	~((A • B) • (~D • ~C))
(b)	It is not both true that Ann is rich if and only if Chris is rich and that Betty is rich if and only if Dirk isn't.	~((A ≡ C) • (B ≡ ~D))
(c)	If it is not both so that Ann is rich if and only if Betty is and that Betty is rich if and only if Charlie is, then neither Ann nor Betty is rich.	~((A ≡ B) • (B ≡ C)) ⊃ (~A • ~B)
(d)	If neither Ann nor Betty is rich then it's not both the case that either Ann or Charlie is rich and that either Betty or Dirk is rich.	(~A • ~B) ⊃ ~((A ∨ C) • (B ∨ D))
(e)	It is not both the case that Ann and Betty are not both rich and that Chris and Dirk are not both rich.	~(~(A • B) • ~(C • D))

Exercise B.9 Neither nor, Not both

(a)	Either Ann is not happy or Betty and Charlie are not both happy.	~A ∨ ~(B • C)
(b)	It is not the case that neither Ann nor Betty is happy.	~(~A • ~B)
(c)	It is not the case that Charlie and Dirk are not both happy.	~~(C • D)
(d)	It would be a lie to say that Evelyn and Ann are both not happy.	~(~E • ~A)
(e)	It is neither the case that Ann is not happy nor that Betty is not happy.	~~A • ~~B

Exercise B.10 Neither nor, Not both

(a)	Ann is happy but Betty and Evelyn are not both happy.	A • ~(B • E)
(b)	If neither Betty nor Evelyn is happy then Charlie and Garry are not both happy.	(~B • ~E) ⊃ ~(C • G)
(c)	If Betty and Evelyn are not both happy then neither Charlie nor Garry is happy.	~(B • E) ⊃ (~C • ~G)
(d)	Neither Ann nor Betty nor Evelyn is happy.	(~A • ~B) • ~E
(e)	Neither Garry nor Betty nor Evelyn is happy.	(~G • ~B) • ~E ~G • (~B • ~E)

Exercise C. Exclusive-Disjunction

(a)	Either Ann or Betty is happy but not both.
(b)	Either Betty or Charlie is happy but they aren't both happy.
(c)	Either Charlie or Dirk is happy but not both.
(d)	If either Ann or Charlie is happy though not both, then Betty or Dirk is happy.
(e)	Either Betty is not happy or Dirk is not happy but not both.

$(A \lor B) \bullet \sim(A \bullet B)$

$(B \lor C) \bullet \sim(B \bullet C)$

$(C \lor D) \bullet \sim(C \bullet D)$

$[(A \lor C) \bullet \sim(A \bullet C)] \supset (B \lor D)$

$(\sim C \lor \sim D) \bullet \sim(\sim C \bullet \sim D)$

Exercise D de Morgan's laws

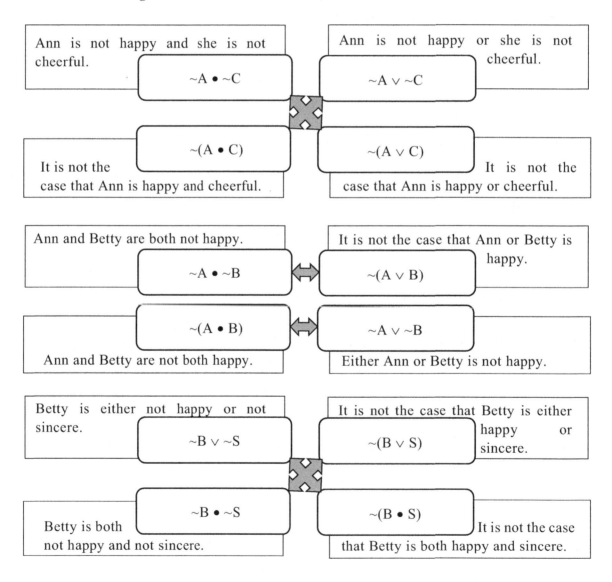

Exercise E.1 Neither nor, Not both

(a)	Charlie and Ann are not both depressed.	~(C • A)	~C ∨ ~A
(b)	Neither Ann nor Betty is depressed.	~A • ~B	~(A ∨ B)
(c)	Ann and Betty are not both depressed.	~(A • B)	~A ∨ ~B
(d)	Neither Betty nor Evelyn is depressed.	~B • ~E	~(B ∨ E)
(e)	Charlie and Garry are both not depressed.	~C • ~G	~(C ∨ G)

Exercise E.2 Neither nor, Not both

(a)	Neither Ann nor Betty is depressed.	~A • ~B	~(A ∨ B)
(b)	Both Charlie and Garry are not depressed.	~C • ~G	~(C ∨ G)
(c)	Betty and Evelyn are not both depressed.	~(B • E)	~B ∨ ~E
(d)	Neither Betty nor Evelyn is depressed, though Ann is.	(~B • ~E) • A	~(B ∨ E) • A
(e)	If Ann is depressed then Betty and Charlie are not both depressed.	A ⊃ ~(B • C)	A ⊃ (~B ∨ ~C)

Exercise E.3 Neither nor, Not both

(a)	Either Ann is not depressed or Betty and Charlie are not both depressed.	~A ∨ ~(B • C)	~A ∨ (~B ∨ ~C)
(b)	It is not the case that neither Ann nor Betty is depressed.	~(~A • ~B)	~~(A ∨ B)
(c)	It is not the case that Charlie and Dirk are not both depressed.	~~(C • D)	~(~C ∨ ~D)
(d)	It would be a lie to say that Evelyn and Ann are both not depressed.	~(~E • ~A)	~~(E ∨ A)
(e)	It is neither the case that Ann is not depressed nor that Betty is not depressed.	~~A • ~~B	~(~A ∨ ~B)

Exercise E.4 Neither nor, Not both

(a)	Amy and Chad are not both happy.	~(A • C)	~A ∨ ~C
(b)	Evelyn and Garry are both not depressed.	~E • ~G	~(E ∨ G)
(c)	Neither Dirk nor Garry is depressed.	~D • ~G	~(D ∨ G)
(d)	Amy and Ben are not both happy.	~(A • B)	~A ∨ ~B
(e)	Ben and Chad are both not happy.	~(B • C)	~(B ∨ C)

Exercise E.5 Neither nor, Not both

(a) Neither Garry nor Evelyn is depressed.	

~G • ~E	~(G ∨ E)
A • (~B • ~C)	A • ~(B ∨ C)
~(B • C) • G	(~B ∨ ~C) • G
D • (~G • ~E)	D • ~(G ∨ E)
~E ⊃ (~A • ~B)	~E ⊃ ~(A ∨ B)

(a) Neither Garry nor Evelyn is depressed.

(b) Amy is happy but neither Ben nor Chad is.

(c) Ben and Chad are not both happy and Garry is depressed.

(d) Dirk is depressed but neither Garry nor Evelyn is.

(e) Amy and Ben are both not depressed as long as Evelyn is not depressed.

Exercise E.6 Neither nor, Not both

(a) If neither Ben nor Amy is happy then Dirk and Evelyn are not both depressed.

1	(~B • ~A) ⊃ ~(D • E)
2	~(B ∨ A) ⊃ (~D ∨ ~E)*

(b) If Ben and Chad are not both happy then Evelyn and Garry are both not depressed.

1	~(B • C) ⊃ (~E • ~G)
2	(~B ∨ ~C) ⊃ ~(E ∨ G)*

(c) Neither Amy nor Ben is happy if and only if Chad and Ben are not both happy.

1	(~A • ~B) ≡ ~(C • B)
2	~(A ∨ B) ≡ (~C ∨ ~B)*

(d) If neither Amy nor Ben is happy and Chad is not happy then neither Evelyn nor Dirk is depressed.

1	[(~A • ~B) • ~C] ⊃ (~E • ~D)
2	[~(A ∨ B) • ~C] ⊃ ~(E ∨ D)*

(e) If Amy and Ben are not both happy then either Evelyn is not depressed or Garry and Dirk are not both depressed.

1	~(A • B) ⊃ [~E ∨ ~(G • D)]
2	(~A ∨ ~B) ⊃ [~E ∨ (~G ∨ ~D)]*

*Two different symbolizations of the antecedent and two different symbolizations of the consequent are provided. It is, of course, possible to offer two more symbolizations with alternate symbolizations of the antecedent and consequent.

There are other
ways of inserting
parentheses.

Exercise F.1 All-Some-None-Not-All

(a) All four are on a diet.

(b) At least one of the four is on a diet.

(c) Someone from the group is on a diet.

(d) Not all are on a diet.

(e) Nobody in the group is on a diet.

$(A \bullet B) \bullet (C \bullet D)$
$(A \vee B) \vee (C \vee D)$
$(A \vee B) \vee (C \vee D)$
$\sim((A \bullet B) \bullet (C \bullet D))$ $(\sim A \vee \sim B) \vee (\sim C \vee \sim D)$
$\sim((A \vee B) \vee (C \vee D))$ $(\sim A \bullet \sim B) \bullet (\sim C \bullet \sim D)$

Exercise F.2 All-Some-None-Not-All

(a) All the boys in this group are busy.

(b) There is a girl in this group who is busy.

(c) Not all girls are busy.

(d) Nobody in this group is busy.

(e) Not everybody in this group is busy.

$(J \bullet K) \bullet L$
$(A \vee B) \vee C$
$\sim((A \bullet B) \bullet C)$ $(\sim A \vee \sim B) \vee \sim C$
$((\sim A \bullet \sim B) \bullet (\sim C \bullet \sim J)) \bullet (\sim K \bullet \sim L)$ $\sim(((A \vee B) \vee (C \vee J)) \vee (K \vee L))$
$\sim(((A \bullet B) \bullet (C \bullet J)) \bullet (K \bullet L))$ $((\sim A \vee \sim B) \vee (\sim C \vee \sim J)) \vee (\sim K \vee \sim L)$

Exercise F.3 All-Some-None-Not-All

(a) Some, but not all, of the boys in this group are busy.

(b) Not all girls in this group are not busy but at least one girl is not busy.

(c) Neither all girls nor all boys in this group are busy.

$((J \vee K) \vee L) \bullet \sim((J \bullet K) \bullet L)$ $((J \vee K) \vee L) \bullet ((\sim J \vee \sim K) \vee \sim L)$
$\sim(\sim A \bullet (\sim B \bullet \sim C)) \bullet (\sim A \vee (\sim B \vee \sim C))$
$\sim(A \bullet (B \bullet C)) \bullet \sim(J \bullet (K \bullet L))$ $\sim[A \bullet (B \bullet C)) \vee (J \bullet (K \bullet L))]$

Example 3

[3cbb] $\sim(\sim(A \vee B) \bullet \sim(W \vee J))$

[3dbb] $\sim\sim(A \vee B) \vee \sim\sim(W \vee J)$

Exercise G.1 Symbolizations

(a) Either both Ann and Betty are on a diet, or neither of them is.

$$(A \bullet B) \vee (\sim A \bullet \sim B)$$
$$(A \bullet B) \vee \sim(A \vee B)$$

(b) Either both Ann and Betty are on a diet, or not both of them are.

$$(A \bullet B) \vee \sim(A \bullet B)$$
$$(A \bullet B) \vee (\sim A \vee \sim B)$$

(c) Not both Larry and Martin are getting fat, though both Martin and Newt are getting fat.

$$\sim(L \bullet M) \bullet (M \bullet N)$$
$$(\sim L \vee \sim M) \bullet (M \bullet N)$$

(d) It is both the case that neither Ann is on a diet nor Larry is getting fat and that neither Betty nor Charlie is on a diet.

$$(\sim A \bullet \sim L) \bullet (\sim B \bullet \sim C)$$
$$\sim(A \vee L) \bullet \sim(B \vee C)$$

(e) It is not the case that neither Ann nor Charlie is on a diet.

$$\sim(\sim A \bullet \sim C)$$
$$\sim\sim(A \vee C)$$

Exercise G.2 Symbolizations

(a) Either neither Ann nor Charlie is on a diet or neither Betty nor Charlie is on a diet.

$$(\sim A \bullet \sim C) \vee (\sim B \bullet \sim C)$$
$$\sim(A \vee C) \vee \sim(B \vee C)$$

(b) It is not the case that not both Martin and Newt are getting fat.

$$\sim\sim(M \bullet N)$$
$$\sim(\sim M \vee \sim N)$$

(c) Neither is it the case that if Larry is getting fat then Ann is on a diet nor that if Martin is getting fat then Betty is on a diet.

$$\sim(L \supset A) \bullet \sim(M \supset B)$$
$$\sim((L \supset A) \vee (M \supset B))$$

(d) Neither is it the case that Ann or Betty is on a diet nor that Betty or Charlie is on a diet.

$$\sim(A \vee B) \bullet \sim(B \vee C)$$
$$\sim((A \vee B) \vee (B \vee C))$$

(e) It is not both the case that neither Ann nor Betty is on a diet and that neither Betty nor Charlie is on a diet.

$$\sim[(\sim A \bullet \sim B) \bullet (\sim B \bullet \sim C)]$$
$$\sim[\sim(A \vee B) \bullet \sim(B \vee C)]$$
$$\sim(\sim A \bullet \sim B) \vee \sim(\sim B \bullet \sim C)$$
$$\sim\sim(A \vee B) \vee \sim\sim(B \vee C)$$

Exercise G.3 Symbolizations

(a) Neither Ann nor Charlie nor Betty is on a diet if Martin and Newt are not both getting fat.

$$\sim(M \bullet N) \supset ((\sim A \bullet \sim C) \bullet \sim B)$$
$$(\sim M \vee \sim N) \supset \sim((A \vee C) \vee B)$$

(b) It is not both the case that Ann and Betty are not both on a diet and that Betty and Charlie are not both on a diet.

$$\sim(\sim(A \bullet B) \bullet \sim(B \bullet C))$$
$$\sim(\sim A \vee \sim B) \vee \sim(\sim B \vee \sim C)$$

(c) Neither is it the case that neither Larry nor Martin is getting fat nor is it the case that neither Martin nor Newt is getting fat.

$$\sim(\sim L \bullet \sim M) \bullet \sim(\sim M \bullet \sim N)$$
$$\sim(\sim(L \vee M) \vee \sim(M \vee N))$$

Exercise G.4 Symbolizations

(a)   Katrina and Mary are never both nice.

$$\sim(K \bullet M)$$
$$\sim K \lor \sim M$$

(b)   Katrina and Susan are never both nice, either.

$$\sim(K \bullet S)$$
$$\sim K \lor \sim S$$

(c)   Either Jennifer is nice or Mary is nice, but never both.

$$(J \lor M) \bullet \sim(J \bullet M)$$
$$(J \lor M) \bullet (\sim J \lor \sim M)$$

(d)   Both Jennifer and Katrina are nice but neither Susan nor Donna is nice.

$$(J \bullet K) \bullet (\sim S \bullet \sim D)$$
$$(J \bullet K) \bullet \sim(S \lor D)$$

(e)   Amy and Susan aren't both nice, but it's not the case that neither of them is nice.

$$\sim(A \bullet S) \bullet \sim(\sim A \bullet \sim S)$$
$$(\sim A \lor \sim S) \bullet (\sim\sim A \lor \sim\sim S)$$

Exercise G.5 Symbolizations

(a)   If Jennifer is nice, then Lucy is nice provided that Donna is nice.

$$J \supset (D \supset L)$$

(b)   Lucy is nice if Jennifer is nice, provided that Donna is nice.

$$D \supset (J \supset L)$$

(c)   If neither Amy nor Betty is nice, then neither Mary nor Susan is nice provided that Lucy isn't nice.

$$(\sim A \bullet \sim B) \supset (\sim L \supset (\sim M \bullet \sim S))$$
$$\sim(A \lor B) \supset (\sim L \supset \sim(M \lor S))$$

(d)   Lucy isn't nice if neither Mary nor Betty is nice, provided that Amy and Susan aren't both nice.

$$\sim(A \bullet S) \supset ((\sim M \bullet \sim B) \supset \sim L)$$
$$(\sim A \lor \sim S) \supset (\sim(M \lor B) \supset \sim L)$$

(e)   Jennifer and Lucy aren't both nice just in case either neither Mary nor Jennifer is nice or neither Katrina nor Lucy is nice.

$$\sim(J \bullet L) \equiv ((\sim M \bullet \sim J) \lor (\sim K \bullet \sim L))$$
$$(\sim J \lor \sim L) \equiv (\sim(M \lor J) \lor \sim(K \lor L))$$

Exercise G.6 Symbolizations

(a)   Jennifer, Katrina, Mary, and Lucy are all nice.

$$(J \bullet K) \bullet (M \bullet L)$$

(b)   At least one of these four girls is nice.

$$(J \lor K) \lor (M \lor L)$$

(c)   At least one of these four girls is not nice.

$$(\sim J \lor \sim K) \lor (\sim M \lor \sim L)$$

(d)   Not all four girls are nice.

$$\sim((J \bullet K) \bullet (M \bullet L))$$
$$(\sim J \lor \sim K) \lor (\sim M \lor \sim L)$$

(e)   None of these four girls is nice.

$$(\sim J \bullet \sim K) \bullet (\sim M \bullet \sim L)$$
$$\sim((J \lor K) \lor (M \lor L))$$

Solutions to Unit 1.5 Exercises

Exercise A.1 "Only If"

(a) Trippy is a cat only if Trippy can meow.

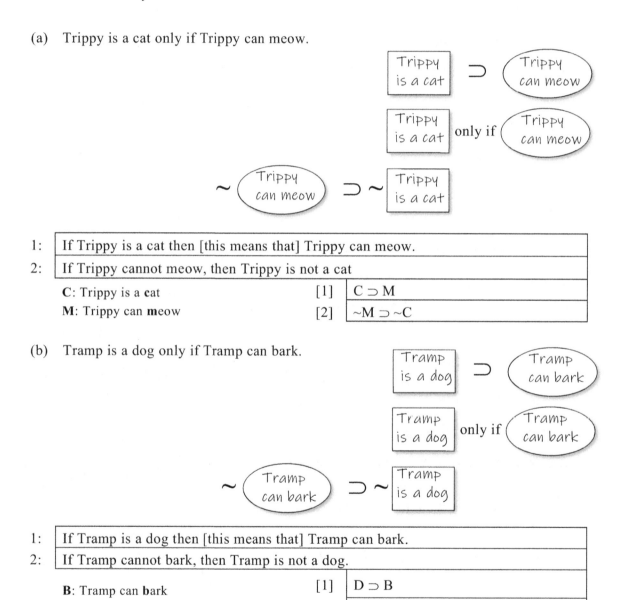

| 1: | If Trippy is a cat then [this means that] Trippy can meow. |
| 2: | If Trippy cannot meow, then Trippy is not a cat |

| **C**: Trippy is a **c**at | [1] | C ⊃ M |
| **M**: Trippy can **m**eow | [2] | ~M ⊃ ~C |

(b) Tramp is a dog only if Tramp can bark.

| 1: | If Tramp is a dog then [this means that] Tramp can bark. |
| 2: | If Tramp cannot bark, then Tramp is not a dog. |

| **B**: Tramp can **b**ark | [1] | D ⊃ B |
| **D**: Tramp is a **d**og | [2] | ~B ⊃ ~D |

Exercise A.2 "Only If"

(a)   Truppy is a fish only if Truppy can swim.

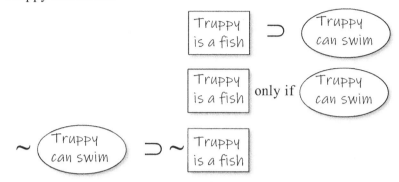

1:	If Truppy is a fish then [this means that] Truppy can swim.
2:	If Truppy cannot swim, then Truppy is not a fish.

H: Truppy is a fish	[1]	H ⊃ S
S: Truppy can **s**wim	[2]	~S ⊃ ~H

(b)   It rains only if it is cloudy.

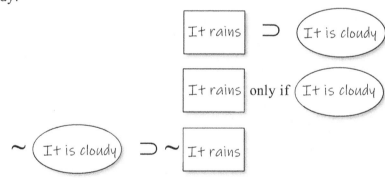

1:	If it rains then [this means that] it is cloudy.
2:	If it is not cloudy, then it does not rain.

C: It is **c**loudy	[1]	R ⊃ C
R: It **r**ains	[2]	~C ⊃ ~R

Exercise A.3 "Only If"

(a)   It snows only if it is cloudy.

1:	If it snows then [this means that] it is cloudy.
2:	If it is not cloudy, then it does not snow.

C: It is cloudy	[1]	S ⊃ C
S: It snows	[2]	~C ⊃ ~S

(b)   It snows only if it is very cold.

1:	If it snows then [this means that] it is very cold.
2:	If it is not very cold, then it does not snow.

V: It is very cold	[1]	S ⊃ V
S: It snows	[2]	~V ⊃ ~S

(c)	Ken will pass logic only if Ken works very hard.

1:    If Ken passed logic [this means that] Ken worked very hard.

2:	If Ken doesn't work very hard, then Ken will not pass logic.

P: Ken passes logic	[1]	P ⊃ W
W: Ken works very hard	[2]	~W ⊃ ~P

(d)   Ken will like logic only if Ken grasps "only if".

1:	If Ken likes logic [this means that] Ken has grasped "only if".
2:	If Ken doesn't grasp "only if", then Ken will not like logic.

L: Ken likes logic	[1]	L ⊃ G
G: Ken grasps "only if"	[2]	~G ⊃ ~L

Exercise A.4 "Only If"

(a) Adam will be healthy only if he goes on a diet.

(b) Ben will be healthy only if he exercises regularly.

(c) Adam will go on a diet only if Ben goes on a diet.

(d) Ben will go on a diet only if Charlie goes on a diet.

H ⊃ A	~A ⊃ ~H
L ⊃ E	~E ⊃ ~L
A ⊃ B	~B ⊃ ~A
B ⊃ C	~C ⊃ ~B

Exercise A.5 "Only If"

(a) Charlie will go on a diet only if Ben goes on a diet.

(b) Ben will exercise only if he goes on a diet.

(c) Ben will be healthy only if he goes on a diet.

(d) Only if Adam goes on a diet will Charlie go on a diet.
Paraphrase: Charlie will go on a diet only if Adam goes on a diet.

C ⊃ B	~B ⊃ ~C
E ⊃ B	~B ⊃ ~E
L ⊃ B	~B ⊃ ~L
C ⊃ A	~A ⊃ ~C

Exercise A.6 "Only If"

(a) You will get an A for this course *if* you get 95% on all your quizzes. ● true ○ false

(b) You will get an A for this course *only if* you get 95% on all your quizzes. ○ true ● false

(c) You will get an A for this course *if* you work hard. ○ true ● false

(d) You will get an A for this course *only if* you work hard. ● true ○ false

Exercise A.7 "Only If" – Complex Terms

(a) A only if B

Ann is sick only if Betty is sick	A ⊃ B ~B ⊃ ~A

(b) ~A only if ~B

Ann is not sick only if Betty is not sick.	~A ⊃ ~B ~~B ⊃ ~~A

(c) (A • B) only if (C • D)

Ann and Betty are both sick only if Charlie and Dirk are both sick.	(A • B) ⊃ (C • D) ~(C • D) ⊃ ~(A • B)

(d) $(A \lor B)$ only if $(C \lor D)$

Ann or Betty is sick only if Charlie or Dirk is sick.	$(A \lor B) \supset (C \lor D)$ $\sim(C \lor D) \supset \sim(A \lor B)$

(e) $(A \supset B)$ only if $(B \supset A)$

Only if it is the case that if Ann is sick then so is Betty, is it the case that if Betty is sick then so is Ann.	$(A \supset B) \supset (B \supset A)$ $\sim(B \supset A) \supset \sim(A \supset B)$

(f) $(A \equiv B)$ only if $(C \equiv D)$

Only if it is the case that Ann is sick just in case Betty is sick, is it the case that Charlie is sick if and only if Dirk is sick.	$(A \equiv B) \supset (C \equiv D)$ $\sim(C \equiv D) \supset \sim(A \equiv B)$

(g) $\sim(A \bullet B)$ only if $\sim(C \bullet D)$

Ann and Betty are not both sick only if Charlie and Dirk are not both sick.	$\sim(A \bullet B) \supset \sim(C \bullet D)$ $\sim\sim(C \bullet D) \supset \sim\sim(A \bullet B)$

(h) $(\sim A \bullet \sim B)$ only if $(\sim C \bullet \sim D)$

Neither Ann nor Betty is sick only if neither Charlie nor Dirk is sick.	$(\sim A \bullet \sim B) \supset (\sim C \bullet \sim D)$ $\sim(\sim C \bullet \sim D) \supset \sim(\sim A \bullet \sim B)$

Exercise A.8 "Only If" – Complex Terms

(a)   Ann will go on a diet only if she isn't healthy.

$A \supset \sim H$

$\sim\sim H \supset \sim A$

(b)   Betty will be healthy only if either she goes on a diet or starts exercising regularly.

$L \supset (B \lor E)$

$\sim(B \lor E) \supset \sim L$

(c)   Ann will go on a diet only if both Betty and Charlie go on a diet.

$A \supset (B \bullet C)$

$\sim(B \bullet C) \supset \sim A$

(d)   Betty will either go on a diet or start exercising regularly only if Ann goes on a diet.

$(B \lor E) \supset A$

$\sim A \supset \sim(B \lor E)$

(e)   Charlie will go on a diet only if Betty goes on a diet but Ann does not.

$C \supset (B \bullet \sim A)$

$\sim(B \bullet \sim A) \supset \sim C$

Exercise A.9 "Only If" – Complex Terms

(a)	Betty will exercise only if she does not go on a diet.	E ⊃ ~B ~~B ⊃ ~E
(b)	Only if Charlie and Betty are on a diet will Ann go on a diet. Paraphrase: Ann will go on a diet only if Charlie and Betty are on a diet.	A ⊃ (C • B) ~(C • B) ⊃ ~A
(c)	Only if Betty either is healthy or starts exercising will Charlie go on a diet. Paraphrase: Charlie will go on a diet only if Betty either is healthy or starts exercising.	C ⊃ (L ∨ E) ~(L ∨ E) ⊃ ~C
(d)	Ann and Betty will be healthy only if they both go on a diet.	(H • L) ⊃ (A • B) ~(A • B) ⊃ ~(H • L)
(e)	Neither Ann nor Betty will go on a diet only if neither of them will be healthy.	(~A • ~B) ⊃ (~H • ~L) ~(~H • ~L) ⊃ ~(~A • ~B)

Exercise B.1 Symbolization

(a) Amy will go out with Chris only if Chris is nice and does not go out with Betty.

M ⊃ (C • ~E)	~(C • ~E) ⊃ ~M

(b) Amy will go out with Dirk only if Betty goes out with him, provided, however, that Dirk is nice.

D ⊃ (Y ⊃ K)	D ⊃ (~K ⊃ ~Y)

(c) Chris will be nice only if either Amy or Betty goes out with him.

C ⊃ (M ∨ E)	~(M ∨ E) ⊃ ~C

(d) Amy will go out with Chris or Dirk only if the boys are both nice.

(M ∨ Y) ⊃ (C • D)	~(C • D) ⊃ ~(M ∨ Y)

(e) Amy or Betty will go out with Dirk only if, first, neither goes out with Chris, and, second, Dirk is nice.

(Y ∨ K) ⊃ ((~M • ~E) • D)	~((~M ∨ E) • D) ⊃ ~(Y ∨ K)

Exercise B.2 Symbolization

(a) Either Amy or Betty will go out with Chris; however, Amy will go out with Chris only if she does not go out with Dirk, and Betty will go out with Chris if she does not go out with Dirk.

$(M \lor E) \bullet ((M \supset {\sim}Y) \bullet ({\sim}K \supset E))$	$(M \lor E) \bullet (({\sim}{\sim}Y \supset {\sim}M) \bullet ({\sim}K \supset E))$

(b) Either if Chris is nice then Amy will go out with him only if Betty doesn't or if Dirk is nice then Betty will go out with him only if Amy doesn't.

$(C \supset (M \supset {\sim}E)) \lor (D \supset (K \supset {\sim}Y))$	$(C \supset ({\sim}{\sim}E \supset {\sim}M)) \lor (D \supset ({\sim}{\sim}Y \supset {\sim}K))$

(c) Dirk will be nice only if, first, Amy is nice and goes out with him and, second, Betty is nice but goes out with Chris.

$D \supset ((A \bullet Y) \bullet (B \bullet E))$	${\sim}((A \bullet Y) \bullet (B \bullet E)) \supset {\sim}D$

(d) Neither Amy nor Betty will go out with Chris if Dirk is nice, but if Dirk is not nice then Amy or Betty will go out with Chris only if he is nice.

$(D \supset ({\sim}M \bullet {\sim}E)) \bullet ({\sim}D \supset ((M \lor E) \supset C))$	$(D \supset {\sim}(M \lor E)) \bullet ({\sim}D \supset ({\sim}C \supset {\sim}(M \lor E)))$

Exercise B.3 Symbolization

(a) Neither Amy nor Betty is nice, but Chris will go out with at least one of them only if Dirk will go out with at least one of them.

$({\sim}A \bullet {\sim}B) \bullet ((M \lor E) \supset (Y \lor K))$	${\sim}(A \lor B) \bullet ({\sim}(Y \lor K) \supset {\sim}(M \lor E))$

(b) Neither Chris nor Dirk is nice; however, Amy will go out with at least one of them and Betty will also go out with at least one of them.

$({\sim}C \bullet {\sim}D) \bullet ((M \lor Y) \bullet (E \lor K))$

(c) Neither Chris nor Dirk is nice; however, Amy will go out with one of them and Betty will go with the other.
Paraphrase: Neither Chris nor Dirk is nice; however, Amy will go out with one of them (i.e. Amy will go out with Chris or Dirk though not both), and Betty will go with the other (i.e. if Amy goes out with Chris, Betty will go out with Dirk, and if Amy goes out with Dirk, Betty will go out with Chris).

$({\sim}C \bullet {\sim}D) \bullet [((M \lor Y) \bullet {\sim}(M \bullet Y)) \bullet ((M \supset K) \bullet (Y \supset E))]$

Exercise C.1 Necessary and Sufficient Conditions

(a)   It hails only if it is cloudy.

Being cloudy is   ● necessary   for hail.
                           ○ sufficient

(b)   It rains if it drizzles.

Drizzle is   ○ necessary   for rain.
                           ● sufficient

(c)   Pully is a hamster only if Pully has cheek pouches.

Having cheek pouches is   ● necessary   for Pully's being a hamster.
                           ○ sufficient

(d)   Pully is a hamster if Pully has cheek pouches.

Having cheek pouches is   ○ necessary   for Pully's being a hamster.
                           ● sufficient

Exercise C.2 Necessary and Sufficient Conditions

(a)   Pully is a hamster if and only if Pully has cheek pouches.

Having cheek pouches is   ● necessary   for Pully's being a hamster
                           ● sufficient

(b)   Susan will pass logic if she makes 55% on the test.

Making 55% on the test is ○ necessary   for Susan's passing logic
                           ● sufficient

(c)   Susan will not get an A if she makes 85% on the test.

Making 85% on the test is ○ necessary   for Susan's not getting A
                           ● sufficient

(d)   Susan will get an A+ if but only if she makes 100% on the test.

Making 100% on the test is ● necessary   for Susan's getting A+
                           ● sufficient

Exercise C.3 Necessary and Sufficient Conditions

(a)   Jack will get a B only if he gets 100% on the project.

Getting 100% on the project is ● necessary   for Jack's getting B
                                ○ sufficient

(b)   Jack will get a B if he gets 100% on the project.

Getting 100% on the test is   ○ necessary   for Jack's getting B
                                ● sufficient

(c)   Tim will lose weight only if he goes on a diet.

Tim's going on a diet is   ● necessary   for his losing weight
                                ○ sufficient

(d)   Jane will go on a diet if she loses weight.

Jane's losing weight is   ○ necessary   for her going on a diet
                                ● sufficient

Exercise C.4 Necessary and Sufficient Conditions

(a)   Logi is a mammal **if** *Logi is a hamster.*   ● true   ○ false

Logi is a mammal **only if** *Logi is a hamster.*   ○ true   ● false

Logi's being a hamster   is   ● sufficient   for Logi's being a mammal.
                                ○ necessary

(b)   Ann will be angry **if** *Stan forgets about the anniversary.*   ● true   ○ false

Ann will be angry **only if** *Stan forgets about the*   ○ true   ● false
anniversary.

Stan's forgetting about the anniversary   is   ● sufficient   for Ann's anger
                                                ○ necessary

(c)   John is an adult **only if** *he is 28 years old*   ○ true   ● false

John is an adult **if** *he is 28 years old*   ● true   ○ false

John's being 28 years old   is   ● sufficient   for his being an adult.
                                    ○ necessary

Exercise C.5 Necessary and Sufficient Conditions

(a)   You will win the lottery **if** *you buy the ticket.*   ○ true   ● false

You will win the lottery **only if** *you buy the ticket.*   ● true   ○ false

Your buying the ticket   is   ○ sufficient   for your winning the lottery.
                                ● necessary

(b)   Ben is a father **only if** *Ben is a man.*   ● true   ○ false

Ben is a father **if** *Ben is a man.*   ○ true   ● false

Ben being a man   is   ○ sufficient   for Ben's being a father.
                         ● necessary

(c)   It hails **if** *it is cloudy.*   ○ true   ● false

It hails **only if** *it is cloudy.*   ● true   ○ false

Being cloudy   is   ○ sufficient   for hail.
                      ● necessary

Exercise C.6 Necessary and Sufficient Conditions

(a) If   Aristo is a Maine Coon   then   Aristo is a cat

Aristo is a cat	if	Aristo is a Maine Coon
Aristo is a Maine Coon	only if	Aristo is a cat
Aristo's being a Maine Coon	is a sufficient condition of	being a cat
Aristo's being a cat	is a necessary condition of	being a Maine Coon

(b) If   it rains   then   it is cloudy

It is cloudy	if	it rains
It rains	only if	it is cloudy
Its raining	is a sufficient condition of	its being cloudy
Its being cloudy	is a necessary condition of	ts raining

Exercise C.7 Necessary and Sufficient Conditions

(a) If   Burr barks   then   Burr is a dog

Burr is a dog	if	Burr barks
Burr barks	only if	Burr is a dog
Burr's barking	is a sufficient condition of	Burr's being a dog
Burr's being a dog	is a necessary condition of	Burr's barking

(b) If   Pum is a hamster   then   Pum has cheek pouches

Pum has cheek pouches	if	Pum is a hamster
Pum is a hamster	only if	Pum has cheek pouches
Pum's being a hamster	is a sufficient condition of	Pum's having cheek pouches
Pum's having cheek pouches	is a necessary condition of	Pum's being a hamster.

Exercise C.8 Necessary and Sufficient Conditions

(a) If   ABCD is a square   then   ABCD is a rectangle

ABCD is a rectangle	if	ABCD is a square
ABCD is a square	only if	ABCD is a rectangle
ABCD's being a square	is a sufficient condition of	its being a rectangle
ABCD's being a rectangle	is a necessary condition of	its being a square

(b) If   ABC is a triangle   then   ABC is a polygon

ABC is a polygon	if	ABC is a triangle
ABC is a triangle	only if	ABC is a polygon
ABC's being a triangle	is a sufficient condition of	its being a polygon
ABC's being a polygon	is a necessary condition of	its being a triangle

Exercise C.9 Necessary and Sufficient Conditions

(a) It rains **only if it's cloudy**

Being cloudy is   ● necessary   for rain.
             ○ sufficient

(b) It rains if it drizzles.

It drizzles **only if it rains.**

Rain is   ● necessary   for drizzle.
       ○ sufficient

(c) Daphie is a sheltie only if Daphie is a dog.

Daphie is a dog **if Daphie is a sheltie**.

Daphie's being a sheltie is   ○ necessary   for Daphie's being a dog.
                      ● sufficient

(d) Mela is a cat if Mela is a Russian blue.

Mela is a Russian blue **only if Mela is a cat.**

Mela's being a cat is   ● necessary   for Mela's being a Russian Blue.
                ○ sufficient

Exercise C.10 Necessary and Sufficient Conditions

(a) ABCD is a polygon **if it is a rhombus**.

ABCD's being a rhombus is   ○ necessary   for its being a polygon.
                    ● sufficient

(b) ABCD is a polygon if it is a parallelogram.

ABCD is a parallelogram **only if ABCD is a polygon**.

ABCD's being a polygon is   ● necessary   for its being a parallelogram.
                  ○ sufficient

(c) ABCD is a rectangle only if it is a polygon.

ABCD is a polygon **if it is a rectangle.**

ABCD's being a rectangle is   ○ necessary   for its being a polygon.
                    ● sufficient

(d) ABCD is a square **only if it is a polygon.**

ABCD's being a polygon is   ● necessary   for its being a square.
                  ○ sufficient

Solutions to Unit 1.6 Exercises

Exercise A.1 "Unless"

(a) Ann will go on a diet unless her doctor objects to her going on a diet.

If Ann's doctor does not object to her going on a diet then she will go on a diet.	~D ⊃ A
Either Ann's doctor objects to her going on a diet or she will go on a diet.	D ∨ A

(b) Betty will go on a diet unless Evelyn forbids her to do so.

If Evelyn does not forbid Betty to go on a diet, Betty will go on a diet.	~E ⊃ B
Either Evelyn forbids Betty to go on a diet or Betty will go on a diet.	E ∨ B

(c) Charlie will go on a diet unless Garry goes on a diet.

If Garry does not go on a diet then Charlie will go on a diet.	~G ⊃ C
Either Garry goes on a diet or Charlie will.	G ∨ C

(d) Garry will go on a diet unless Charlie goes on a diet.

If Charlie does not go on a diet then Garry will go on a diet.	~C ⊃ G
Either Charlie goes on a diet or Garry will.	C ∨ G

Exercise A.2 "Unless"

(a)   Betty will go on a diet unless Ann's doctor objects to Ann's going on a diet.

If Ann's doctor does not object to Ann's going on a diet, Betty will go on a diet.	$\sim\!D \supset B$
Either Ann's doctor objects to Ann's going on a diet or Betty will go on a diet.	$D \vee B$

(b)   Betty will not go on a diet unless Ann goes on a diet.

If Ann does not go on a diet, Betty will not go on a diet.	$\sim\!A \supset \sim\!B$
If Ann goes on a diet or Betty will not go on a diet.	$A \vee \sim\!B$

(c)   Betty and Ann will both go on a diet unless Ann's doctor objects to Ann's going on a diet.

If Ann's doctor does not object to Ann's going on a diet, Betty and Ann will both go on a diet.	$\sim\!D \supset (B \bullet A)$
Either Ann's doctor objects to Ann's going on a diet or Betty and Ann will both go on a diet.	$D \vee (B \bullet A)$

(d)   Ann will go on a diet unless Charlie or Garry goes on a diet.

If it is not the case that Charlie or Garry goes on a diet (i.e. if neither Charlie nor Garry goes on a diet), Ann will go on a diet.	$\sim\!(C \vee G) \supset B$
Either Ann's doctor objects to Ann's going on a diet or Betty will go on a diet.	$(C \vee G) \vee B$

Exercise A.3 "Unless" – Complex Terms

(a) $\sim\!A$ unless C

Ann is not happy unless Charlie is sad.	$C \vee \sim\!A$ $\sim\!C \supset \sim\!A$

(b)   A unless $\sim\!C$

Ann is happy unless Charlie is not sad.	$\sim\!C \vee A$ $\sim\!\sim\!C \supset A$

(c) $\sim\!B$ unless $\sim\!D$

Betty is not happy unless Dirk is not sad.	$\sim\!D \vee \sim\!B$ $\sim\!\sim\!D \supset \sim\!B$

(d) $(C \vee D)$ unless $(A \bullet B)$

Either Charlie or Dirk is sad unless Ann and Betty are both happy.	$(A \bullet B) \vee (C \vee D)$ $\sim\!(A \bullet B) \supset (C \vee D)$

Exercise A.4 "Unless" – Complex Terms

(a) (C • D) unless (A ∨ B)

Charlie and Dirk are both sad unless either Ann or Betty is happy.	(A ∨ B) ∨ (C • D) ~(A ∨ B) ⊃ (C • D)

(b) (A ⊃ B) unless (B unless A)

Betty is happy if Ann is happy, unless Betty is happy unless Ann is happy.	(A ∨ B) ∨ (A ⊃ B) (~A ⊃ B) ∨ (A ⊃ B) ~(A ∨ B) ⊃ (A ⊃ B) ~(~A⊃B) ⊃ (A ⊃ B)

(c) (A ≡ B) unless (A ≡ ~B)

Ann is happy just in case Betty is happy, unless Ann is happy just in case Betty is not happy.	(A ≡ ~B) ∨ (A ≡ B) ~(A ≡ ~B) ⊃ (A ≡ B)

Exercise A.5 Symbolizations

(a) Ann will not go on a diet unless Betty goes on a diet.

~B ⊃ ~A B ∨ ~A ~A ∨ B

(b) Unless Ann goes on a diet, Betty will not go on a diet.

~A ⊃ ~B A ∨ ~B ~B ∨ A

(c) Betty will not go on a diet unless Charlie and Garry both go on a diet.

~(C • G) ⊃ ~B (C • G) ∨ ~B ~B ∨ (C • G)

(d) Ann will not go on a diet unless either Charlie or Garry goes on a diet.

~(C ∨ G) ⊃ ~A (C ∨ G) ∨ ~A ~A ∨ (C ∨ G)

Exercise A.6 Symbolizations

(a) Ann will go on a diet just in case Betty goes on a diet, unless Ann's doctor objects to Ann's going on a diet.

~D ⊃ (A ≡ B) D ∨ (A ≡ B) (A ≡ B) ∨ D

(b) Ann will go on a diet, unless Garry does not go on a diet but Betty does go on a diet.

~(~G • B) ⊃ A (~G • B) ∨ A A ∨ (~G • B)

(c) Neither Charlie nor Garry will go on a diet unless Betty and Ann both go on a diet.

~(B • A) ⊃ (~C • ~G) (B • A) ∨ (~C • ~G) (~C • ~G) ∨ (B • A)

(d) Either Ann or Betty will not go on a diet unless either Charlie or Garry goes on a diet.

~(C ∨ G) ⊃ (~A ∨ ~B) (C ∨ G) ∨ (~A ∨ ~B) (~A ∨ ~B) ∨ (C ∨ G)

Exercise B.1. Symbolizations

(a)   Amy will go out with Dirk unless Betty goes out with him, provided, however, that Dirk is nice.

D ⊃ (~K ⊃ Y)	D ⊃ (K ∨ Y)	D ⊃ (Y ∨ K)

(b)   Chris will not be nice unless either Amy or Betty goes out with him.

~(M ∨ E) ⊃ ~C	~C ∨ (M ∨ E)

(c)   Amy will go out with Dirk if and only if he is nice, unless Dirk goes out with Betty.

~K ⊃ (Y ≡ D)	(Y ≡ D) ∨ K

(d)   Amy or Betty will go out with Dirk, unless he is not nice or one of the girls goes out with Chris.

~(~D ∨ (M ∨ E)) ⊃ (Y ∨ K)	(Y ∨ K) ∨ (~D ∨ (M ∨ E))

Exercise B.2 Symbolizations

(a)   Either Amy or Betty will go out with Chris; however, Amy will go out with Chris unless she goes out with Dirk, and Betty will go out with Chris if she does not go out with Dirk.

(M ∨ E) • ((~Y ⊃ M) • (~K ⊃ E))	(M ∨ E) • ((M ∨ Y) • (~K ⊃ E))

(b)   Either if Chris is nice then Amy will go out with him unless Betty does or if Dirk is nice then Betty will go out with him unless Amy does.

(C ⊃ (~E ⊃ M)) ∨ (D ⊃ (~Y ⊃ K))	(C ⊃ (M ∨ E)) ∨ (D ⊃ (K ∨ Y))

(c)   Dirk will not be nice unless, first, Amy is nice and goes out with him and, second, Betty is nice and Betty goes out with Chris.

~((A • Y) • (B • E)) ⊃ ~D	~D ∨ ((A • Y) • (B • E))

(d)   Neither Amy nor Betty will go out with Dirk unless he is nice, but if Dirk is nice then Amy or Betty will go out with Dirk unless Chris is nice.

(~D ⊃ (~Y • ~K)) • (D ⊃ (~C ⊃ (Y ∨ K)))
(~(Y ∨ K) ∨ D) • (D ⊃ ((Y ∨ K) ∨ C))

Made in the USA
Las Vegas, NV
25 July 2024

92912568R00136